No. 2735
$18.95

62 HOME
REMOTE CONTROL
AND
AUTOMATION PROJECTS

DELTON T. HORN

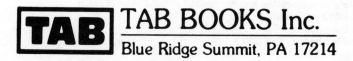

TAB BOOKS Inc.
Blue Ridge Summit, PA 17214

FIRST EDITION

FIRST PRINTING

Copyright © 1986 by TAB BOOKS Inc.

Printed in the United States of America

Library of Congress Cataloging in Publication Data

Horn, Delton T.
    62 home remote control and automation projects.

    Includes index.
    1. Dwellings—Automation. 2. Dwellings—Electronic
equipment. I. Title. II. Title: Sixty-two
home remote control and automation projects.
TH4812.H67 1986   643'.6   86-5899
ISBN 0-8306-0735-8
ISBN 0-8306-2735-9 (pbk.)

Contents

Projects   v

Introduction   viii

1 The Basics of Remote Control and Automation   1
Definitions—Simple Remote Control—Simple Automation—
Applications for Control Systems—Mechanical Devices—Using
Motors—Sensors—Chapter Summary

2 Building and Customizing the Projects   25
Safety Precautions—Finding Parts—Substituting Electronic
Components—Customizing the Projects

3 Lighting   35
Relay Switching—Triac Remote Control—Light Dimmer—Remote
Lamp Dimmer—Multiple Light Dimmer—Automated Guest
Greeter—Photosensitive Automatic Light Switching—Time-Acti-
vated Automation—Sequential Controller—Cross-Fader

4 Doors and Windows   57
Door and Window Indicators—Automatic Door Opener—Complete
Entry Alarm System

5 Temperature Control   69
Temperature Sensors—Probe Assemblies—Simple Electronic
Thermostat—Boiler Controller—Temperature Equalizer—Heater
Humidifier—Air Conditioner Humidity Control

6 Liquid Control   91
Liquid Probes—Plant Monitor—Flood Alarm—Second Flood
Alarm—Moisture Detector—Sump Pump Controller—Second
Sump Pump Controller

7 Stereo and TV Projects   **101**

Stereo Automatic Shut-Off—Advanced Auto Shut-Off—VOX
Recorder Controller—VOX Relay—Sound Compressor Circuit—
Recorder Timer Switch—Auto-Off Circuit—Remote Control Mute

8 Telephone Projects   **115**

Telephone - Activated Relay—Improved Telephone - Activated
Relay—Off-Hook Alarm—Telephone Recorder Controller—
Autodialer—Automatic Caller—Chapter Summary

9 Controlling Motors   **127**

Dc Motors—Ac Motors—The Universal Motor—Motor Controllers—Speed Control

10 Electronic Switching   **145**

Relays—Transistor Switches—Other Semiconductor Switching
Devices—Dc Controlled Switches—Touch Switches

11 Timers   **163**

The 555 Timer—Multiple 555 ICs—Precision Timers—The 2240
Programmable Timer—Cascading Timers—24 Hour Clocks

12 Wireless Control   **193**

Light Beam Control—Carrier Current Control—Tone Encoding—
Touch-Tone Encoding—Radio Control

13 Computer Control   **253**

Programming—Input Signals—D/A Conversion—A/D Conversion

Index   **269**

Projects

1   Relay Switching   35

2   Triac Remote Control   39

3   Light Dimmer   41

4   Remote Lamp Dimmer   42

5   Multiple Light Controller   43

6   Automated Guest Greeter   46

7   Photosensitive Automatic Light Switching   48

8   Time-Activated Automation   48

9   Sequential Controller   54

10   Cross-Fader   55

11   Automatic Door Opener   62

12   Complete Entry Alarm System   67

13   Simple Electronic Thermostat   75

14   Boiler Controller   75

15   Temperature Equalizer   81

16   Heater Humidifier   82

17 Air Conditioner Humidity Control 86

18 Plant Monitor 91

19 Flood Alarm 94

20 Another Flood Alarm 94

21 Moisture Detector 95

22 Sump Pump Controller 95

23 Another Sump Pump Controller 99

24 Stereo Automatic Shut-Off 101

25 Advanced Auto Shut-Off 102

26 VOX Recorder Controller 103

27 VOX Relay 105

28 Sound Compressor 107

29 Recorder Timer Switch 108

30 Auto-Off Circuit 110

31 Remote Control Mute 113

32 Telephone-Activated Relay 115

33 Improved Telephone-Activated Relay 116

34 Off-Hook Alarm 121

35 Telephone Recorder Controller 121

36 Autodialer 123

37 Automatic Caller 123

38 Motor Controller 133

39 Speed Control 140

40 & 41 Touch Switches 160

42 Latching Light-Controlled Relay 200

43 Adjustable Light-Controlled Relay 200

44 Another Light-Controlled Relay 202

45 Light Interruption Detector 203

46 Light-Beam Transmitter   204

47 Light-Beam Receiver   205

48 Infrared Transmitter   207

49 Infrared Receiver   207

50 Multifunction Infrared Transmitter   208

51 Multifunction Infrared Receiver   212

52 Fiberoptic Transmitter   215

53 Fiberoptic Receiver   216

54 Carrier Frequency Generator   221

55 First Carrier-Current Transmitter   223

56 Second Carrier-Current Transmitter   224

57 Third Carrier-Current Transmitter   225

58 First Carrier-Current Receiver   225

59 Second Carrier-Current Receiver   226

60 Tone Decoder   226

61 Third Carrier Current Receiver/Tone Decoder   226

62 Low-Power AM Transmitter   251

Introduction

MOST ELECTRONICS EXPERIMENTERS ENJOY PROJECTS FOR various remote control and automation applications. Such applications are fascinating, educational, practical, and economical. They are also a great way to impress your friends and family with your hobby.

This book features 62 remote control and automation projects. Most can be easily adapted in countless ways to suit other applications. Experimenting is strongly encouraged. The emphasis in this book has been on the practical. While theoretical and general topics are briefly covered, you might also want to read *Handbook of Remote Control & Automation Techniques—2nd Edition* by John E. Cunningham and Delton T. Horn (TAB book 1777) for more background information.

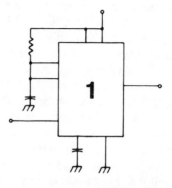

The Basics of
Remote Control and Automation

T HE PURPOSE OF THIS BOOK IS TO PRESENT A COLLECTION of practical projects for remote control and automation applications. To fully understand the projects, and to allow you to customize them to your own individual applications, we'll start out with two chapters on fundamental principles before getting into the actual projects. If you feel you already have a good grounding in this area, you may skip ahead to Chapter 3.

Obviously, we can't go into too much detail in just two chapters. If you want to learn more about the underlying principles in this area, I recommend that you read *Handbook Of Remote Control & Automation Techniques—2nd Edition* by John E. Cunningham and Delton T. Horn (TAB book 1777).

DEFINITIONS

The first thing we need to do is to define just what we mean by "remote control" and "automation." "Remote control" refers to a system that allows an action in one area to be controlled from a separate location. There may or may not be interconnecting wires. "Automation" refers to a system that can operate partially, or totally without human supervision and control. In practical applications, the distinction between these two concepts is somewhat blurred. The goal of both is similar. The idea is to reduce unnecessary human effort. Remote control and automation offer greater convenience over direct manual control.

SIMPLE REMOTE CONTROL

Virtually all remote control systems are made up of three sections, as illustrated in Fig. 1-1. The "Control Initiator" is the remote switch or switches. It is manually activated. The switching information is then transmitted via the "Signal Path" line to the "Controlled Device." Note that in some systems, the "Signal Path" may not exist as actual wires. The switching information may be transmitted as light beams, sound waves, or radio waves.

The "Controlled Device," of course, is whatever we want to control from the remote location. In most cases, an "Indicator" of some sort will be necessary. In most remote control applications, the operator will not be able to see the controlled device. Indicators are used to tell the remote operator the current condition(s) of the Controlled Device. For example, a LED on the remote control panel might light up to indicate that the Controlled Device is receiving power.

Remote Control systems may range from the simple to the complex. A simple application is treated three different ways in Fig. 1-2. A light is to be turned on or off from a remote location.

The simplest approach is shown in Fig. 1-2A. The power cable is simply extended, so the switch can be located wherever we want it. This is more properly remote switching, rather than true

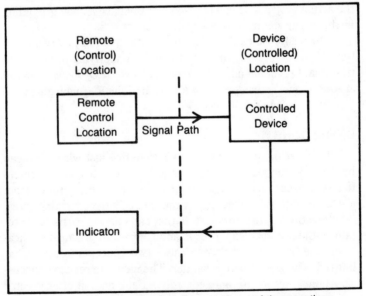

Fig. 1-1. Most remote control systems are made up of three sections.

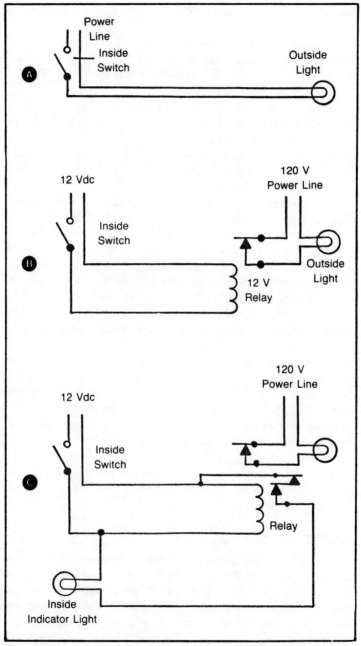

Fig. 1-2. There are usually several possible approaches to a simple remote control application.

3

remote control. The power for the controlled device is carried right to the control point.

Remote switching can certainly be useful. It is quite commonly used in simple systems. For example, in most homes the outside porch light is controlled from a switch inside the house. This is a form of remote switching.

In many applications, remote switching is not practical or desirable. If the distance from the control initiator to the controlled device is very great, remote switching could be a nuisance. Heavy power cables would need to be strung between the two devices. Because of the high power flowing through the signal lines, there is always a risk of fire or electric shock.

While remote switching is perfectly adequate in some applications, in other applications, we may well prefer true remote control. In a remote control system, the systems full supply voltage is not carried by the signal line. Only a much smaller signal voltage is transmitted from the control initiator to the controlled device.

The most basic approach to true remote control is to use a relay, as illustrated in Fig. 1-2B. Much lighter wire is needed for the signal path. (The wire can even be eliminated altogether in some systems.) Adding multiple remote control switches is much easier than with a remote switching system.

A further improvement is shown in Fig. 1-2C. In this circuit, a latching relay is used, so a continuous signal does not need to be transmitted. A brief pulse is used to open or close the relay contacts. The relay will then latch itself into the new state, until it receives another control pulse. This reduces power drain, and lowers the signal line's requirements even further.

The circuit in Fig. 1-2C also adds the refinement of an indicator light at the remote control location. The inside light is lit when the outside light is lit. There's no need to peek out a window, or go outside to see if the light is on.

SIMPLE AUTOMATION

Automation eliminates the need for a human operator, either at the device, or at a remote location. Many systems can be set up to perform some or all of their functions automatically, without human supervision. A washing machine which switches itself from one cycle to the next is an example of an automation system.

Automation systems may be either open loop or closed loop. In an open-loop system, the controller pays no attention to the state of the controlled device. Many open-loop systems involve a timer. A typical example is illustrated in Fig. 1-3. Here the light will be turned on or off at a specific time preset on the timer. Notice that the timer will not check to see whether the light is already on or off. It will just send its control signal blindly, at the preset time. The type of system also cannot react to any failures in the system. For example, if the light bulb burns out, the timer will continue to try to turn it on and off at the preset intervals.

In a closed-loop system, the condition of the controlled device is monitored by the controller. A typical closed-loop system is a thermostat, as illustrated in Fig. 1-4. The room temperature is continually monitored by the thermostat. If the temperature drops below a preset point, the thermostat tells the furnace to come on. The furnace generates heat into the room. When the temperature detected by the thermostat exceeds a specific level, the thermostat tells the furnace to shut down. In other words, the output of the controlled device (heat from the furnace) is monitored by the controller (thermostat). The controller controls the controlled device, and the controlled device controls the controller. Operation is cyclic, which is why this is called a closed-loop system.

The return monitor signal from the controlled device back to the controller is often called an error signal. The system will try to keep the error voltage at a specific fixed level, and will automatically correct any deviation (error) from the standard.

In some applications, open-loop system will do the job just fine. In others, a closed-loop system may be required. Why not just use closed-loop systems all the time? For one thing, closed-loop sys-

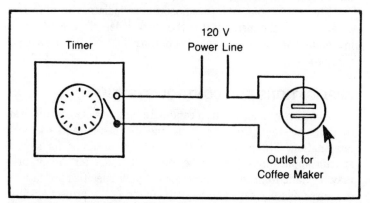

Fig. 1-3. Many open-loop automation systems incorporate a timing device of some sort.

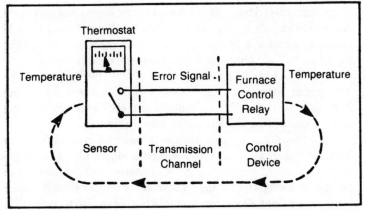

Fig. 1-4. A thermostat is an example of a closed-loop automation system.

tems tend to be more complex and expensive than open-loop systems. If we don't need to monitor the controlled device, why bother?

Closed-loop systems must be carefully designed to prevent instability, or oscillation. As an example, let's consider a thermostat in a large room. The thermostat is located at a distance from the furnace register. When the temperature in the room drops, the thermostat tells the furnace to generate more heat. It takes quite some time to heat the entire room. By the time the temperature near the thermostat is high enough for it to turn the furnace off, the area near the furnace register will be too hot.

Similarly, when the furnace shuts down, and the temperature starts to drop, it may be some time before the thermostat notices the change and turns on the furnace.

The whole point of a thermostat is to maintain an even temperature. But the instability of the system described here results in a room that is alternately too hot or too cold, never hitting a happy medium.

APPLICATIONS FOR CONTROL SYSTEMS

Almost anything can be a candidate for a remote control or automation system. Consider your specific needs, and use your imagination. The projects in this book are designed for several specific applications that may be commonly called for. Adaptations may be made to fit the requirements of your specific applications, of course. No law says you have to construct the project systems exactly as they are described here. Moreover, if you use your imagination, and some logical thought, many of these circuits can be used in very different applications. To use one simple example, a circuit for controlling a light bulb, could also be used to control a hot-plate, assuming the current capability of the circuit is not exceeded. You might be able to use the same techniques I've used for an automatic door opener to design a robotic arm. You'd be surprised how adaptable the basic principles of remote control and automation are.

Of course, any electrically powered device is an obvious potential control application. Some typical electrical remote control and/or automation applications include:

- ☐ outdoor lighting on/off
- ☐ indoor lighting on/off
- ☐ lighting level
- ☐ fans
- ☐ air conditioning
- ☐ furnaces/heaters
- ☐ stereo/radio on/off
- ☐ stereo/radio volume
- ☐ TV on/off
- ☐ TV volume
- ☐ TV/stereo/radio station select
- ☐ intercom systems
- ☐ burglar/fire alarms
- ☐ electric coffee pot/oven
- ☐ water heater

Clearly, this list could go on and on.

Less obvious applications include the physical manipulation of objects. Such applications include:

- ☐ garage door opening/closing
- ☐ other door opening/closing
- ☐ window opening/closing
- ☐ draperies opening/closing
- ☐ locks
- ☐ sump pumps
- ☐ lawn sprinklers

Let your imagination be your guide. What would you like to accomplish from a remote location or automatically? For the best results, you should design your control system to maximize flexibility. A good design permits you to add new features indefinitely.

You're never boxed in.

Start out with something relatively simple. Just control one or two specific functions at first. Later you can add as many functions as you like, and can afford. If you start out planning too comprehensive a system, you're almost sure to run into trouble. The initial expense may be inordinately high. The project may be too intimidating taken as a whole, and may never be completed. The more complex a system is, the more likely it is that mistakes will creep in. On the other hand, if you start simple, and work on one function at a time, you can make sure it is working 100% before moving on to the next function. Don't complicate your life. The point of remote control and automation is to make things easier on you.

This advice is not trivial. Most experimenters (including myself, I must confess) tend to get stars in their eyes, and can get themselves in deeper than expected. I have known several experimenters whose grandiose schemes have died in the throes of their own over-complexity. It's happened to me on a few occasions. I'd like to think that I've learned my lesson by now, but, to be perfectly honest, I doubt if star-prone eyes are ever fully curable. We can all stand periodic reminding of the KISS formula—Keep It Simple, Stupid!

MECHANICAL DEVICES

Electrical switching, and even changing voltages and resistances are fairly obvious types of control. Any operation that is controlled by electrical signals is probably a good choice for remote control or automation.

But other operations may not be electrically controlled. Suppose we want an automatic door opener. The door itself is not electrically controlled. Some kind of electrical to mechanical energy converter is needed.

Most readers of this book will probably face their greatest problems with the mechanical interfaces. The electronic circuitry generally isn't too complex, but the mechanical devices used in some control systems may be quite unfamiliar to the average electronics experimenter. Therefore, in this section, we will examine the basics of mechanical devices in some detail.

The first step in designing a mechanical system is the same as in designing an electronic circuit—define the purpose. Exactly what do you want the system to do? Ask yourself a series of questions. What do you want moved? How heavy is it? How far should it move? How fast should it move? How much power will it take to achieve the desired movement? Clearly, to answer these questions meaningfully, we will need to use some standard units of measurement.

"What do you want moved?" No quantitative measurement is needed for this question. It is purely descriptive.

"How heavy is it?" Any standard units of weight can be used, as long as they are consistent. We'll use the pound as our standard, although the gram could be used as well.

"How far should it move?" Again, we have a choice of standards for distance—the metric system, or the English system. We will use the foot as our basic standard.

"How fast should it move?" Speed is a comparison of distance over time. We will define speed in terms of feet-per-second.

"How much power will it take to achieve the desired movement?" This is probably the most significant question, and the one most people are likely to be at a loss to answer.

Let's consider a simple example. We need to lift a twenty pound weight straight up. Clearly we must exert a twenty pound force in the upward direction, but this doesn't tell us how much energy, or power is required for the task. We need to know how far up the weight is to be moved. Certainly more energy will be needed to lift the weight ten feet than it would be to lift the same weight five feet.

Remember that speed was defined by the distance/time ratio. Similarly, mechanical energy, or force can be measured by using a weight/distance ratio. That is, force is measured in foot-pounds. The formula is simple enough:

$$\text{Force} = \text{Weight} \times \text{Distance} = \text{pounds} \times \text{feet}$$

To lift our twenty pound weight ten feet, we need $20 \times 10 = 200$ foot-pounds of energy.

Power includes speed, in addition to force. Obviously, it will take more energy to move that twenty pound weight ten feet in one second than in ninety seconds. This time we can use the force/time ratio. That is:

$$\text{Power} = \text{Force/Time} = \text{foot-pounds/seconds}$$

Let's return to our example. To lift our twenty pound weight ten feet in five seconds. We have already determined that force = 200 foot-pounds, so:

$$\text{Power} = 200/5 = 40 \text{ foot-pounds/second}$$

Foot-pounds-per-second is a useful and clear measurement of power. However, other standards exist. Electrical power, as you know, is measured in watts. Foot-pounds-per-second can be converted to watts, or vice versa:

1 watt = 0.7376 foot-pounds-per-second
1 foot-pound-per-second = 1.356 watt

Great, but there's still another standard measurement of power to deal with. Motors are generally rated in horsepower. To continue with the conversion formulae:

1 watt = 0.00134 horsepower
1 horsepower = 746 watts
1 foot-pound-per-second = 0.0018 horsepower
1 horsepower = 550 foot-pounds-per-second

All mechanical devices of the type we are dealing with here are technically "machines." In this context, the word "machine" has a slightly different meaning than we are used to. A machine is a device that transforms the magnitude or direction of a mechanical force. By this definition, a computer, for example, is not a machine.

In working with any machine, it is vital to always remember the law of energy conservation. All of the energy in a system must come from somewhere, and all of the energy in a system must go somewhere. Energy can neither be created nor destroyed.

The ratio of the force exerted by a machine to the force applied to it is called the mechanical advantage. This is an important concept, as you will soon see. Mechanical advantage may be positive, or negative (mechanical disadvantage).

One of the simplest machines is the lever. As shown in Fig. 1-5, a lever consists of three basic parts:

☐ INPUT—energy is applied to the machine here
☐ FULCRUM—the lever is supported here
☐ OUTPUT—energy is exerted by the machine here

We can divide the lever itself into two sections. The distance from the input to the fulcrum is the power arm, or force arm. The

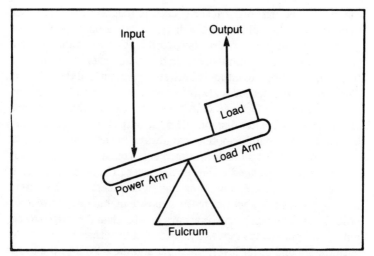

Fig. 1-5. A simple lever consists of three parts—the power arm, the fulcrum, and the load arm.

distance from the fulcrum to the output is the load arm or weight arm. This is also indicated in Fig. 1-5.

The relative lengths of the power arm and the load arm determine the mechanical advantage:

Mechanical Advantage = power arm/load arm

For example, let's say the power arm is 4 times the length of the load arm:

Mechanical Advantage = 4/1 = 4

The force at the output will be four times the force at the input. But isn't this a violation of the law of energy conservation? No. There is a price to be paid for the increase in force. The input must be moved four times as far as we want the output to move. Since power is the ratio of force and distance, we can see that the power at the input is the same as the power at the output. (Friction, and other losses are being ignored here for simplicity.) Some of the input distance has simply been transformed into output force.

Usually when we think of a lever, we think of a first-order lever. This is the type shown in Fig. 1-5. The fulcrum is between the input and the output. This type of lever also performs a direction transformation. The output moves in the opposite direction as

11

the input. The first-order lever is used to magnify the force used to move the output object, or the distance the output object moves.

Other types of levers are also possible, by rearranging the position of the various components. In a second-order lever, as illustrated in Fig. 1-6, the output is between the input and the fulcrum. The force at the output is always greater than the force at the input with this type of lever. Of course, this means, the input must always move a greater distance than the output. In a second-order lever input and output motion are always in the same direction.

There is a third possible arrangement. You've probably already guessed that it is called a third-order lever. This type of lever is illustrated in Fig. 1-7. This time the input is between the output and the fulcrum. It operates in the opposite manner as the second-order lever. The input force is always greater than the output force, but the output always moves a greater distance than the input. As with the second-order lever, the input and the output of the third-order lever always move in the same direction.

Notice that physically second-order levers and third-order levers are identical. The only difference is which part is used as the input and which is used as the output.

Another simple machine that is frequently useful in control applications is the pulley. A typical pulley application is illustrated in Fig. 1-8. This system is used to change the direction of force. A downward force on one end of the cord causes an upward force on the other end.

Pulleys can also be used to magnify a lever. This is again thanks to the law of conservation of energy. In a pulley system the ten-

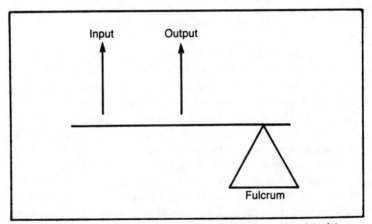

Fig. 1-6. In a second-order lever, the output is between the input and the fulcrum.

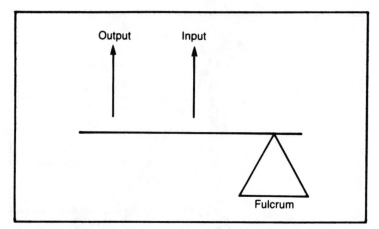

Fig. 1-7. The third-order lever is similar to the second-order lever, except the input and output are reversed.

sion, or force, is the same along the entire cord. Figure 1-9 shows how multiple pulleys can be used to create a mechanical advantage. Since the tension is the same throughout the cord, the four strands of cord supporting the load will have approximately four times the force being exerted on the single strand input. (Friction losses will waste some of the output force, but in most cases, these losses will be minimal and can be ignored.)

In practical mechanical systems, certain losses must be con-

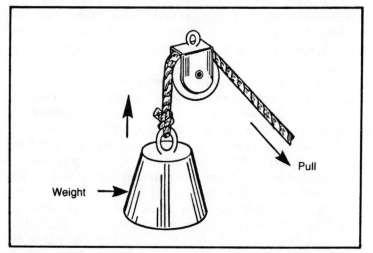

Fig. 1-8. A pulley is another simple machine that is frequently useful in control applications.

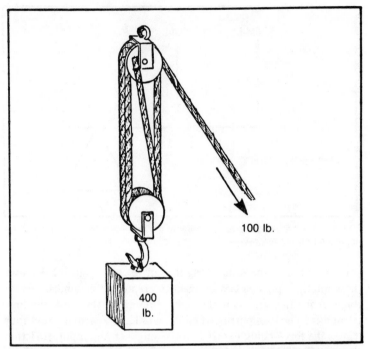

Fig. 1-9. Multiple pulleys can be used to create a mechanical advantage.

sidered. Two of the most important factors are *friction* and *inertia*. As one object is moved against another object or substance, some of the energy will be consumed as heat at the point of contact. This is called friction. If you roll a ball down a very long, smooth hallway, it will eventually come to a stop, even if it doesn't hit anything. This is due to friction.

Friction exists in all mechanical systems outside a pure vacuum. There is even friction against the surrounding air, which is the main reason why an arrow fired over an open field will fly just so far before gravity takes over, and it falls to the ground.

In many control systems friction won't present a significant problem. In others, it will make the system require an increase in the supplied power to make up for the lost energy. In some systems, however, friction can be a very significant factor, limiting motion, causing premature wear of parts, or possibly even creating a fire hazard (waste energy is converted to heat by friction). Methods for dealing with potential friction problems will be discussed along with the appropriate projects.

Inertia is a physical property that can be considered somewhat

14

similar to electrical resistance. Mechanical systems tend to resist changes in motion. An object at rest tends to stay at rest, and an object in motion tends to resist any changes in speed or direction (including stopping).

If an object is at rest, the force required to set it into motion (ignoring friction) is:

Force = Mass of Object × Desired Acceleration

Lower accelerations (speeds) require less power. This allows the use of smaller (and less expensive) motors and other components. A slower system will tend to be less trouble-prone, with fewer snarled or broken cords, jammed motors, and other problems. In most home control applications high speed operation is not a priority. Why complicate your life by trying to make things move faster than absolutely necessary?

USING MOTORS

Most mechanical energy in control systems will probably come from some sort of motor. A motor, of course, is yet another type of energy transformer. It converts electrical energy (voltage) into mechanical energy as rotary motion.

Motors always produce rotary motion (the armature spins), and the speed of rotation will usually be too high for practical control applications. Speeds in a control system should usually be rather slow to increase safety, and to reduce the power requirements. In this section we will explore means of transforming the high-speed rotary motion of a motor into useful mechanical energy.

One useful, but simple method for changing the speed of rotary motion is to use a pulley and belt arrangement, as shown in Fig. 1-10. Notice that the pulleys have significantly different sizes. The relative diameters indicate their relative speeds of rotation. For example, if the small pulley is attached to the shaft of a motor, the larger pulley will turn at a significantly lower rate.

The exact ratios can be easily calculated. The amount of speed reduction is inversely proportional to the pulley diameters. That is:

$$rpm1/rpm2 = D2/D1$$

where rpm1 is the speed of pulley 1, and D1 is its diameter. Pulley 2's speed is indicated as rpm2, and its diameter is D2.

Let's say we have a motor that has a rotary speed of 100 rpm. A 1-inch diameter pulley is connected to the motor's shaft. The other pulley has a diameter of four inches. We now know three of the values in the equation. It just takes some simple algebra to find the fourth:

$$100/rpm2 = 4/1$$
$$100/rpm2 = 4$$
$$100 = 4rpm2$$
$$100/4 = rpm2 = 25$$

The small pulley will make 100 complete revolutions in a minute, while the larger pulley will make just 25. The larger pulley rotates at one fourth the rate of the small pulley.

In designing control systems, we will usually know the motor's speed, and the desired speed, and will need to find appropriate pulley sizes. For instance, a motor might have a speed of 500 rpm. We need to slow this down to 100 rpm. The first step is to arbitrarily select a size for pulley 1. Let's use 1-inch again, just because it happens to be a convenient value. Once again, we just plug the known values into the equation:

$$500/100 = D2/1$$
$$500/100 = D2$$
$$5 = D2$$

The second pulley should have a diameter of five inches.

It probably won't ever come up, but the same technique can also be used to speed up rotary motion. In this case pulley 1 (the

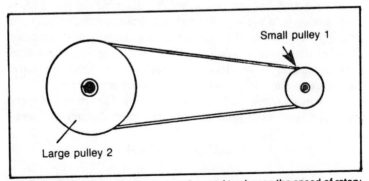

Fig. 1-10. A pulley and belt system can be used to change the speed of rotary motion.

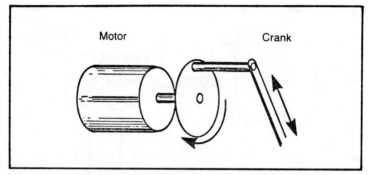

Fig. 1-11. A simple method for converting rotary motion into linear motion is to use a crank.

one attached to the motor shaft) would have a larger diameter than pulley 2. The two pulleys should be carefully aligned to prevent the belt from climbing up one side of a pulley and slip off, or wear out prematurely.

Belts and pulleys are a good method for transferring mechanical energy from one part of a system to another. The belt is flexible enough to absorb shocks, smoothing out the force applied to the motor. Another advantage is that if something jams up the system, the belt will probably slip or break. That might not sound like an advantage, but a belt is much easier and cheaper to replace than a burnt-out motor.

Belts and pulleys are great if we need the mechanical energy in rotary form (movement in a circle). But in many (if not most) practical applications, we will need linear (straight line) rather than rotary motion. Fortunately, it is possible to convert rotary motion into linear motion (and vice versa, if desired) although it often requires some ingenuity.

One fairly simple technique for converting rotary motion into linear motion is to use a crank, as shown in Fig. 1-11. As the shaft turns, the rod connected to the crank will move back and forth. Obviously a fairly slow rotary motion is needed for most practical applications. Slow rotary motion will allow the rod to move back and forth smoothly and at a reasonable speed.

Another approach is to use a capstan, or drum, with a cord wrapped tightly around it as shown in Fig. 1-12. As the drum turns, the cord is moved linearly. This arrangement can be used in many of the same sort of applications that might call for pulleys.

A variation of the capstan approach is illustrated in Fig. 1-13. Here one end of the cord is attached directly to the drum, or spool.

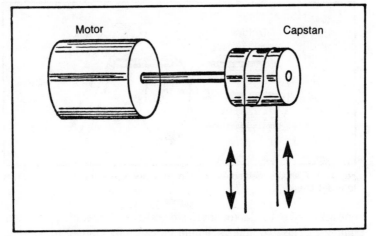

Fig. 1-12. The rotary motion of a capstan or drum translates into linear motion of an attached cord.

As the spool is turned, the cord is wound, or unwound.

SENSORS

Most practical home control systems will require some sort of sensor mechanism to monitor the controlled device. There are countless types of sensors. Almost any condition can be electrically sensed. Of course, electrical signals can be sensed directly. In many control applications we may only need to determine whether or not the supply voltage is currently reaching the controlled device. Obviously, this can be sensed with a simple circuit that turns on (or off) when the voltage is present. For example, a relay can be used as a simple voltage sensor.

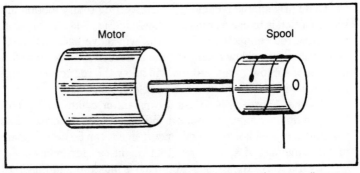

Fig. 1-13. This is a variation on the simple capstan-based rotary-to-linear motion converter of Fig. 1-12.

It isn't much more complicated to sense for a voltage that exceeds a specific pre-set limit, or strays outside a specific range of acceptable values. Current flow can also be easily monitored. Things get a bit more tricky when we want to electrically monitor nonelectrical conditions. Fortunately, the problem is rarely insurmountable, or even unduly difficult.

Many control systems involve mechanical motion of some kind. This means that physical positions often need to be sensed. Generally, the easiest approach is to use a special mechanical switch. There are several types of switches suitable for position sensing.

A magnetic reed switch can be used to indicate proximity. They are often used in burglar alarm systems to indicate whether a door or window is open or shut. This type of switch is illustrated in Fig. 1-14. It is in two parts. One part simply contains a permanent magnet. This section is mounted on the moving object (such as a door). The other part contains a reed switch which responds to a magnetic field. This section is mounted on the fixed object (such as the door jam). Wires connect the switch to the circuitry. When the magnet is brought in close proximity to the switch, the switch closes its contacts (or opens its contacts, depending on the specific design).

Another switch that is useful for mechanical sensing applications is the snap-action switch, shown in Fig. 1-15. A small lever touches the object to be sensed. When the object moves, it moves

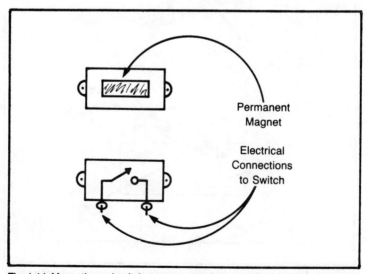

Permanent
Magnet

Electrical
Connections
to Switch

Fig. 1-14. Magnetic reed switches are very useful sensor devices in many control applications.

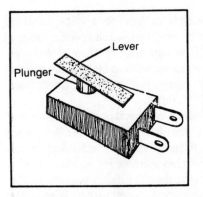

Fig. 1-15. Snap-action switches can be used to detect a relatively small movement.

the lever, activating the switch. This type of switch is designed so that only a very small force is needed to actuate it.

Still another handy switch for mechanical applications is the mercury switch, illustrated in Fig. 1-16. It is basically a small glass tube with two internal electrodes that do not touch each other. A small globule of mercury is contained in the tube. If the switch is positioned so that the mercury rolls down to touch both electrodes,

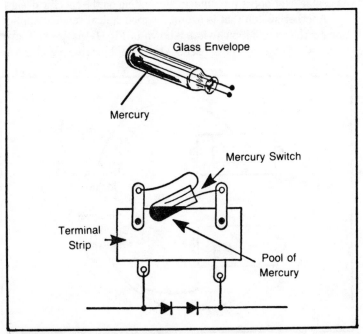

Fig. 1-16. The mercury switch is often called a tilt switch because it can sense the angle of the switch body.

electrical contact is made (the switch is closed). Otherwise, the switch is open. This type of switch is useful for sensing angular position. It is often called a tilt switch.

Switches are great for simple on/off or yes/no sensing. In some control applications, we may need to monitor a continuous range of mechanical positions. Multiple switches could be used, but this is not an elegant solution and often results in undue expense and complexity.

Sometimes we can use the mechanical motion we want to monitor to turn the shaft of a potentiometer. This results in a variable resistance that corresponds to the mechanical position. A simple voltage divider circuit converts the variable resistance into a variable voltage. A simple system of this type is illustrated in Fig. 1-17.

Another continuous mechanical position sensor is shown in Fig. 1-18. The voltage drop across a forward-biased diode is more or less constant. (About 0.7 volt for a silicon diode.) A string of diodes can be used as a precision voltage divider. The cord is made of two parts, an insulated cord that extends to the object being monitored (perhaps a door being opened and closed). At the end of the insulated cord is a length of uninsulated conductive wire, terminating in a weight. The wire passes through a series of conductive rings at junctions between the diodes.

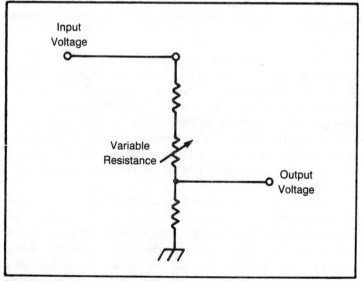

Fig. 1-17. A simple voltage divider can convert a variable resistance into a variable voltage.

21

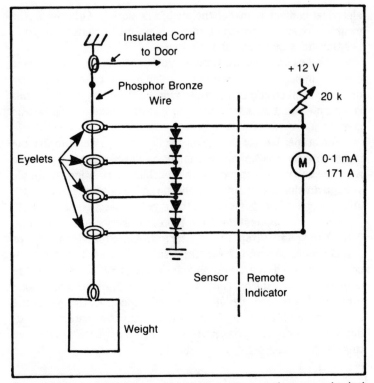

Fig. 1-18. A string of diodes can be used to create a continuous mechanical position sensor device.

As the object is moved, the weight is raised and lowered. At one extreme, the wire is in contact with all the rings, shorting out all the diodes. As the object starts to move away from this extreme, the cord drops through the rings. The insulated section passes through some of the rings, so those diodes are no longer shorted, and their voltage drop(s) can be sensed electrically. As the object moves further from the original extreme position, more and more of the diodes are switched into the circuit, resulting in a larger voltage drop.

Many other types of sensors are available for various special purposes. Light can be measured with *photoresistors, phototransistors,* or *photocells.* Sound can be detected with a microphone and a simple VOX (Voice-Operated switch) circuit. A *thermistor* is a component that varies its resistance in response to the ambient temperature. Several *gas sensors* have been put on the market to serve as electric "noses."

22

A *crystal* can often be used as a pressure sensor. This is the approach used in ceramic cartridges in inexpensive record players. Mechanical pressure along the y axis of a crystal will cause a voltage to be generated across its x axis. This is called the piezoelectric effect.

Another effect that can be used in monitoring applications is the *Hall effect*. If a current flows through a conductor under the influence of a magnetic field at right angles to the direction of current flow, a voltage drop will be produced. Hall effect magnetic sensors are commercially available.

Almost anything can be electrically sensed. In some oddball applications a little more creativity may be required because no commercially manufactured device may be available for the task (at least, not at a reasonable price). Various types of sensors will be used in the projects throughout this book. They will be discussed as we come to them.

CHAPTER SUMMARY

In this chapter I have tried to give you a very quick introduction to basic remote control and automation techniques. This discussion has been rather general and simplified, however, most of the important concepts we will be using in the projects have been presented.

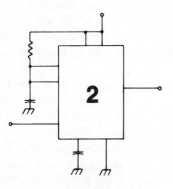

Building and
Customizing the Projects

R EMOTE CONTROL AND AUTOMATION PROJECTS ARE OFTEN somewhat different in their construction requirements than most electronic projects. Therefore, this chapter will give you a few tips on putting together practical home control projects. In addition, every home control application is different from every other home control application. Some degree of customization is almost inevitable. This chapter will also give you some suggestions on customizing the projects from this book to suit your own individual applications.

SAFETY PRECAUTIONS

Many of the projects described in this book involve ac house current. I can not possibly over-stress the importance of safety precautions in these projects. Taking short-cuts could be fatal! There is absolutely no excuse for that.

Use proper housings for all ac-powered circuits. Never leave hot circuitry exposed during operation. Insulated housings are a must. Never use a metal housing as a termination for either end of the ac line. Use a proper ground. All wires carrying ac voltages must be properly and thoroughly insulated. Wrap any exposed junctions in several layers of black electrician's tape. And make sure it is really electrician's tape, and not just black plastic tape. Always remember, it is better to have too much insulation than to risk having too little.

Use wires that are heavy enough to safely carry the current called for by the circuit. When in doubt, use a heavier gauge wire. Ac power lines should be at least 18 or 16 gauge. Do not use 20 gauge or lighter wire for ac applications. Use strain relief devices for all external wires and cables to lessen the possibility of eventual breakage, or shorting.

Fuses are **not** optional! Use all fuses called for in the projects. They are there for a reason. A fuse protects both the circuitry, and the operator. Leaving out a 50-cent fuse is false economy. It could be fatal. Who wants to die to save half a buck?

Never, ever substitute a higher rated fuse. This defeats the purpose of the fuse. If you can't find the specified fuse value, substitute a lesser rated fuse. If it is insufficient, all you will lose is the fuse—it might blow too soon. **Never** use a higher rated fuse. It might not blow in time. Some expensive component in the circuit might end up blowing to protect the fuse. And you could run a risk of severe injury, or even death. It's not worth it!

Also make absolutely certain that all mechanical parts have sufficient clearance. Try to make it impossible for any passing idiot to stick his fingers where they could get crushed by the moving parts. If it is possible to do something stupid, believe me, sooner or later, someone will do it. Nothing is ever completely foolproof—fools can be surprisingly ingenious. But try to come as close to the ideal of foolproof as you can.

Sometimes a moving part must move in the same area as humans. For example, consider an automatic door. It is an extremely good idea for all moving parts to move slowly, giving people a chance to get out of the way. Where serious injury might be a real possibility, visual and/or audible alarms should be used whenever the device is in motion.

Always make certain that all moving parts have sufficient clearance, and can't get hung up on anything. Remember, only a fool compromises where safety is concerned. Adequate safety should be your number one concern at all times.

FINDING PARTS

Remote control and automation projects often call for some unusual parts. Specialized sensors can often be rather difficult to locate. The normal outlets for electronic components usually won't carry the necessary mechanical parts. In many cases the specific mechanical component you need may not be available at all. You may need to customize it from something designed for an entirely different purpose. As always, ingenuity is required.

I will assume that you already know how to find standard electronic components. This section will give you a few hints on how to start looking for the "oddball" parts. Surplus stores are usually a good place to start. Most cities have at least one government/military surplus outlet. The government unloads millions of dollars of perfectly good equipment as surplus every year. In some cases it has been used, but parts can be easily cannibalized and reused by the experimenter. Other times, the equipment is brand new and unused, but obsolete for some reason. A lot of equipment from World War II, Korea, and Vietnam is still available in the surplus market. These are often excellent buys for the experimenter. Finally, many items have no business being sold for surplus at all. I recently bought some high quality screwdrivers that had apparently never been used for a quarter apiece. Apparently, the government buys a certain number of screwdrivers (or whatever) each year. Whatever hasn't been used by the end of the year is sold as surplus, and then they go out and buy a new batch of identical screwdrivers for next year. It's ridiculous. But the experimenter can take advantage of this form of governmental waste.

Industrial surplus is also available from some outlets, especially mail-order surplus houses. While there are some bargains to be found in industrial surplus (particularly when a manufacturer goes out of business), government surplus usually leads in under-priced high quality.

There are advantages and disadvantages to buying surplus by mail. Mail-order houses are usually able to offer slightly lower prices, because of lower overhead costs (although, this is sometimes offset by shipping and handling costs). Mail-order houses are often able to stock a larger variety of items than a walk-in store. Shopping mail order does have its disadvantages. There is the inevitable shipping delay, of course. Some mail-order houses have minimum order limits.

A lot of experimenters are overly cautious about shopping by mail for fear of rip-offs. Actually, rip-offs are relatively rare, but they do occasionally occur. Fortunately, current FTC and postal regulations on mail-order sales are quite strict. If you do run into a problem with a mail-order dealer, contact the local Postmaster.

The biggest disadvantage of buying surplus items by mail order is that you can't actually see them before you buy them. Catalog and flyer descriptions can be misleading. This isn't always an indication of criminal intent. It is often very hard to adequately describe an item. In some cases even photographs may not tell you enough. This is particularly a problem when you intend to cannibalize a piece of equipment for needed parts, or to use it for something other than its original purpose. Some surplus items are "whatzits." You can't use them for their original purpose, because there's no way to determine what the original purpose was. Once I bought some round circuit boards that were apparently part of a missile guidance system. Who cares? I got several expensive components off of them. Buying "whatzits" by mail order is a true "pig in the poke," which may be a great bargain, or may be worthless junk.

Buying surplus by mail is admittedly a gamble. Fortunately, if you don't buy things completely blindly, you should get more bargains than duds. Let the buyer beware.

Addresses for mail-order surplus houses can be found in the ads in the back of experimenter-oriented magazines. To get you started, here are three industrial surplus companies:

American Design Components
39 Lispenard St.
New York, NY 10013

C & H Sales
2176 E. Colorado Blvd.
Pasadena, CA 91107

Herback & Rademan, Inc.
401 E. Erie Ave.
Philadelphia, PA 19134

Old household appliances can be another good source of parts, especially mechanical assemblies. Think about each of the functions an appliance performs. Often these functions can be turned to other ends. Try not to consider the appliance's primary functions, so much as its secondary functions. For example, a refrigerator's primary function is keeping foods cool. Many modern refrigerators include an automatic defrost feature, which will usually have some sort of sensor and/or timer which could be used in many other control applications. All refrigerators have a door switch to turn the little light on and off. Such switches can be extremely useful in control projects. A thermostat is also a part of every refrigerator. A lot of useful goodies can be cannibalized from the secondary functions.

Hit the yard sales for used appliances. You can often pick up some great bargains. In many cases, the unit will need some repair to perform its primary function, but one or more of the secondary functions may be working perfectly—ready for you to cannibalize it.

Automotive junkyards and surplus dealers are another excellent source for mechanical parts. Ignore the original application, just think about whether or not this object can be used to perform the operation you have in mind. A little bit of creative shopping and salvaging can save you literally hundreds of dollars in a complete control system.

SUBSTITUTING ELECTRONIC COMPONENTS

Occasionally it may be necessary to substitute a component value when the specified value is not available. In most cases, high-precision component values are not necessary, which means there is some leeway in substituting values.

A close standard value can often be directly substituted. For example, a 0.2 μF capacitor may be called for. If a 0.22 μF or 0.25 μF capacitor is used, there will probably be no noticeable difference in circuit operation. However, if a specific capacitor type (mylar, ceramic, electrolytic, tantalum, etc.) is called for, try to stick with the specified type. It is called for because of certain characteristics that are important in the circuit's operation. If no capacitor type is specified, you can probably use whatever is available. Ceramic discs are reliable, widely available, and relatively inexpensive, so they are generally the best choice for nonpolarized capacitances.

Resistance values can also be altered somewhat in most cases with minimal or no noticeable difference in circuit operation. If an exact value is required, it will be noted in the text. Except when a precision resistor is required, only standard resistance values are used in this book. They are all readily available. Sometimes, you can use the next standard resistance value. For example, if 12 kΩ is called for, you may be able to get away with a good 10 kΩ or 15 kΩ resistor. When such substitutions are made, it is a good idea to breadboard the modified circuit first to ensure there will be no nasty surprises when you wire the permanent version. I'd say such a change won't matter about 85% of the time. Other times, it could affect circuit operation. Just test it first, before soldering.

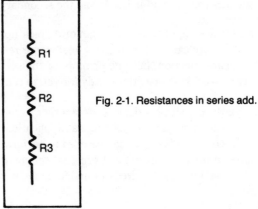

Fig. 2-1. Resistances in series add.

In many cases you can create a hard-to find value by combining components that you have on hand. Resistors can be strung along in series, as shown in Fig. 2-1, to create a larger resistance. The total resistance can be calculated simply by adding together the individual series values:

$$R_t = R1 + R2 + R3 \ldots + R_n$$

As an example, let's say we have three 180-ohm resistors in series. The total resistance will be equal to:

$$R_t = 180 + 180 + 180 = 540 \text{ ohms}$$

The total resistance for a series combination is always larger than any of the individual series resistances.

Resistors can also be combined in parallel, as illustrated in Fig. 2-2. The formula is slightly more complex for parallel resistances. The reciprocal of the total resistance is equal to the sum of the reciprocals of the individual parallel resistances:

$$1/R_t = 1/R1 + 1/R2 + 1/R3 \ldots + R_n$$

For example, if three 100-ohm resistors are combined in parallel, the total resistance will work out to:

$$1/R_t = 1/100 + 1/100 + 1/100 =$$
$$3/100 = 1/33.3$$
$$R_t = 33.3$$

The total resistance of a parallel combination is always less than any of the individual parallel resistances.

If only two resistances are combined in parallel, a slightly different formula can be used:

$$R_t = (R1 \times R2)/(R1 + R2)$$

For example, if R1 = 100 ohms, and R2 = 220 ohms;

$$R_t = (100 \times 220)/(100 + 220) =$$
$$22000/320 =$$
$$68.75 \text{ ohms}$$

If both parallel resistances are equal, the total combined value will be equal to exactly one half the value of either of the parallel resistances. For example, if R1 = R2 = 100 ohms:

$$R_t = (100 \times 100)/(100 + 100) =$$

$$10000/200 =$$
$$100/2 =$$
$$50 \text{ ohms}$$

Of course, series and parallel combinations can be used together, as shown in Fig. 2-3. First you'd solve for the series value of R_a and R_b (R_{ab}). Then you'd find the parallel value of R_c and R_{ab} (R_{abc}). Finally, you'd find the series combination of R_d and R_{abc} (R_t).

Fig. 2-2. The reciprocal of the equivalent value of resistances in parallel is equal to the sum of the reciprocals of the individual resistances.

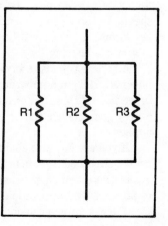

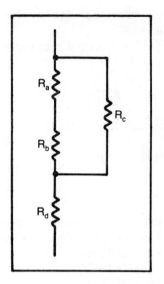

Fig. 2-3. In practical circuits, both series and parallel combinations are often found.

Capacitances can also be combined in series or parallel arrangements, but the formulas are reversed. For capacitances in series, use this formula:

$$1/C_t = 1/C1 + 1/C2 + 1/C3 \ldots + 1/C_n$$

And, for capacitances in parallel, simply add the individual values:

$$C_t = C1 + C2 + C3 \ldots + C_n$$

Often semiconductors can be substituted. Similar ICs (op amps, for example) can often be substituted by comparing their spec sheets. In some cases, identical IC devices are available in different forms. A 747 dual op amp, for instance, is two 741 op amps in a single housing.

Any time you make any kind of IC substitution, check and double check the pin numbering. Similar devices may bring different functions out to different pins. If you wire an IC wrong, there is a very good chance that it will be destroyed as soon as power is applied.

If you are not sure about whether a substitution can be made, try the circuit out first in breadboard form, before soldering. If you are not sure and an expensive IC is involved, I'd advise you not to attempt the substitution. You could destroy the IC.

Transistors can usually be substituted. Just use any good semiconductor substitution guide. In virtually all of the projects in this book, general-purpose substitution transistors can be used.

All in all, you shouldn't have much problem in finding any of the electronic components for these projects.

CUSTOMIZING THE PROJECTS

You should certainly feel free to customize any or all of the projects to suit your own individual applications. In the section on finding mechanical parts, I said, "Ignore the original intended application, and try to determine if this object can be used for the application you have in mind." The same advice applies to circuitry. A circuit that responds to changes in lighting level could be made to respond to changes in temperature by substituting a thermistor for the original photoresistor. Often considerable customization can be achieved simply by changing a sensor, or the input signal.

Block diagrams can be a big help. Determine what each stage in the circuit needs to do, then find a circuit that serves that function. This is far easier than designing a complex circuit from scratch. Most (if not all) complex circuits are simply made up of several relatively simple stages. As always, use your imagination.

I strongly recommend breadboarding any circuit changes before permanently soldering them. Occasionally what works on paper may not work the same way in actual practice. It's better to find out early on, when it is easy to make additional changes and reuse the components, than after everything has been soldered together. Don't invite frustration.

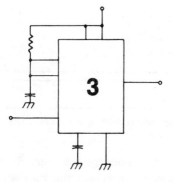

Lighting

O NE OF THE MOST BASIC TYPES OF REMOTE CONTROL AND
automation applications is the control of electric lighting. In
many cases it would be very convenient to be able to turn lights
on and off from a remote location. For example, an indoor porch
light is often controlled from inside. Automatic control of lighting
is also frequently a handy thing to have. Perhaps the porch light
could come on automatically at dusk, and maybe turn off at
midnight.

Almost anyone could use some type of lighting control system,
so we will start out with this type of project. Another reason to
start with lighting projects is their relative simplicity. An electrical signal needs to be turned on and off, or, in some cases, attenuated (a light dimmer). Nothing fancy is required, and there are
almost never any mechanical parts to complicate the projects.

The lighting control projects in this chapter range from the very
simplest to some fairly sophisticated applications. Both remote control and automation applications are covered.

PROJECT 1—RELAY SWITCHING

The most obvious type of lighting control application is to permit the lights to be turned on and off from a remote location. A
very direct approach is shown in Fig. 3-1. This is more properly
remote switching rather than remote control. The power-supply

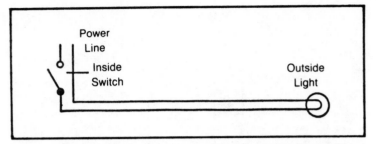

Fig. 3-1. Remote switching is the simplest approach to "remote control," but it is extremely limited.

voltage passes through both the controlled device (light) and the remote switch, and all the connecting wire between them.

In some cases, remote switching is perfectly adequate. It has the advantages of being very simple and inexpensive. Virtually every home has some remote switching. If the switch for your porch light is inside, this is a form of remote switching.

However, remote switching is not always ideal. The connecting wires carry a live ac voltage. This means there is some degree of shock and/or fire hazard, especially if the wire is not enclosed in a wall or other structure. Fairly heavy wire with good, thick insulation must be used.

There are a great many occasions when the connecting wire will have to be strung where people may be able to come in contact with it, or through a path that would be far easier with a lighter and more flexible wire. It would be highly desirable if the connecting wires between the controller and the controlled device did not have to carry the full supply voltage.

The solution to these problems, of course, is a true remote control system. In a true remote control system, the connecting wire only carries a small control signal voltage. The control signal voltage is usually dc, rather than ac, further reducing the shock hazard.

Probably the simplest approach to remote control in such an application is to use relays. An extremely simple circuit is illustrated in Fig. 3-2. The dc power source may be either a battery, or a small ac-driven dc power supply. Only the small voltage and current needed to trigger the relay coil needs to flow through the connecting wires between the controller and the light. Instead of the full ac power needed to light a 100-watt bulb, the same job can be done by sending a small (typically under 1/2 watt) dc control signal.

Remote relay switching of this type can be used to control any ac-powered device, providing, of course, that the relay's switch contacts can handle the necessary power.

The simple circuit shown in Fig. 3-2 is certainly functional, but it definitely has its limitations. One problem is that there is no indicator device to tell the controller the current condition of the controlled device. Is the light already on, or is it off? Sometimes a remote indicator isn't necessary. We might be able to glance out the window to see if the porch light is on or not. However, such visibility isn't always possible, or desirable.

An improved remote relay switching circuit is illustrated in Fig. 3-3. The relay in this circuit has two sets of contacts. One controls the ac light, exactly as before. The other connects the dc control signal to a third wire between the controller and controlled locations. This third wire runs back to the controller location, to a small dc light bulb (a flashlight bulb, or perhaps a LED). The remote indicator light will be lit when the relay contacts are closed.

Actually, this isn't the ideal type of remote indication. All the indicator light tells you is that power is reaching the relay. It does not tell you if the outdoor light is actually lit or not. The outdoor bulb could be broken, or burnt out. There could be a break in a wire past the relay.

In most simple lighting applications, this won't really be much of a problem. Just go outside and do a visual check every week or two.

If the light is critical, however, you will need a true feedback indicator to actually monitor the light itself. The circuit for one solution is shown in Fig. 3-4. A photovoltaic cell monitors the outdoor light bulb. When the light is on, the photocell will generate

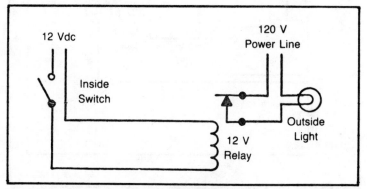

Fig. 3-2. In a true remote control system, only a small control signal is sent from the remote controller to the controlled device.

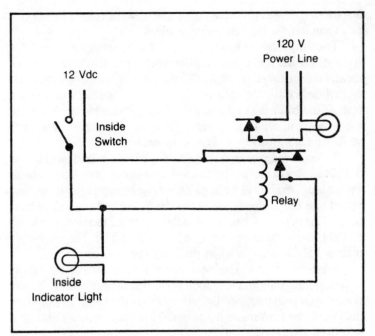

Fig. 3-3. This improved relay circuit includes a remote indicator.

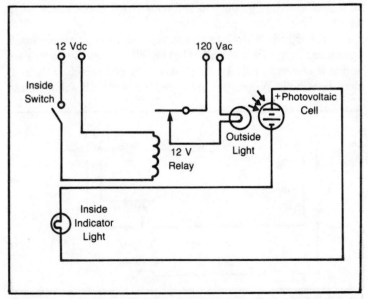

Fig. 3-4. A better remote indication can be achieved with a true output sensor device.

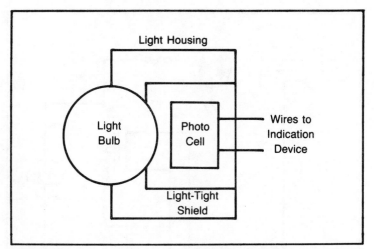

Fig. 3-5. The photocell used as a sensor must be shielded from any external light to prevent false indications.

a voltage and turn on the indicator lamp. For this system to work, the photocell must be shielded from any outside light, as shown in Fig. 3-5.

PROJECT 2—TRIAC REMOTE CONTROL

Another approach to remote switching control of lights, or ac-powered appliances is shown in Fig. 3-6. A triac and a transformer are used as switching elements. The complete parts list is given in Table 3-1.

The remote switch is used to short out the secondary (6.3 volt) winding of the transformer. This causes a high current to flow through the primary (120 volt) winding, which actuates the triac and energizes the load. Once the triac starts conducting, current will stop flowing through the primary winding of the transformer. As a result, the winding is not likely to burn out.

Potentiometer R1 is a shunting resistor. A small magnetizing current will flow through the primary winding of the transformer, even when the remote switch in the secondary circuit is open. While quite small, this magnetizing current may be large enough to trigger the triac, if the shunt resistance was not present. R1 should be adjusted for the highest resistance that will not cause false triggering.

Because of the amount of power flowing through this part of the circuit, an ordinary light-duty potentiometer can not be used

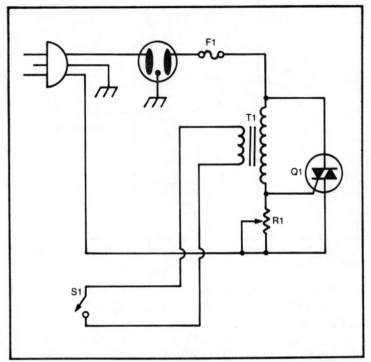

Fig. 3-6. A triac can be used for remote control of lights, or low-power ac devices.

for R1. This component should be rated for at least 2 watts.

To prevent damage from overheating, a heat sink should be used on the triac. A 3 × 3 × 1/16-inch cooling fin (copper or aluminum) should be adequate for the GE-X12 specified.

Note that a five amp "fast-blow" fuse is shown in the schematic. Do not under any circumstances omit this component. Do not use a larger fuse, or a "slow-blow" type fuse. Because only an extremely tiny current flows to the remote switch, very light-duty bell wire may be used between the controlled device and the remote controller. The chief advantage of this circuit is no power supply is needed at the remote location.

Table 3-1. Parts List for the Triac Remote Controller Circuit of Fig. 3-6.

Q1	GE-X12 (or similar) Triac
T1	Power transformer—secondary 6.3 V, 1 A
R1	50-Ω 2-W potentiometer
F1	5-A fuse and holder (3AG type)

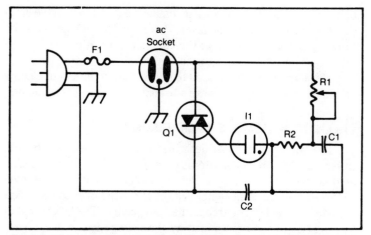

Fig. 3-7. While not a true remote control device, this simple light dimmer circuit can be a nice addition to a control system.

PROJECT 3—LIGHT DIMMER

While this project is not truly a remote control or automation device, it is closely related. In addition, it will be used in the remote control project described in the next section.

Lamp dimmers are always popular projects. They permit you to adjust the amount of light to suit you. Brighter light would be suitable for reading, while a dimmer light might be desirable for a romantic dinner. A simple light dimmer circuit is shown in Fig. 3-7. The parts list is given in Table 3-2.

The load (light being driven) should not exceed 400 watts. A heat sink is not absolutely required for the triac in this project, but it certainly wouldn't hurt, and could prevent premature circuit failure. Potentiometer R1 is used to control the amount of power reaching the socket, and therefore, the brightness of the lamp plugged into the socket.

There is a minor compromise involved in this circuit. The neon

Table 3-2. Parts List for the Light-Dimmer Circuit of Fig. 3-7.

Q1	RCA 40502 (or similar) Triac
I1	NE-2 Neon lamp
R1	50 kΩ potentiometer
R2	15 kΩ 1/2-W resistor
C1, C2	0.068 μF 250 V capacitor
F1	1-A fuse and holder (3AG type)

bulb will not trip the triac until it conducts enough to turn the lamp on at a moderately bright level. Potentiometer R1 needs to be turned past this point to turn the lamp on. Then it can be backed off to a dimmer glow, if desired.

This circuit should be used to adjust the brightness of electrical lamps only. Do not try to use it to control the speed of ac motors.

PROJECT 4—REMOTE LAMP DIMMER

The lamp dimmer just described is modified for remote control in Fig. 3-8. An optoisolator is used. A small dc voltage is generated at the remote location. Potentiometer R1 controls the level of this dc voltage. The signal voltage is carried over the connecting wires to the light source in the optoisolator. The brightness of this light source is determined by the voltage fed to it.

The light source and a photoresistor are enclosed in a light-

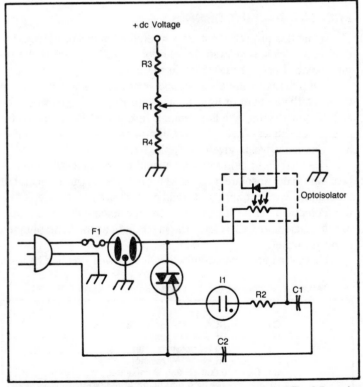

Fig. 3-8. By adding an optoisolator, the light dimmer circuit of Fig. 3-7 can be adapted for remote control.

tight housing. Only light from the internal light source reaches the photoresistor. Therefore, its resistance is proportional to the brightness of the internal light source, which is dependent on the dc control voltage.

The photoresistor of the optoisolator takes the place of the potentiometer in Fig. 3-7. Otherwise, the circuit functions in exactly the same way as before, but under remote control.

PROJECT 5—MULTIPLE LIGHT CONTROLLER

So far the remote control projects we have described in this chapter have been designed to control just a single light or ac socket.

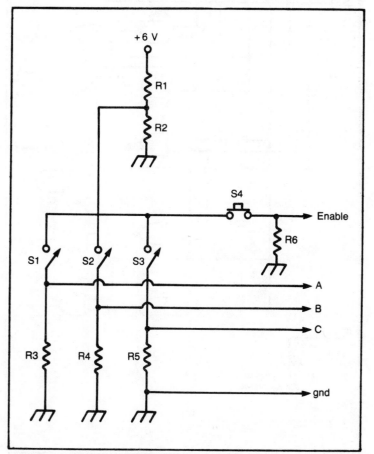

Fig. 3-9. This is the remote controller section of the multiple light controller project.

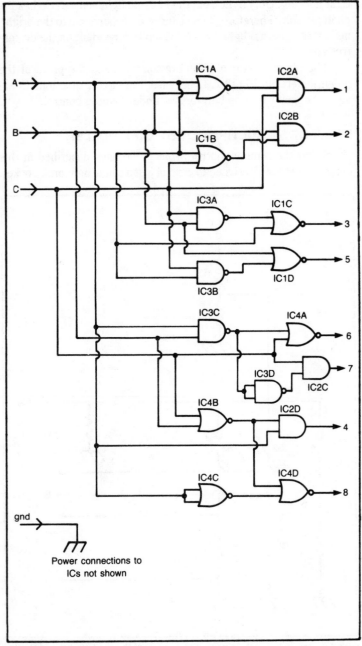

Fig. 3-10. The digital data in the multiple light controller project is received and decoded by this circuit.

44

In some applications we may want individual control over several different devices.

Of course, we could just build a number of independent circuits of the type already discussed, but that would be rather inelegant at best. It could also be unnecessarily expensive. A better solution is illustrated in Figs. 3-9, 3-10, and 3-11. The schematic is broken into three parts for clarity. The circuit is not as complicated as it may appear. The parts list for this multiple light controller project is given in Table 3-3.

Figure 3-9 shows the remote controller section. The receiver/decoder section is shown in Fig. 3-10. Finally, the output switching circuit is shown in Fig. 3-11. This last section is repeated for each individual ac socket to be controlled.

As the system is set up here, five control lines between the controller and the controlled devices can operate up to eight independent output devices. The signal lines are configured as follows:

☐ 1 = common (ground)
☐ 2 = enable
☐ 3, 4, 5 = encoded digital data

When an enable signal (logic 1 on the ENABLE line) is received

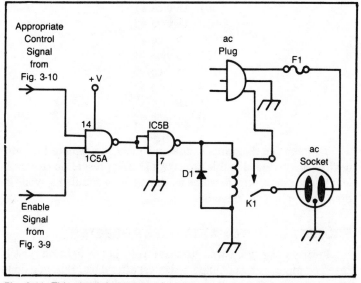

Fig. 3-11. This circuit is repeated for each ac device to be controlled by the multiple light controller project.

IC1, IC4	CD4001 quad NOR gate
IC2	CD4081 quad AND gate
IC3, IC5*	CD4011 quad NAND gate
D1*	1N4001 diode
K1*	Latching relay to suit load
F1*	Fuse to suit load
S1, S2, S3	SPST switch
S4	Normally Open SPST pushbutton
R1	820 Ω resistor
R2	4.7 kΩ resistor
R3-R6	1 kΩ resistor

*repeat for each of up to eight controlled devices

by the decoder, it looks at the current digital data (lines 3 - 5), and activates the appropriate latch. If the selected device was previously off, it will now be turned on. If it was already on, the new activation process will turn it off.

The eight controlled devices are controlled by three digital (binary) bits, which are encoded as follows:

> 001 Device #1
> 010 Device #2
> 011 Device #3
> 100 Device #4
> 101 Device #5
> 110 Device #6
> 111 Device #7
> 000 Device #8

To keep the diagrams simple and clear, no remote indicator devices are included in this project. It should present no real problem to add some, which can be as simple or as detailed as your individual application demands.

PROJECT 6—AUTOMATED GUEST GREETER

Perhaps you don't want to leave your porch light on, just in case you might get an unexpected guest after dark. But, you don't want the guest to have to wait outside in the dark until you can answer the door. The circuit shown in Fig. 3-12 offers a clever solution. The parts list for this project is given in Table 3-4. When the doorbell is rung, the porch light will go on for a predetermined period of time.

Ordinarily, the doorbell is activated with a SPST switch. In this project, we replace the doorbell switch with a DPST (or DPDT) switch. One section (pole) of the switch is connected directly to the doorbell in the usual manner. The second half (pole) sends a trigger signal to a timer. When triggered, the timer's output goes high, activating the output relay for a period of time determined by resistor R1 and capacitor C1. The formula for the time period is:

$$T = 1.1 \, RC$$

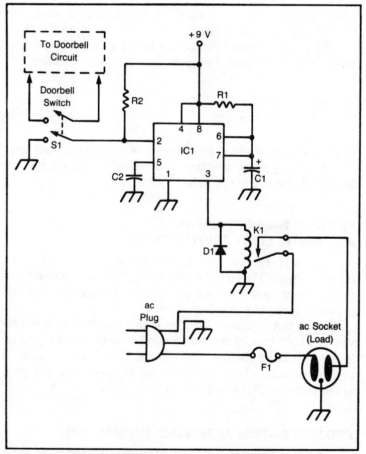

Fig. 3-12. This circuit will automatically turn on a light when the doorbell is rung.

47

```
IC1    555 timer
D1     1N4002 diode
K1     Relay to suit load
F1     Fuse to suit load
S1     Normally Open DPST momentary push-button (doorbell switch—
          see text)
C1     250 μF 35 V electrolytic capacitor (see text)
C2     0.01 μF capacitor
R1     1 MΩ resistor (see text)
R2     10 kΩ resistor
```

where T is the time in seconds. R1 is the resistance in ohms, and C1 is the capacitance in farads.

For this application, I think a time period of four to five minutes would probably be best. I suggest these component values:

R1 = 1 Meg (1,000,000 ohms)
C1 = 250 μF

which give a time period of 275 seconds, or about 4.6 minutes.

Of course, you can substitute other values for these components to allow different time periods.

PROJECT 7—PHOTOSENSITIVE AUTOMATIC LIGHT SWITCHING

Naturally, there isn't much point in leaving a porch light on during daytime. The circuit shown in Fig. 3-13 will automatically turn the light on at dusk and off at dawn. The parts list for this project is given in Table 3-5.

Notice that a timer is included in this circuit. This is to prevent the light from blinking on and off in response to a passing cloud, or moving shadow. The timer's delay is set for about 2 minutes (actually 112 seconds) with the component values given in the parts list (R1 = 680 kΩ, C1 = 150 μF).

PROJECT 8—TIME ACTIVATED AUTOMATION

Another popular approach to automation is to have the lights

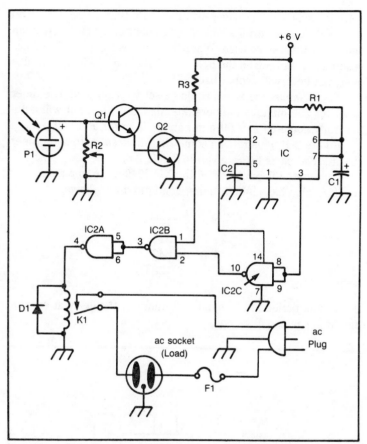

Fig. 3-13. Lights can automatically be turned on when it is dark with this circuit.

**Table 3-5. Parts List for the Photosensitive
Automatic Light Switcher Circuit of Fig. 3-13.**

IC1	555 timer
IC2	CD4011 quad NAND gate
Q1, Q2	NPN transistor (2N2222 or similar)
D1	1N4002 diode
P1	Photocell
K1	Ac relay to suit load
F1	Fuse to suit load
C1	150 μF 25 V electrolytic capacitor (see text)
C2	0.01 μF capacitor
R1	680 kΩ resistor (see text)
R2	5 kΩ potentiometer (sensitivity)
R3	100 kΩ resistor

automatically switch on and off at specific times. One way to do this is illustrated in Fig. 3-14. Any 24-hour clock circuit with an alarm function can be used. When the alarm is triggered, the timer is activated, turning on the light. After the timer's delay period is over, the light will switch back off.

For example, the alarm could be set for 7:00 p.m. The timer is set for 200 minutes (3 hours, 20 minutes). The light will automatically come on at 7:00 p.m., and will go off at 10:20 p.m.

Figure 3-15 illustrates a somewhat different automatic timer circuit. The parts list is given in Table 3-6.

This circuit is built around the XR-2240 programmable timer IC. This chip has eight outputs, configured as follows:

1T	16T
2T	32T
4T	64T
8T	128T

If the time period (T) is equal to 3 minutes, the delay at each of the output pins will be equal to:

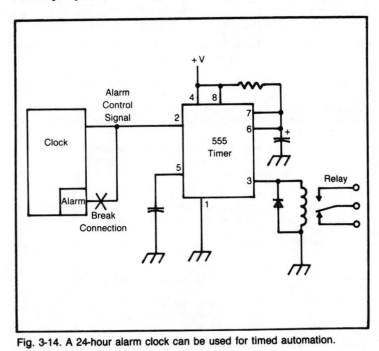

Fig. 3-14. A 24-hour alarm clock can be used for timed automation.

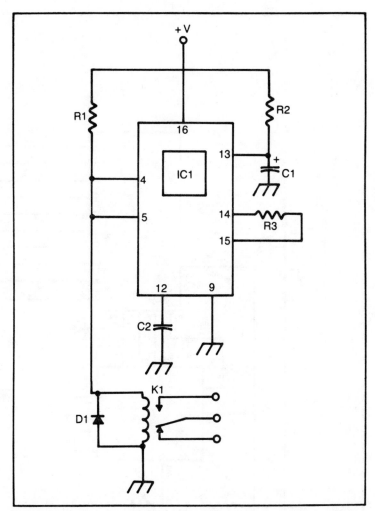

Fig. 3-15. This 24-hour timer automation circuit is built around the XR2240 programmable timer IC.

<table>
<tr><td rowspan="8">**Table 3-6.**
Parts List for the
Automatic Timer
Circuit of Fig. 3-15.</td><td>IC1</td><td>XR2240 programmable timer</td></tr>
<tr><td>D1</td><td>1N4002 diode</td></tr>
<tr><td>K1</td><td>Relay to suit application</td></tr>
<tr><td>C1</td><td>500 μF 35 V electrolytic capacitor</td></tr>
<tr><td>C2</td><td>0.01 μF capacitor</td></tr>
<tr><td>R1</td><td>10 kΩ resistor</td></tr>
<tr><td>R2</td><td>120 kΩ resistor</td></tr>
<tr><td>R3</td><td>22 kΩ resistor</td></tr>
</table>

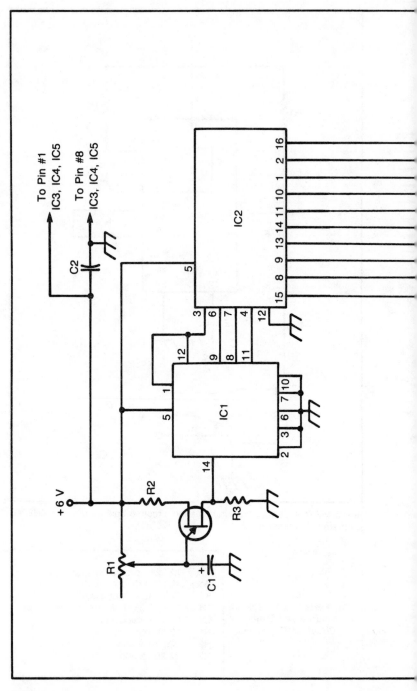

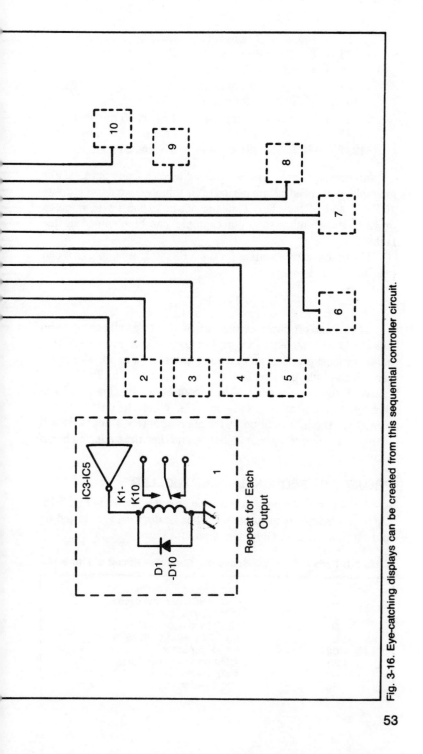

Fig. 3-16. Eye-catching displays can be created from this sequential controller circuit.

53

$$1T = 1 \times 3 = 3 \text{ minutes}$$
$$2T = 2 \times 3 = 6 \text{ minutes}$$
$$4T = 4 \times 3 = 12 \text{ minutes}$$
$$8T = 8 \times 3 = 24 \text{ minutes}$$
$$16T = 16 \times 3 = 48 \text{ minutes}$$
$$32T = 32 \times 3 = 96 \text{ minutes} = 1 \text{ hour, } 36 \text{ minutes}$$
$$64T = 64 \times 3 = 192 \text{ minutes} = 3 \text{ hours, } 12 \text{ minutes}$$
$$128T = 128 \times 3 = 384 \text{ minutes} = 6 \text{ hours, } 24 \text{ minutes}$$

Intermediate times can be obtained by combining outputs. For example, if we need a time period of 57 minutes, we'd use outputs 16T, 2T, and 1T together. Time periods up to 255 T (765 minutes or 12 hours, 45 minutes in our example) can be obtained in this fashion.

The time period equation for the XR2240 is as simple as it can possibly be. It is simply:

$$T = RC$$

The on and off times for this circuit won't be quite as neat and precise as with an actual clock, but they will be more than adequate for most practical automation purposes. After all, who really cares if the light goes on at 6:57 or 7:02, instead of 7:00?

With the component values shown here, the timer will run through approximately a 24-hour cycle. When the circuit is first turned on, the light will be lit for approximately 4 hours. It will then be turned off for about 20 hours, and then the cycle will begin again.

PROJECT 9—SEQUENTIAL CONTROLLER

A rather novel type of automation circuit is shown in Fig. 3-16. Up to ten independent lights (or other ac devices) are turned on and off in sequence. Only one is on at a time.

Table 3-7. Parts List for the Sequential Controller Circuit of Fig. 3-16.

IC1	74C90 decade counter
IC2	74C41 BCD-decimal decoder
IC3, IC4, IC5	CD4049 hex inverter
Q1	UJT (2N4891 or similar)
C1	5 μF 25 V electrolytic capacitor
C2	0.1 μF capacitor
R1	1 MΩ potentiometer (rate)
R2	1 kΩ resistor
R3	100 Ω resistor

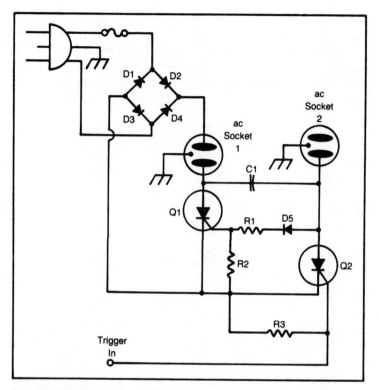

Fig. 3-17. This is the circuit for the cross-fader project.

While not suitable for applications such as the porch light situations discussed with the last few projects, this circuit can be useful, especially as an eye-catching display or warning device. Fairly short delay times should be used for such applications. The parts list for this project is given in Table 3-7.

PROJECT 10—CROSS-FADER

Another unusual automation circuit is shown in Fig. 3-17. The

Table 3-8. Parts List for the Cross-Fader Circuit of Fig. 3-17.

Q1, Q2	C106B (or similar) SCR
D1-D5	1N4003 diode
R1	47 kΩ resistor
R2, R3	4.7 kΩ resistor
C1	0.5 μF 250 V capacitor
F1	2-A fuse and holder (3AG type)

55

parts list is given in Table 3-8.

This circuit is a cross-fader between two lights. One light will gradually be faded down to full off, as the other one is faded up to full on. This circuit should not be used for anything except lighting. Do not under any circumstances attempt to drive an ac motor with this circuit. Each of the two lighting loads should not exceed 100 watts.

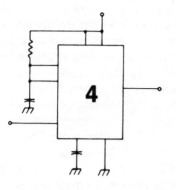

Doors and Windows

I N THIS CHAPTER WE WILL EXPLORE THE CONTROL OF DOORS and windows. The techniques described in this chapter can also be applied to many other applications. As always, apply ample doses of imagination.

DOOR AND WINDOW INDICATORS

If we are going to control an entrance (such as a door or window), we absolutely need to know the condition of the entrance. Trying to open a door that's already open, or close a window that is already closed is not just futile, it could be dangerous, either to the control machinery, or any nearby people, or both. Not having an indication device for a light could be inconvenient. For a controlled door or window it could be dangerous.

There are several approaches you could take to monitoring an entrance. The most basic and direct, of course, is to use one of the magnetic reed switches designed for this purpose. These switches come in two parts. One part, which is mounted on the moving door or window pane itself, contains a small permanent magnet. No electrical connections are made to this unit. It moves with the door or window.

The other section is mounted on the doorjamb or window frames, so that it is lined up with the magnet unit when the door or window is closed. This section contains a small magnetically-sensitive reed switch. Electrical connections are made to this stationary unit in the same way as for any other switch. When the door or window is shut, the magnetic field of the moving section activates the stationary switch unit. A typical installation is illustrated in Fig. 4-1.

Magnetic reed switches are available in both Normally Open (NO) and Normally Closed (NC) versions. The "normal" condition is defined as the state of the unactivated switch, away from the magnet. That is, for a NO switch, the switch is closed when the door or window is shut, or open when the door or window is opened. A NC switch works in just the reverse fashion.

These magnetic switches can be used in circuits in the same way as any SPST switch, so it is no problem to use them to activate any indication device you might choose.

Magnetic reed switches are widely marketed for use in bur-

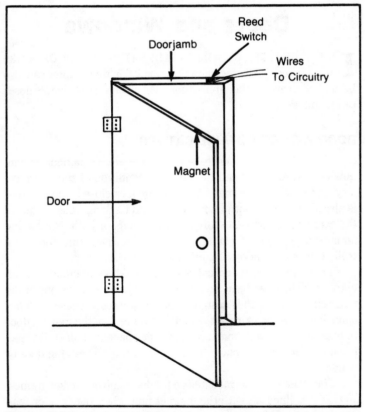

Fig. 4-1. This is a typical installation using a magnetic reed switch to monitor a door.

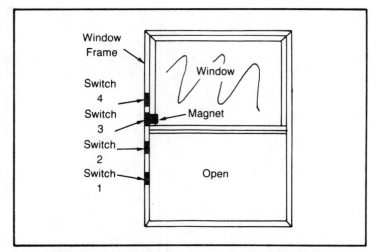

Fig. 4-2. Multiple switch units can monitor multiple window positions.

glar alarm systems, and are available from almost all electronics and hardware dealers.

Simple switches are fine for simple "yes - no" or "open - shut" indications. But in some applications, we might need more detailed information. For example, we might need to know how wide a door is opened. Is it fully open? Is it half open? A quarter of the way open? Three quarters?

One solution would be to mount multiple stationary switch units, so that the magnet comes into contact with each as the door or window moves through its range. A simple window installation is shown in Fig. 4-2.

Doors usually present more of a problem, because most of the door's movement is away from the doorjamb. One possible arrangement is shown in Fig. 4-3. An extension arm with several switch units mounted on it extends from the doorjamb, over the door. This may work in some cases, but it may be highly undesirable, impractical and/or dangerous in others.

If only coarse resolution is required, you may be able to get away with a multiple switch system. But if more than three or four positions are monitored, the system rapidly becomes unwieldy and expensive. In addition, in this system no allowance is made for the door or window to be positioned between monitoring points. In the example shown in Fig. 4-4, all of the switches would be open. The indicator devices would have no idea of what the window's position might be. Obviously, this is not good.

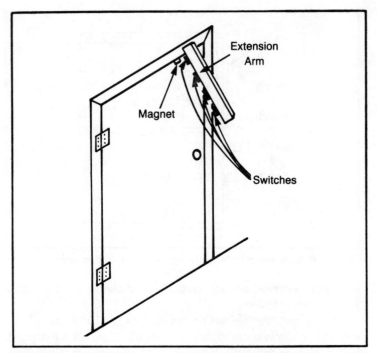

Fig. 4-3. An extension arm over a doorway can be used to monitor various positions.

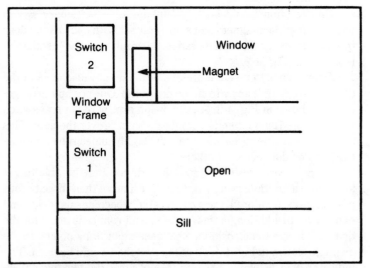

Fig. 4-4. The multiple switch unit monitoring system runs into problems with in-between positions.

In many practical applications, a true continuous monitoring system must be devised. One convenient solution for doors is illustrated in Fig. 4-5. An insulated cord is attached to the moving edge of the door. At the end of the cord is a length of conductive wire. The phosphor bronze wire sold in hardware stores for hanging pictures will do the job nicely. The cord and wire terminates with a weight.

The wire passes through a series of conductive rings, or eyelets. As the door moves, the weight is raised and lowered. In its highest position, the conductive wire passes through all of the rings. As the weight drops due to the movement of the door, the insulated section of the cord passes through some of the rings.

Two silicon diodes are connected between each pair of rings. The entire string of diodes is forward biased. When the conductive wire passes through a pair of rings, the associated diodes will be shorted out. When the insulated cord passes through one or more

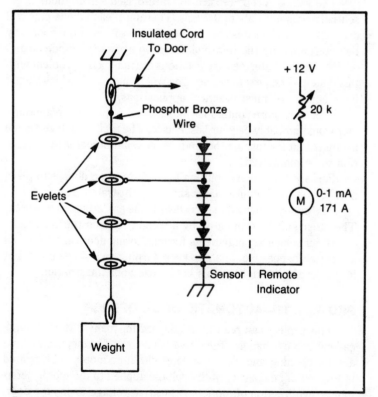

Fig. 4-5. A diode string can be used to monitor a door's position.

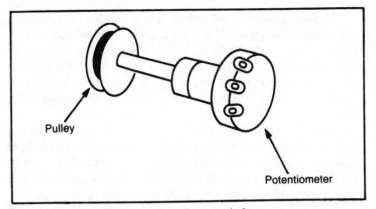

Fig. 4-6. Pulley mounted on a potentiometer shaft.

rings, some of the diodes will be an effective part of the monitoring circuit.

The voltage drop across a forward-biased silicon diode is essentially constant—about 0.7 volt. Therefore, each diode pair will drop 1.4 volt unless it is shorted out. The position of the door may be determined by the total voltage drop across the diode string.

Notice that intermediate positions are not such a problem with this system. The next lower position will be indicated, which should be adequate for most practical applications.

If an even more continuous indication is required, a potentiometer would probably be your best choice. The trick is to devise some arrangement for turning the shaft of the potentiometer by the motion to be monitored.

Perhaps the easiest solution for monitoring a door is to place a pulley on the potentiometer shaft, as illustrated in Fig. 4-6.

The pulley is turned by a cord with one end attached to a door. The other end is terminated by a weight to keep the cord taut.

Other sensor arrangements for monitoring doors and windows are certainly possible. I hate to keep harping on a single point, but it is relevant throughout this book—use your imagination.

PROJECT 11—AUTOMATIC DOOR OPENER

This project can readily be adapted for many different applications, just by changing the activating device. The mechanical linkage for opening and closing a door with a dc motor is illustrated in Fig. 4-7. The polarity of the voltage applied to the motor determines the direction of motion. A positive voltage opens the door, and a negative voltage closes it.

The control circuitry is shown in Fig. 4-8. When the switch is closed, the door is opened (a positive polarity voltage is applied to the motor). The door will remain open as long as the switch is held closed. Once the switch is released, the timer is triggered, holding the door open for a period determined by capacitor C1, resistor R1, and potentiometer R2. The following component values are suggested:

C1	100 μF
R1	18 kΩ
R2	50 kΩ potentiometer

By adjusting the potentiometer, the time delay can be anything from about 20 seconds to approximately 75 seconds.

After the timer completes its cycle, the reverse voltage is fed to the motor, closing the door. Notice that a diode string indicator (as shown in Fig. 4-5) is used. When the door is fully open, the posi-

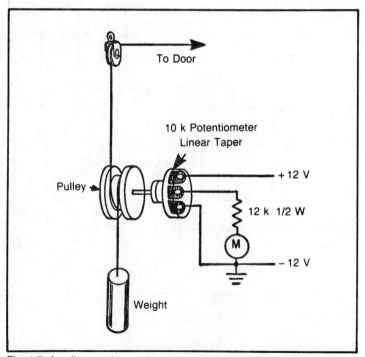

Fig. 4-7. A pulley can be used to mechanically control a potentiometer.

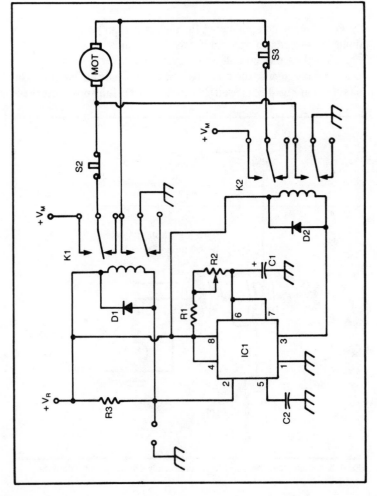

Fig. 4-8. The control circuitry for an automatic door.

Table 4-1. Parts List for the Automatic Door Opener (Fig. 4-8).

IC1	555 timer
D1, D2	1N4002 diode
K1, K2	DPDT dc relay to suit motor
MOT	Dc motor
S1	Normally-Open SPST switch (see text)
S2	Normally-Closed SPST snap action switch (positioned so it opens when the door is fully opened)
S3	Normally-Closed SPST snap action switch (positioned so it opens when the door is fully closed)
C1	100 μF 35 V electrolytic capacitor (see text)
C2	0.01 μF capacitor
R1	18 kΩ resistor (see text)
R2	50 kΩ potentiometer (see text)
R3	100 kΩ resistor

tive voltage is cut off from the motor. Similarly, when the door is fully closed, no additional negative voltage will be fed to the motor. This prevents damage to the motor and the mechanical linkage system. The parts list for this automatic door opener circuit is shown in Table 4-1.

Table 4-2. Parts List for the Complete Entry Alarm System (Fig. 4-9).

IC1	CD4001 quad NOR gate
IC2	CD4049 hex inverter
IC3	CD4011 quad NAND gate
Q1	NPN transistor (2N2222 or similar)
D1-D6	1N914 diode
D7	1N4002 diode
K1	Relay to suit alarm device
S1, S2, S3, S6, S8	Normally-Open SPST switches
S4, S5, S7	Normally-Closed SPST switches
C1, C2, C4, C5, C6, C10, C11, C12, C13	0.01 μF capacitor
C3, C7, C8	0.1 μF capacitor
C9, C15	10 μF 35 volt electrolytic capacitor
C14	50 μF 35 volt electrolytic capacitor
R1, R2, R4, R5, R11, R13, R14	1 MΩ resistor
R3, R6, R7, R9, R10, R12	100 kΩ resistor
R8, R15, R17	3.3 MΩ resistor
R16	10 kΩ resistor

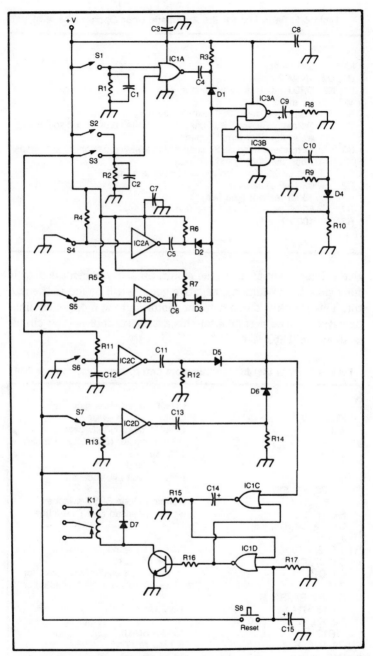

Fig. 4-9. The sensors described in this chapter can be used for a complete entry alarm system.

66

Almost any switching device can be used, depending on the desired application. A remotely located switch permits remote control. A push-button on the doorjamb could be used. A pressure sensitive switch under a mat in front of the door could also be used. When someone steps on the mat, the door will automatically open, just like the automated doors at the supermarket.

While I can't think of any practical application, this circuit could be activated by a timer or clock of some type.

PROJECT 12—COMPLETE ENTRY ALARM SYSTEM

An alarm system might not seem entirely appropriate for a book on remote control and automation projects, but it is related. This project illustrates additional uses for the door and window monitors presented earlier in this chapter. Also, this circuitry could be adapted for other control projects.

The circuit is illustrated in Fig. 4-9. The parts list is given in Table 4-2. Notice that both NO and NC switches are supported. Additional stages may be added as desired to monitor as many entrances as you need. Switches S1 through S5 will turn on the alarm after a delay of approximately 30 seconds. Switches S6 and S7 trigger the alarm instantly. Once triggered, the alarm may be reset by momentarily closing the RESET switch (S8).

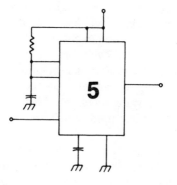

Temperature Control

R EMOTE CONTROL, AND ESPECIALLY AUTOMATION TECH-
niques can be very useful for providing a more comfortable
environment. Probably the most widespread form of environmental control is the control of temperature. A thermostat is an automatic device for controlling heating and/or air conditioning
equipment. A thermostat can be a simple automated switch, or it
can be a highly sophisticated device, with plenty of special features.
This chapter offers several projects for automating temperature
control in a variety of ways.

TEMPERATURE SENSORS

There are several approaches to electrically monitoring temperature. The most commonly used temperature sensors in electronic circuits are thermocouples, diodes, and thermistors. We will
briefly discuss each of these in the next few pages.

Thermocouples

Perhaps the simplest electrical temperature sensor is the ther-
mocouple. It consists of nothing more than a junction of two wires
made of different metals. When the junction is heated, a voltage
proportional to the applied temperature is developed across the
junction. This is known as the *Seebeck effect*. The developed voltage can then be measured and used to control many different circuits, as desired.

Diode Temperature Sensors

A standard silicon diode can also be used as a temperature sensor. If a small forward bias is applied to the diode, the voltage drop across the diode will respond to changes in temperature at a rate of about 1.25 mV (0.00125 volt) per degree Fahrenheit.

A simple diode temperature sensor circuit is illustrated in Fig. 5-1. If you are familiar with electronics theory, you should recognize this circuit as a variation on the Wheatstone bridge. Wheatstone bridges are widely used in measurement circuits of many different types.

The supply voltage for this circuit should be between +1 and +1.5 volt. Almost any silicon diode may be used in this type of application, including the popular and inexpensive 1N914 diode.

Thermistor

In modern circuits, probably the most popular type of temperature sensor is the thermistor, or *therm*al res*istor*. All resistance elements are temperature sensitive to some extent. A thermistor is specifically designed to emphasize the effects of temperature on

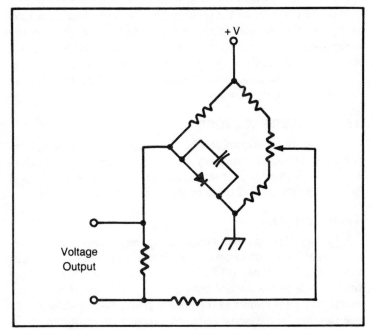

Fig. 5-1. A diode can be used as a simple temperature sensor.

70

the component's resistance in a predictable manner.

There are two types of thermistors—NTC and PTC. NTC thermistors, which are the more common, have a *negative temperature coefficient*. This means that resistance decreases as temperature increases. PTC thermistors, on the other hand, have a *positive temperature coefficient*, and operate in the opposite manner—resistance increases as the temperature increases. Both types can be useful in various applications.

Thermistors are very handy for temperature sensing applications, but they have their definite limitations. In most cases, the temperature-resistance curves are not linear. Temperature measurement scales (Fahrenheit and Celsius), however, are linear systems. This means it is difficult to design a thermistor-based circuit that is linear over a wide range. Difficult, but not entirely impossible. Many electronic thermometer circuits have been designed around thermistors.

NTC thermistors can exhibit negative resistance characteristics under some circumstances, leading to thermal runaway, and possible self-destruction of the thermistor.

Remember that Ohm's law specifies the interrelationships of resistance, current, and voltage:

$$R = E/I$$
$$E = RI$$
$$I = E/R$$

where R is the resistance, I is the current, and E is the voltage.

Consider the simple series circuit of Fig. 5-2. A NTC thermistor is in series with a fixed resistor. For simplicity, we will ignore the thermal drift of the fixed resistance. We will assume the applied voltage is 10 volts, and the fixed resistance is 1 kΩ (1000 ohms). The resistance of the thermistor, of course, is dependent on the temperature. The higher the temperature, the lower the resistance, because this is a NTC device.

At some temperature, the thermistor will have a resistance of 10 kΩ (10,000 ohms). The total resistance of the circuit is 11 kΩ (1 kΩ + 10 kΩ). Therefore, the current flowing through the circuit will be equal to:

$$I = E/R = 10/11000 \approx 0.00091 \text{ amp} = 0.91 \text{ mA}$$

The voltage drop across the fixed resistance is approximately equal to:

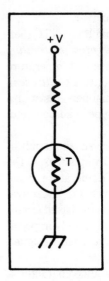

Fig. 5-2. A NTC thermistor can be susceptible to thermal runaway.

$$E = RI = 1000 \times 0.00091 \approx 0.91 \text{ volts}$$

And the thermistor will drop about:

$$E = RI = 10000 \times 0.00091 \approx 9.1 \text{ volts}$$

Because of the negative temperature coefficient, the resistance of the thermistor will drop as the ambient temperature increases. At some higher temperature, the thermistor's resistance will be 1 kΩ (1000 ohms), making the total resistance in the circuit equal to 2000 ohms. Now the current flowing through the circuit is about:

$$I = 10/2000 = 0.005 \text{ amp} = 5 \text{ mA}$$

Note that the current increases with the temperature.

The voltage drop across the two resistances will be equal, because of their equal values:

$$E = 1000 \times 0.005 = 5 \text{ volts}$$

What do these two examples tell us? As the temperature increases, the current flow and the voltage drop across the thermistor also increases. So what?

Well, what happens to the voltage dropped across a resistance element? It is dissipated as heat. The higher the voltage drop, the greater the heat produced. Therefore, as the ambient temperature increases, the resistance of the thermistor drops, and the voltage dropped across its increases. The voltage drop will cause the thermistor to generate heat. Obviously, this increases the temperature sensed by the component, further reducing its resistance, which increases the voltage dropped across it, increasing the generated heat, and so on and so on.

As long as the current is relatively small, this self-heating effect probably won't be too terribly significant. It may result in a slight loss in accuracy, but no real harm will be done. However, when large currents flow through a NTC thermistor, the effect can be quite large, resulting in thermal runaway. The sensed temperature will become totally meaningless, and the circuitry could be damaged from overheating.

PTC thermistors are not subject to thermal runaway. As the temperature increases, so does the resistance, reducing the voltage drop, thereby decreasing the amount of heat generated. In fact, PTC thermistors are often used as temperature regulators. When power is applied, the thermistor will heat itself until a stable level is reached. A fairly constant temperature will be maintained despite any minor changes in the ambient temperature or thermal load.

Thermistors are not suited for monitoring rapid temperature fluctuations. If a thermistor is moved from one temperature extreme to another, it cannot respond instantly, because of inertia. The mass of the thermistor's body must heat up or cool down to match the new ambient temperature. Obviously, this takes a finite amount of time. It should be equally obvious that the larger the thermistor's body, the greater the time required for it to respond to a change in ambient temperature. For a small disc or bead thermistor, the response time will typically be just a few seconds. Large thermistors, of course, will have a longer response time. Some heavy-duty thermistors have a body that is one-inch in diameter. These units might require up to two minutes to respond to a change in the ambient temperature.

PROBE ASSEMBLIES

In most applications, the temperature sensing element should be housed in some kind of protective probe assembly. This is especially true if the temperature of a liquid is to be measured. Any conductive liquid (such as water) could shunt out the connecting leads, resulting in false readings. Nonconductive liquids could soften the epoxy protecting the delicate active element. Corrosive liquids could damage the leads and/or the sensor body.

Except for hermetically sealed glass body thermistors, liquid can creep inside the component itself, seeping through minute openings between the leads and the epoxy coating. This could result in misreadings, and eventual corrosion of the sensing element.

While these problems are most prevalent when the sensors are immersed in a liquid, they can show up in other applications too. Even measuring air temperature could be problematic if the humidity is high. Also, an unshielded temperature sensor could be cooled by passing winds. This is desirable, of course, if you want to monitor the wind chill. But if you're interested in the actual temperature, it could be a significant problem. High winds, or contact with other objects could damage a delicate temperature sensor.

The solution to all these problems is not particularly difficult. We simply have to house the sensor in some sort of probe assembly. A typical probe housing is illustrated in Fig. 5-3.

The probe itself is usually a tube of glass or stainless steel, welded shut at one end. A temperature insulating handle is often placed on the opposite end of the probe. The sensor is inserted in the tip of the probe. Often a bit of epoxy will be used to improve mechanical strength, and to improve the thermal contact between the sensor and the external probe housing.

The connecting leads are soldered to the sensor and brought out through the back end of the probe. Generally, another dab of

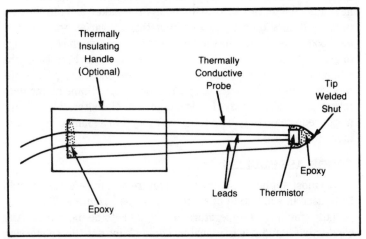

Fig. 5-3. For most practical applications, the temperature sensor should be enclosed in a probe housing.

epoxy here would be a good idea, to relieve strain on the connecting wires, and to prevent them from being pulled free of the sensor.

For most purposes, a "straight stick" probe, as shown in Fig. 5-3 will do the job just fine. For more permanent setups, a threaded probe could be screwed into a socket or holder.

PROJECT 13—SIMPLE ELECTRONIC THERMOSTAT

A fairly simple electronic thermostat circuit for controlling an electric heating element is shown in Fig. 5-4. The parts list for this project is given in Table 5-1.

The heater load may be rated from 10 mA (0.01 amp) up to about 35 amperes. The triac should be selected to handle the appropriate amount of current. Similarly, the fuse size should be determined by the heater element. With larger heater elements, household type screw-in fuses might be used instead of the light-duty 3AG types found in most electronic circuits. Select the fuse rating conservatively. It is better to use a too small fuse than a too large one.

PROJECT 14—BOILER CONTROLLER

If you have an oil based hot-water heater, this project could save you quite a bit in fuel bills.

In hot-water heaters fueled by oil, the system's water temperature is controlled by a device called an aquastat. Usually there are manual adjustments for water temperature and circulator control. Typically, the circulator is set about 20° lower than the water temperature.

Greatest fuel efficiency can be achieved by using a somewhat lower water temperature setting in summer than in winter. Good "rule of thumb" values are about 180° for winter, and 160° for summer.

Notice that with these recommended values, the water temperature varies inversely with the outside temperature. This project monitors the outside temperature, and automatically adjusts the water temperature accordingly. For best results, the circulator control should be set to about 125° to 135°. Rather than settling for a seasonal approximation, the water heater will respond directly to changes in the weather, maximizing fuel efficiency.

The input section of this project is shown in Fig. 5-5, and the output section is shown in Fig. 5-6. The project is split into two sections just to make the schematics a little easier to work with.

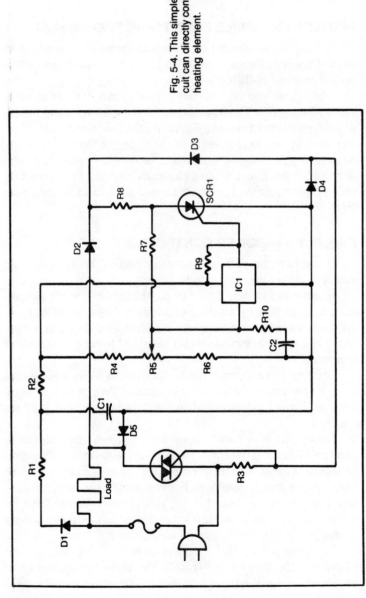

Fig. 5-4. This simple thermostat circuit can directly control an electrical heating element.

Table 5-1. Parts List for the Simple Electronic Thermostat Project (Fig. 5-4).

IC1	LM3911
Q1	Triac (see text)
SCR1	2N5064 (or similar)
D1-D5	1N4004 (or similar)
C1	0.5 μF 200 V capacitor
C2	0.05 μF capacitor
R1	3.3 kΩ resistor
R2	82 kΩ resistor
R3	27 Ω resistor
R4, R6	16.5 kΩ 2 % wirewound resistor
R5	10 kΩ potentiometer
R7	10 MΩ resistor
R8	100 Ω resistor
R9	68 kΩ resistor
R10	1.5 MΩ resistor

All resistors should be 1/2 watt or better.

The parts list for the entire project is given in Table 5-2.

Switch S1 permits the user to select between automatic and manual (override) modes. The relay's (K1) switch contacts are wired in series with the boiler's aquastat. The lower and upper temperature limits are set via potentiometers R32 and R25 respectively. The other trimpots are for calibration purposes. The calibration procedure is as follows:

☐ Set to automatic mode.
☐ Adjust R13 for 4.6 volts at pin #5 of IC2.
☐ Adjust R18 for 4.6 volts at pin #12 of IC2.
☐ Adjust R5 so that the voltage between pins #10 (−) and #5 (+) corresponds to the measured temperature. (1° F = 10 mV) (water monitor sensor).
☐ Adjust R1 so that the voltage between pins #12 (−) and #3 corresponds to the measured temperature. (1° F = 10 mV) (air monitor sensor).

These tests are best performed with both sensors together, at the same temperature, along with an accurate reference thermometer. Place the two sensors and the thermometer in a dry, even temperature location that is protected from significant passing breezes.

☐ Measure the output (pin #6) of IC3. This voltage should correspond to the measured voltage × 2 (1° F = 0.2 volt).

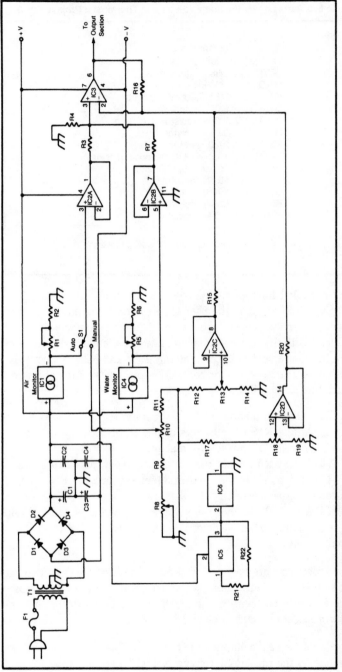

Fig. 5-5. This is the input section of an economical boiler-controller circuit.

78

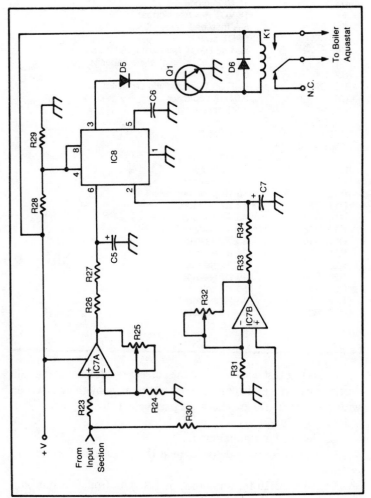

Fig. 5-6. The boiler-controller project circuit is completed here.

79

Table 5-2. Parts List for the Boiler Controller Circuit (Figs. 5-5 and 5-6).

IC1, IC4	AD590 temperature sensor
IC2	LM324 quad op amp
IC3	741 op amp
IC5	LM334 constant current source
IC6	6.9 V temperature stabilized reference voltage
IC7	747 dual op amp
IC8	555 timer
Q1	NPN transistor (Radio Shack RS2017 or similar)
D1-D4	1N4002 diode
D5	1N1202 diode
D6	1N4004 diode
T1	18-VCT 2-A transformer
F1	5-A fuse and holder (3AG)
S1	SPDT switch
K1	12-Vdc DPDT relay with 160-Ω coil
C1, C3	1000 μF 50 V electrolytic capacitor
C2, C4	0.1 μF capacitor
C5, C7	5 μF 35 V electrolytic capacitor
C6	0.01 μF capacitor
R1, R5	5 kΩ trimpot
R2, R6, R24, R28, R31	15 kΩ resistor
R3, R4, R7 R15, R16, R20	100 kΩ resistor
R8	20 kΩ trimpot
R9	33 kΩ resistor
R10	10 kΩ potentiometer
R11, R29	12 kΩ resistor
R12, R17	4.2 kΩ resistor
R13, R18	1.5 kΩ trimpot
R14, R19	8.2 kΩ resistor
R21	27 Ω resistor
R22	4.7 Ω resistor
R23, R30	10 kΩ resistor
R25, R32	50 kΩ potentiometer
R26, R33	18 kΩ resistor
R27, R34	2.2 kΩ resistor

If this last test does not give the correct results, begin the calibration over. If it still does not work out right, something is wrong with the circuit. Doublecheck all part values.

☐ Set S1 for manual mode.

☐ Adjust R8 until the voltage at the junction of R9 and R10 is 4.6 volts.

☐ Adjust R10 for an output of 1.8 volts from IC3 (pin #6).

PROJECT 15—TEMPERATURE EQUALIZER

As Fig. 5-7 illustrates, a thermostat is a closed-loop type of automation circuit. This simply means that there is a continuous, circular path throughout the automation system. The thermostat monitors the room temperature and controls the furnace. The heat from the furnace changes the room temperature, which affects the thermostat. The input (room temperature) and output (heater) are interrelated, affecting each other directly. Because of this interrelationship between the input and the output, the closed-loop system can exhibit some instability or oscillation.

Consider what happens if the thermostat is positioned some distance from the heater duct and there is only limited air circulation in the room. The temperature in the room drops, so the thermostat asks the furnace to put out more heat. Because of the distance from the heater duct to the thermostat, it will be some time before the temperature at the thermostat is high enough for it to shut off the furnace. Part of the room will now be too hot.

When the furnace is finally turned off, the room will begin to cool, especially near any heat leaks, such as doors and windows. Let's assume these leaks are also a significant distance from the thermostat. Again it will be a considerable time before the thermostat can sense the drop in temperature. By this time, part of the room might be too cold.

You can see how the room's overall temperature oscillates from too hot to too cold, and back, without ever hitting a happy medium. You not only don't get the proper benefits of your heating system,

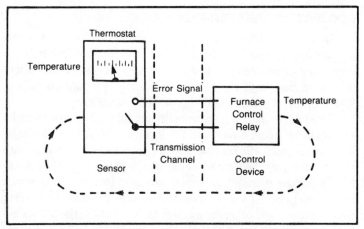

Fig. 5-7. A thermostat is a closed-loop type of automation circuit.

you will also tend to waste quite a bit of fuel or power with the unnecessary oscillations.

Of course, a partial solution is to position the thermostat close to the heating register and significant heat leaks. But the thermostat can still only monitor its own location in the room. Hot or cold spots could still develop in other parts of the room.

A better solution is to increase the motion of the air. Air motion will tend to stabilize the temperature. Warmer air can be moved into cold spots, or vice versa. A fan is a simple device for stimulating air motion. The circuit shown in Fig. 5-8 will control a fan in response to ambient temperature. A special purpose IC (LM3911) is used to sense the temperature. The parts list for this project is given in Table 5-3.

The relay is chosen so that its contacts will safely carry the current drawn by the fan. Similarly, fuse F2's value should be selected specifically for the fan to be used with the system. Typically, this fuse should not be greater than one or two amps, at the very most. Do not, under any circumstance, omit either of the fuses shown in the diagram.

The temperature that switches on the fan is determined by potentiometer R3. Its setting is best determined experimentally for maximum comfort.

Of course, a continuously running fan will stimulate air movement, but at a price of wasted power, and increased ambient noise. Moreover, it could result in chilly drafts in some parts of the room. With this circuit the fan will only be briefly turned on when it is specifically needed.

PROJECT 16—HEATER HUMIDIFIER

In winter months, heaters are put into heavy use, driving utility bills up and humidity down. Obviously, higher utility bills are something of concern to all of us. But why should we care about decreased humidity? For one thing, arid air is a poor conductor, which means a greater build up of static electricity.

The human body is also humidity sensitive. The most healthy environment would have humidity levels in the 30 to 50% range. In winter months, the house is sealed off, limited air exchange with the outdoors, and heating units dry up the humidity of the air. Often the indoor humidity in winter can drop to 10 to 20%, which is extremely dry. This can irritate sensitive membranes, leading to sore throats and other such ailments. In addition, the body's humidity sensitivity can make dry air in the 50° to 70° range seem

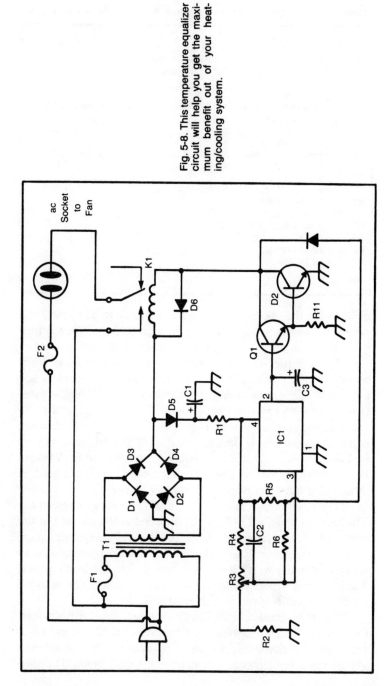

Fig. 5-8. This temperature equalizer circuit will help you get the maximum benefit out of your heating/cooling system.

Table 5-3. Parts List for the Temperature Equalizer Project (Fig. 5-8).

IC1	LM3911 Temperature Sensor Control IC
Q1, Q2	NPN transistor (2N2222 or similar)
D1-D6	1N4002 diode
D7	1N457 diode
K1	24-V relay (contacts current handling should be selected to suit driven fan)
T1	24-V 1/2-A transformer
F1	0.5-A fuse (3AG)
F2	Fuse (3AG) (value determined by driven fan)
C1	100 μF 100 V electrolytic capacitor
C2	0.1 μF 35 V capacitor
C3	5 μF 25 V electrolytic capacitor
R1	12 kΩ resistor
R2, R4	27 kΩ resistor
R3	5 kΩ potentiometer
R5	100 kΩ resistor
R6	10 MΩ resistor
R7	22 kΩ resistor

even colder than normal. Raising the humidity to 30 to 50% will permit a lower thermostat setting for a given degree of comfort.

This project is designed to add humidity to heated air. Before I get to the actual circuitry, let me voice a few warnings. When artificially adding humidity, you shouldn't go overboard and add too much. That can be as bad as too little. Humidity levels greater than about 60% can significantly increase discomfort, and make cold temperatures seem even colder. Also germs tend to thrive in moist air. Some people, having heard about the problems of winter low humidity, add so much artificial humidity that their homes become positively dank. They are doing more harm than good. A little added humidity is good. Too much is bad.

The circuit shown in Fig. 5-9 can add humidity to heated air. The sensor (again, a LM3911 IC) is placed in the air path of the heater's main vent (or vents). When the temperature exceeds a point set by potentiometer R3, a solenoid is activated, opening a spray nozzle. Since the water is sprayed directly into the heating vent, it immediately vaporizes, adding to the air humidity. The parts list for this project is given in Table 5-4.

The spray nozzle should eject a relatively fine mist of water, for easy and quick vaporization. Otherwise, you'll just get a wet heating vent. Suitable nozzles can be inexpensively purchased from almost any large hardware, or plumbing supply store. The sole-

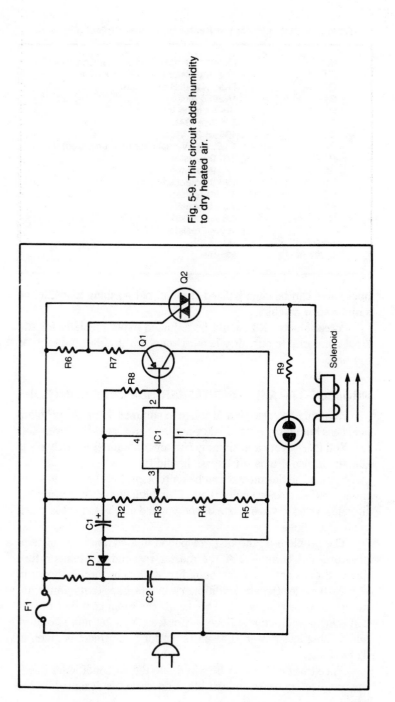

Fig. 5-9. This circuit adds humidity to dry heated air.

Table 5-4. Parts List for the Heater Humidifier Project (Fig. 5-9).

IC1	LM3911 Temperature Sensor Control IC
Q1	PNP transistor (2N3906 or similar)
Q2	Triac (T2302B or similar)
D1	1N2069 diode
I1	NE-2H neon lamp
F1	3-A fuse (3AG)
C1	100-μF 25 V capacitor
C2	1 μF, 200 V capacitor (non-polarized)
R1	270 Ω resistor
R2, R4, R9	27 kΩ resistor
R3	10 kΩ potentiometer
R5	4.7 kΩ resistor
R6	1.2 kΩ resistor
R7	1.8 kΩ resistor
R8	150 kΩ resistor
Solenoid	see text
Spray nozzle	see text

noid valve can be cannibalized from an old washing machine, or similar such machine.

Potentiometer R3 should be adjusted experimentally for the most comfortable humidity level. Do not set it either too high or too low.

PROJECT 17—AIR CONDITIONER HUMIDITY CONTROL

Humidity can also be a problem in summer. Here the problem is excess humidity, which makes hot temperatures seem even hotter. You feel sweaty and clammy. An air conditioner not only cools the air, it also drains off excess humidity.

Setting the thermostat can be a problem. In relatively low humidity, 80° can seem cooler than 77° in high humidity. Setting the thermostat too low is a waste of energy, and may result in too much cooling at times.

The problem is, the body responds to a combination of temperature and humidity. A thermostat responds to temperature alone. It does not sense the humidity at all. The circuit shown in Fig. 5-10 cycles the air conditioner's compressor to minimize humidity, and air stagnation. This keeps the room cool, but the air conditioner will actually have to run less. You get more comfort while using less power. The parts list for this project is given in Table 5-5.

Since this circuit must be wired into the air conditioner itself, the unit used must be compatible. This circuit is designed on the

**Table 5-5. Parts List for the Air
Conditioner Humidity Control Circuit (Fig. 5-10).**

IC1	7805 +5 V regulator IC
IC2, IC3, IC4	7555 timer IC
Q1, Q2	NPN transistor (2N2222 or similar)
D1-D4	1N4004 diode
D5	1N914 diode
D6, D7, D8	LED
K1, K2	DPDT relay (contacts selected to match controlled circuit)
C1	250 μF, 25 V electrolytic capacitor
C2, C4	10 μF 25 V tantalum capacitor
C3, C6, C9	0.01 μF capacitor
C5, C8	0.001 μF capacitor
C7	1000 μF, 10 V electrolytic capacitor
C10	500 μF, 10 V electrolytic capacitor
R1, R7, R8	27 kΩ resistor
R2	33 kΩ resistor
R3, R12, R13	10 MΩ resistor
R4, R14	4.7 kΩ resistor
R5, R15	3.3 kΩ resistor
R6, R16	1 kΩ resistor
R9	470 Ω resistor
R10	1 MΩ potentiometer
R11	220 kΩ resistor

assumption that the air conditioner uses 24-volt dc control circuitry.

Connections to the air conditioner's existing thermostat are indicated on the schematic diagram by small circles containing one of the following letters:

G
R
W
Y

These letters indicate a more or less standard color coding, outlined in Table 5-6. This table also indicates common labelling schemes used in many commercial air conditioner thermostats. The green wire should run to the fan, and the yellow wire should run to the compressor. Appropriate relays should be selected to match the current drawn by the fan and compressor.

A three-position switch (S1) (DP3T) is used to determine the operating mode of the unit. In the NORM position, the air conditioner operates in its normal manner.

In CYCLE A, Potentiometer R10 is used to adjust the compressor on-time. With the component values given in Table 5-5, this

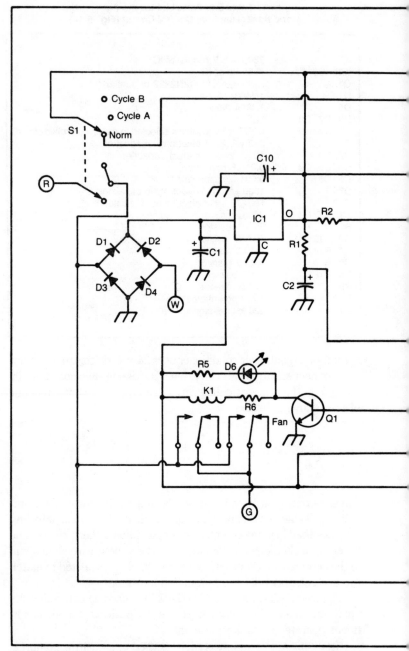

Fig. 5-10. Summer humidity problems can be minimized economically with this circuit.

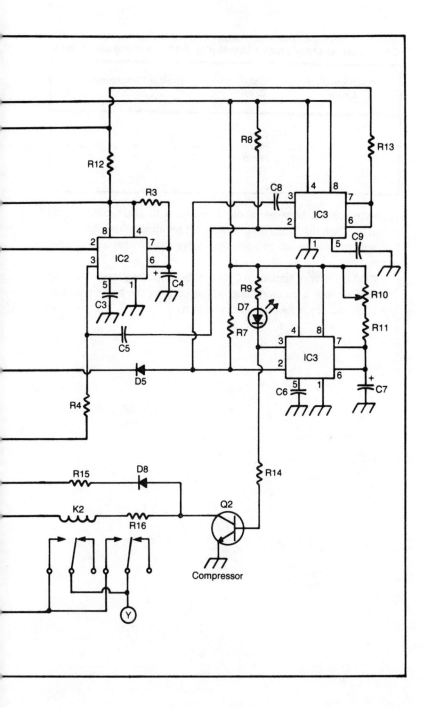

Table 5-6. The Thermostat Connections for the Air Conditioner Humidity Control Circuit (Fig. 5-10) are Summarized Here.

Schematic Label	Cable Color	Typical Thermostat Labels				
G	Green	G	G	G	F	G
R	Red	R	RH	4	M	R5
W	White	W	W	W	H	4
Y	Yellow	Y	Y	Y	C	Y6

time can be set between about 5 minutes to approximately 20 minutes. Then the compressor is shut off for about 20 minutes. The fan will run for about two minutes after the compressor is shut down.

CYCLE B is very similar to CYCLE A, but the compressor off time is twice as long. This mode is good for keeping the home reasonably cool and dry when no one is at home.

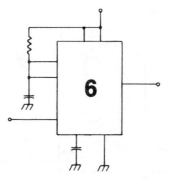

Liquid Control

I N THIS CHAPTER WE WILL LOOK AT A NUMBER OF CIRCUITS
for dealing with liquids. Some of these might not be applications you are likely to immediately consider as likely candidates
for electronic circuitry. The liquids should be kept out of the circuitry itself. If shouldn't have access to anything other than the
probe.

LIQUID PROBES

Many liquids, including water, are electrically conductive. The
liquid is usually more conductive than air. A pair of metallic probes,
(stiff wires or metal rods) are placed where the liquid is expected,
as illustrated in Fig. 6-1. If the liquid level comes up over the ends
of the probes, they are electrically shorted together. The equivalent circuit is shown in Fig. 6-2. It essentially behaves like a switch.
When the probes are dry, the switch is open. Immersing the probes
"closes the switch."

PROJECT 18—PLANT MONITOR

A variation on the basic liquid level sensing probe can remind
you when to water your plants. The circuit is shown in Fig. 6-3.
The parts list is given in Table 6-1.

The probes are buried in the soil near the roots. The amount
of moisture in the soil determines its conductivity (resistance). A

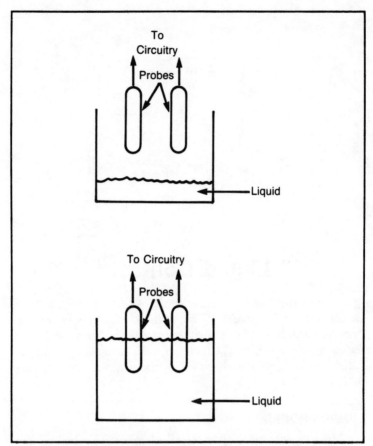

Fig. 6-1. A pair of metallic probes can serve as a liquid detector.

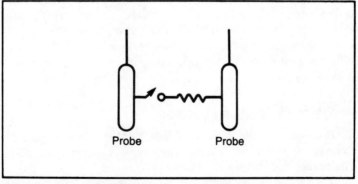

Fig. 6-2. Liquid probes work because of the electrical conductivity of water and also many other liquids.

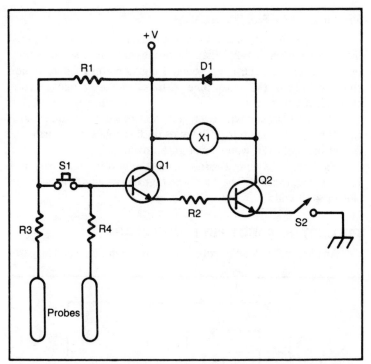

Fig. 6-3. This circuit will remind you when it's time to water your plants.

comparator determines when the resistance exceeds a level set via the potentiometer. When the soil is sufficiently moist, one LED will be lit. If it gets too dry, the other LED will light up. For best visibility, two different color LEDs should be used.

Alternatively, the comparator could trigger an alarm or buzzer when the soil is too dry. The potentiometer setting should be determined experimentally. When the soil is almost, but not quite too dry, adjust the potentiometer until the too dry LED comes on, then back off until the other LED is lit.

Table 6-1. Parts List for the Plant Monitor Circuit of Fig. 6-3.

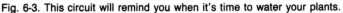

IC1	Op amp (LM741 or similar)
LED1, LED2	LED
R1, R3, R4, R5	100 kΩ resistor
R2	1 MΩ potentiometer
R6	1 kΩ resistor
R7	330 Ω resistor

PROJECT 19—FLOOD ALARM

A simple flooding alarm circuit is shown in Fig. 6-4. The parts list is given in Table 6-2. When the probes are immersed in water, or other liquid, the alarm will sound. Potentiometer R5 determines the frequency of the alarm tone. A fixed resistance may be substituted, if you prefer.

Place the probes wherever you want to guard against flooding. If water comes up over the ends of the probes, the alarm will be set off, until the water level goes down.

This circuit is quite flexible. Even the power supply requirements are noncritical. The supply voltage can be anything between +6 to +12 volts.

PROJECT 20—ANOTHER FLOOD ALARM

An alternative flood alarm circuit is shown in Fig. 6-5. The parts

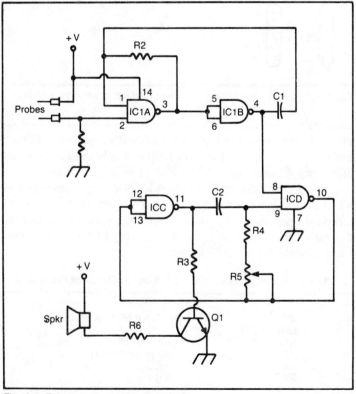

Fig. 6-4. This is a simple flooding alarm.

Table 6-2. Parts List for the First Flood Alarm Circuit of Fig. 6-4.

Q1, Q2	NPN transistor (2N2222 or similar)
D1	1N4002 diode
S1	NO SPST push switch
S2	SPST switch
X1	Alarm device (see text)
R1	33 kΩ resistor
R2-R4	1 kΩ resistor

list is given in Table 6-3. It works in pretty much the same way as the previous circuit. Depressing switch S1 permits you to test the alarm. With switch S2 closed, the alarm cannot operate, so it can be selectively disabled, as desired.

The alarm itself can be almost anything. You can use a bell, buzzer, or Sonalert™. Any sound source that can be activated by an applied voltage will do. If you prefer, a visual indicator, such as a light, can be used in place of the audible alarm.

PROJECT 21—MOISTURE DETECTOR

The circuits shown in Figs. 6-4 and 6-5 are intended to measure an accumulation of water (or other liquid). A depth of at least half an inch is required. The probes could be placed higher for greater depths, but they can't really be placed much lower. Suppose we need to detect a smaller amount of liquid?

The moisture detector circuit of Fig. 6-6 should do the trick. The parts list for this project is given in Table 6-4. The sensor is made up of fine wires spaced an inch or so apart. The alarm can be almost anything, as in the last project. A buzzer, bell, or Sonalert™ can be triggered by this circuit. Nothing is terribly critical here. Almost any PNP transistor and SCR can be used with good results.

PROJECT 22—SUMP PUMP CONTROLLER

One of the primary applications for a flood detector is to control a sump pump to automatically correct the problem. This is unquestionably automation at work. An automated sump pump controller circuit is illustrated in Fig. 6-7. The parts list for this project is given in Table 6-5.

Notice that this circuit has three probes. The OFF probe should be mounted somewhat lower than the ON probe. The COMMON probe should be lined up with the OFF probe, or a little lower.

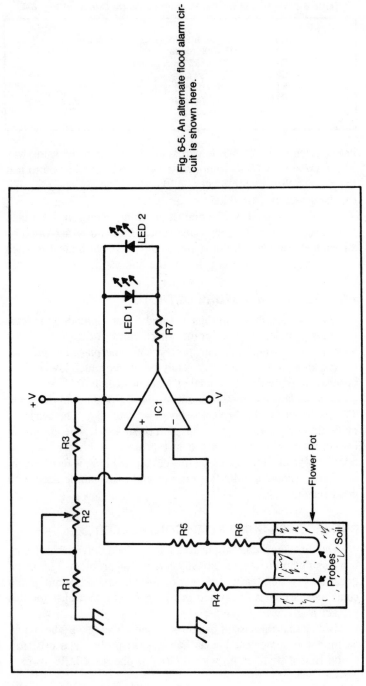

Fig. 6-5. An alternate flood alarm circuit is shown here.

IC1	CD4011
Q1	2N3904 transistor
SPKR	Small speaker
C1	0.1 μF capacitor
C2	0.01 μF capacitor
R1	1 MΩ resistor
R2	3.3 MΩ resistor
R3, R4	10 kΩ resistor
R5	50 kΩ potentiometer
R6	33 Ω resistor

Table 6-3. Parts List for the Second Flood Alarm Circuit of Fig. 6-5.

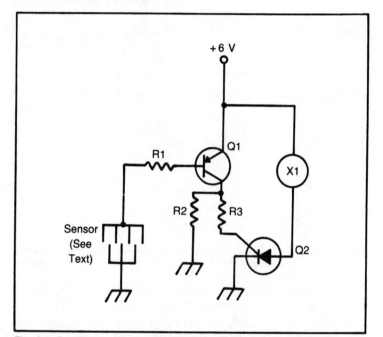

Fig. 6-6. Small amounts of moisture can be detected with this circuit.

Table 6-4. Parts List for the Moisture Detector Circuit of Fig. 6-6.

Q1	PNP transistor (2N3906 or similar)
Q2	SCR
X1	Alarm sounder (buzzer, bell, or Sonalert™)
R1	100 kΩ resistor
R2	10 kΩ resistor
R3	1 kΩ resistor

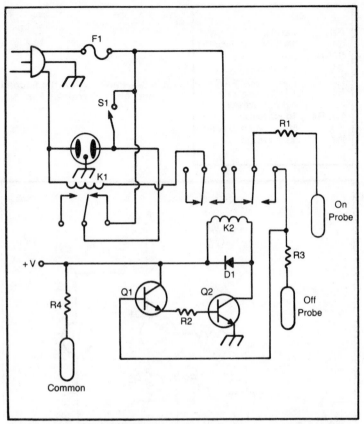

Fig. 6-7. When flooding is detected, this circuit will turn on a sump pump.

If the water rises enough to touch the COMMON and OFF probes, nothing happens. However, when the water reaches the ON probe, the relays are triggered, and the sump pump is turned on.

The pump will presumably lower the water level. When the level drops below the ON probe, nothing will happen. The pump

Table 6-5. Parts List for the First Sump Pump Controller Circuit of Fig. 6-7.

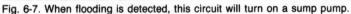

Q1, Q2	NPN transistor (2N2222 or similar)
D1	1N4002 diode
K1	120 Vac SPST relay (contacts determined by load pump)
K2	DPDT dc relay
F1	Fuse (selected to match load pump)
S1	SPST switch
R1-R3	1 kΩ resistor

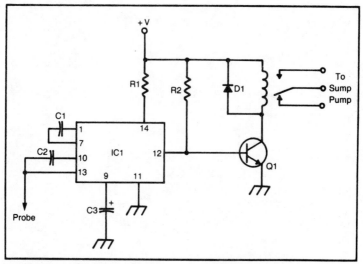

Fig. 6-8. This is an alternate sump pump controller circuit.

Table 6-6. Parts List for the Second Sump Pump Controller Circuit of Fig. 6-8.

IC1	LM1830
Q1	2N3055
D1	1N4002
C1	0.001 μF capacitor
C2	0.05 μF capacitor
C3	25 μF capacitor
R1	470 Ω resistor
R2	2.2 kΩ resistor

will keep running. It is not until the water level drops below the OFF probe that the system will shut down. This will prevent the pump from oscillating on and off with the water level just at the edge of the ON probe.

PROJECT 23—ANOTHER SUMP PUMP CONTROLLER

A different sump pump controller circuit is shown in Fig. 6-8. The parts list is given in Table 6-6. This circuit is a little simpler than the previous project, since it is built around a single IC (the LM1830). This circuit has only a single probe and may tend to oscillate under some circumstances.

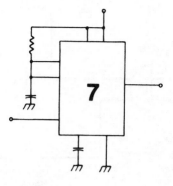

Stereo and TV Projects

H OME ENTERTAINMENT SYSTEMS OFFER A NUMBER OF OP-
portunities for remote control and automation applications.
Many commercial pieces of audio and video equipment come with
remote controllers. This chapter will present several relatively simple projects for increasing your enjoyment of stereo and/or televi-
sion/video equipment.

PROJECT 24—STEREO AUTOMATIC SHUT-OFF

Most automatic record changers feature automatic shut-off after
the last record has been played. This is handy, but power continues
to be applied to the rest of the system. The amplifier, for example,
remains on until you manually turn it off. It's easy to forget it when
no sound is coming out.

If you are recording your records, the tape will keep running
after the last record is over. Rewinding back to the end of the last
selection when you don't know where it is can be an irritating nuisance, even at the best of times.

A simple solution is illustrated in Fig. 7-1. Simply wire an ac
socket in parallel with the turntable's motor. When the motor shuts
itself off, power will be disconnected from this socket. Whatever
is plugged into this socket will be shut down along with the record
changer.

Some tape machines have problems if power is interrupted
while the tape is running. Such machines should not be used with

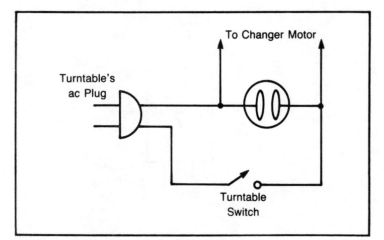

Fig. 7-1. This circuit will shut off a tape recorder after the last record has been played on an automatic turntable.

an auto shut-off system like this. Most modern tape decks, how-ever, have no problem at all, although the tape might need to be slackened slightly by hand before power is reapplied, to prevent tape breakage.

While no fuse is shown in the diagram, adding one certainly wouldn't be a bad idea. The fuse's rating will depend on what is being plugged into the socket. Even if each piece of equipment in your stereo system is independently fused, additional fusing isn't necessarily overkill. You can never have too much over-current pro-tection.

PROJECT 25—ADVANCED AUTO SHUT-OFF

A more deluxe automatic shut-off circuit is shown in Fig. 7-2. Once again, the circuit is placed in parallel with the record changer's motor. When the record changer turns itself off, the DPDT relay is triggered, removing power from the ac socket(s).

Switch S1 is a simple DPDT switch to allow you to set the sys-tem into the automated mode, or the manual mode. In the manual mode, the record changer does not control power to the sockets. This allows maximum flexibility. You don't want to have to run the record player or rewire the system to listen to the FM radio, or a prerecorded tape.

Multiple ac sockets can be wired in parallel. Fusing is advised, although it is not shown here. The two lamps (I1, and I2) and the resistor are optional. These are simply indicators of S1's position.

In the manual mode, I1 is lit, while I2 lights up for the auto mode.

Despite the extreme simplicity of this project (there isn't even a parts list), it can be a very powerful and valuable addition to almost any stereo system.

PROJECT 26—VOX RECORDER CONTROLLER

Do you ever do any dictation into a tape recorder? If so, and if you're like most of us, there are probably a lot of pauses on the tape, as you stop to think. This wastes tape, and can slow up transcription. But turning the recorder on and off manually can be a nuisance and a distraction. Wouldn't it be nice if the tape recorder was smart enough to turn itself on and off at appropriate times?

Well, while I'm not sure it really counts as intelligence on the

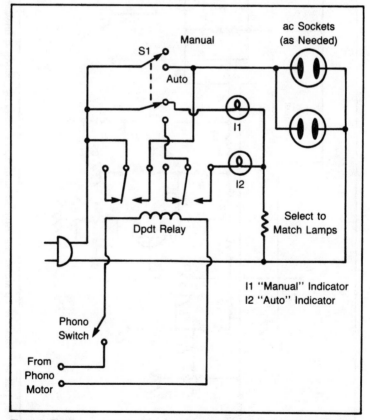

Fig. 7-2. This is a somewhat more sophisticated automatic shut-off circuit for stereo systems.

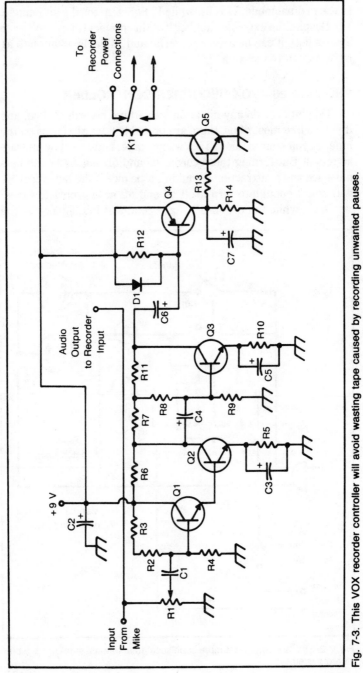

Fig. 7-3. This VOX recorder controller will avoid wasting tape caused by recording unwanted pauses.

104

part of your recorder, the circuit shown in Fig. 7-3 will turn on the recorder whenever you speak into the microphone. When you stop speaking, the system will wait a few seconds then shut off the recorder. This eliminates any long pauses on the tape. The parts list for this circuit is given in Table 7-1.

The recorder is controlled by relay K1. The exact connections and relay required will depend on the specific tape machine you use. This circuit is very easy to use. There is just a single control. Potentiometer R1 controls the sensitivity of the input stage, to allow for any background noise in the area. Just adjust this control so that it activates the recorder when you speak, and shuts it off when you are not speaking into the microphone.

This circuit could easily be adapted to control almost anything by making a sound, such as shouting, or clapping your hands. The next project is specifically designed for such applications.

PROJECT 27—VOX RELAY

A general-purpose VOX (voice-operated switch) circuit is shown in Fig. 7-4, with the parts list given in Table 7-2. Almost any small relay can be activated with this circuit, permitting it to control almost anything. If a larger load is used, the small relay can be used to control a second, larger relay.

Potentiometer R1 controls the sensitivity of the circuit. This

Table 7-1. Parts List for the VOX Recorder Controller Circuit of Fig. 7-3.

Q1, Q2, Q3, Q5	NPN transistor (2N4256 or similar)
Q4	PNP transistor (2N428 or similar)
D1	1N38B diode
C1	0.1 μF capacitor
C2, C3, C5	100 μF 50 V electrolytic capacitor
C4, C6, C7	10 μF 50 V electrolytic capacitor
R1	2 MΩ potentiometer
R2	1 MΩ resistor
R3	100 kΩ resistor
R4	270 kΩ resistor
R5, R10	560 Ω resistor
R6, R9, R11	2.7 kΩ resistor
R7	1.2 kΩ resistor
R8	15 kΩ resistor
R12	33 kΩ resistor
R13	47 kΩ resistor
R14	22 kΩ resistor
K1	Dc relay (see text)

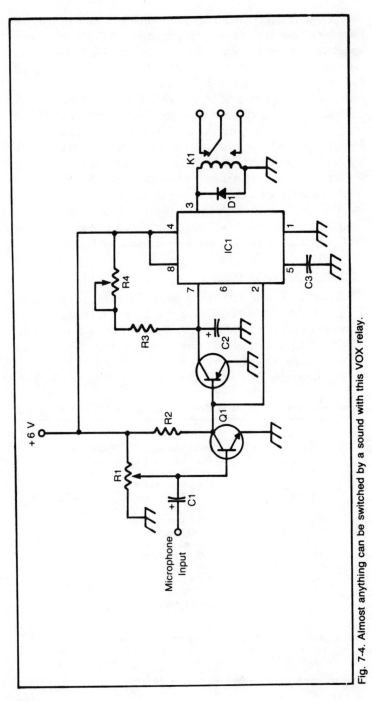

Fig. 7-4. Almost anything can be switched by a sound with this VOX relay.

106

Table 7-2. Parts List for VOX Relay Circuit of Fig. 7-4.

Q1	NPN transistor (2N3904 or similar)
Q2	PNP transistor (2N3906 or similar)
IC1	555 timer IC
D1	1N4002 diode
K1	Relay to suit controlled device
C1	1 μF 10 V electrolytic capacitor
C2	50 μF 10 V electrolytic capacitor
C3	0.01 μF capacitor
R1	10 kΩ potentiometer
R2, R3	1 kΩ resistor
R4	100 kΩ potentiometer

means you can adjust how loud the triggering sound must be. Any loud, sharp sound can be used to activate the VOX circuitry. A good, sharp hand-clap will usually give good results. The sensitivity control should be set high enough that false triggering from background noise won't be a major problem.

The 555 timer introduces a slight delay. By adjusting potentiometer R4, delays from about 0.05 second to approximately five seconds can be set up. For longer delays, a louder sound may be required. At the higher settings of the delay control, a hand-clap will be too short. A shout, or whistle would work better under such circumstances. The advantage of the longer time delay is that it reduces the chances of some stray transient sound accidentally activating the relay at an undesired time.

PROJECT 28—SOUND COMPRESSOR

Have you ever tried recording a panel discussion, or some other event with several people talking from various locations? If you have, you're certainly familiar with the hassles of constantly watching the VU meters, and riding the tape recorder's gain controls. There is always at least one person who constantly bellows, and another one who barely speaks above a whisper. How can you set the gain controls so that both will be recorded clearly without undue distortion? It can especially be a problem when you don't know who is going to speak next. Sometimes even recording a single speaker can lead to problems of this sort. Many people constantly raise and lower the volume of their voices as they speak, often in an unpredictable manner.

Wouldn't it be nice if you had an assistant with incredibly fast reflexes, and no tendency to be distracted or let his mind wander?

You could put this assistant to work riding the gain controls, freeing you for other tasks. As you probably suspect, this project is just such an automated assistant. The official name for this type of circuit is a sound compressor.

The circuit shown in Fig. 7-5 literally compresses the dynamic (volume) range of the signals being recorded. Loud sounds are attenuated to a lower level, and soft sounds are boosted to a higher level. The parts lists for this projects is given in Table 7-3.

The circuit responds to changes in sound level very rapidly. There are three controls, R7, R11, and R18. Potentiometer R7 adjusts the input sensitivity. This control essentially determines the softest sound level that can be recognized by the circuitry.

The average output level to the tape deck is set by potentiometer R18. The output signal will be relatively constant, within a narrow range, and the recorder's gain controls can be set to a good position, and then left alone.

The third control, potentiometer R11 sets the amount of compression. This is the dynamic range control, determining the amount of variation in the output signal to be recorded.

A compression circuit is great for equalizing voice levels, but it should not be used to record music. Music generally depends heavily on dynamic variation for its emotional effect. Compressed music sounds very flat and dull, and extremely uninteresting.

This is an example of using the right tool for the right job. You can't expect a simple circuit to handle every job, of course.

PROJECT 29—RECORDER TIMER SWITCH

Most VCRs (video cassette recorders) include a timer so programs can be recorded unattended. But suppose there is a program coming on the radio that you'd like to record, but you're not going to be home.

You can get a mechanical ac timer, but you probably won't be very satisfied with the results. These mechanical timers are intended primarily for lighting. High accuracy in the timing is not particularly critical, and is definitely not a feature of these devices. They can be off by as much as five to fifteen minutes. For automatic lighting applications, this degree of error will probably be negligible. For recording, the error is quite unacceptable. Either you'll miss part of the program (when the timer runs slow), or you'll record a lot of stuff you're not interested in before the show (when the timer runs fast).

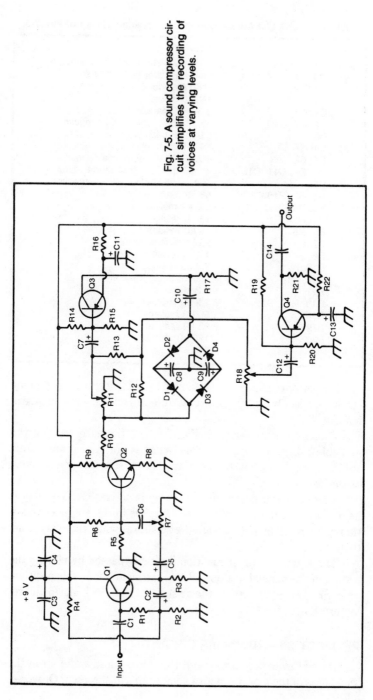

Fig. 7-5. A sound compressor circuit simplifies the recording of voices at varying levels.

109

Table 7-3. Parts List for the Sound Compression Circuit of Fig. 7-5.

Q1, Q2	NPN transistor (2N2923 or similar)
Q3, Q4	PNP transistor (2N397 or similar)
D1, D2	1N914 diode
D3, D4	1N270 diode
C1, C14	0.5 μF capacitor
C2, C7, C12	33 μF 25 V electrolytic capacitor
C3	0.022 μF capacitor
C4	150 μF 25 V electrolytic capacitor
C5, C6	4.7 μF 25 V electrolytic capacitor
C8, C9, C11, C13	47 μF 25 V electrolytic capacitor
C10	100 μF 25 V electrolytic capacitor
R1, R2, R15	56 kΩ resistor
R3, R9	2.2 kΩ resistor
R4, R14	22 kΩ resistor
R5, R6	15 kΩ resistor
R7	25 kΩ potentiometer
R8	120 Ω resistor
R10, R21	3.3 kΩ resistor
R11, R18	100 kΩ potentiometer
R12	8.2 kΩ resistor
R13, R17, R22	1.2 kΩ resistor
R16	560 Ω resistor
R19	33 kΩ resistor
R20	120 kΩ resistor

Far better results can be achieved by using a true time-keeping clock, especially an all-electronic (digital) clock with an alarm feature.

The circuitry is shown in Fig. 7-6, and the parts list is given in Table 7-4. As you can see, this circuit is not very complicated, and only requires a handful of parts. The existing clock does most of the work.

When the alarm goes off, the relay is activated. The relay is held in for 59 minutes. When the switch is in the automatic position, power will be fed through the ac socket while the relay is activated.

The automatic timer function can be bypassed by placing the switch in the manual position. When the switch is in this position, power is applied directly to the ac socket. The clock alarm and relay are ignored.

PROJECT 30—AUTO-OFF CIRCUIT

Do you ever fall asleep with the TV on, and wake up in the wee hours of the morning with a snowy, no-signal screen? Or worse,

110

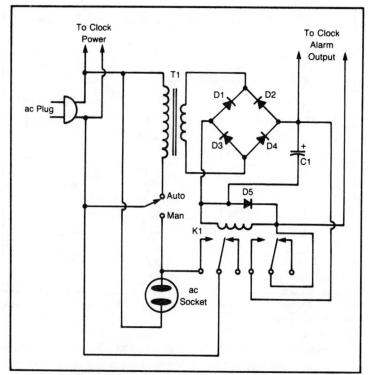

Fig. 7-6. An electronic alarm clock can serve as a recorder timer.

you're rudely awakened when the station signs back on the air—usually much earlier than you want to get up. This is annoying, of course. It also wastes power. Large screen color TVs especially eat up quite a bit of power.

The circuit shown in Fig. 7-7 will automatically disconnect power when the station stops broadcasting. The 555 timer provides a slight delay before shut-off so any momentary signal blanking between programs (common when the station switches between local and network programming) won't turn your TV off on you.

Table 7-4. Parts List for the Recorder Timer Switch Circuit of Fig. 7-6.

T1	12 Vac transformer
D1-D5	1N4002 diode
C1	100 μF 25 V electrolytic capacitor
K1	12 Vdc DPDT relay

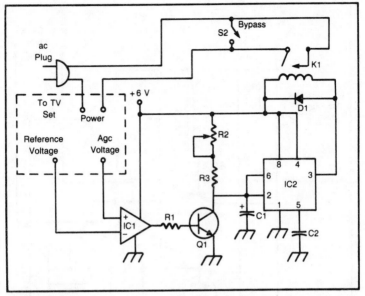

Fig. 7-7. This circuit will automatically turn off the TV when the station goes off the air.

The signal must be absent for a minute or so. The exact delay can be set via potentiometer R2. A bypass switch is provided, so that the TV set can be used normally if desired.

Once the system has shut down, the set will stay off until the reset pushbutton is depressed. The parts list for this project is given in Table 7-5.

This circuit can also be adapted for use with your stereo sys-

Table 7-5. Parts List for the TV Auto-Off Circuit of Fig. 7-7.

IC1	LM339 comparator
IC2	555 timer
Q1	NPN transistor (2N2222 or similar)
D1	1N4002 diode
K1	Dc relay with SPST contacts
S1	N.O. momentary contact SPST switch
S2	SPST switch
C1	10 μF 25 V electrolytic capacitor
C2	0.01 μF capacitor
R1	1 kΩ resistor
R2	1 MΩ potentiometer
R3	390 kΩ resistor

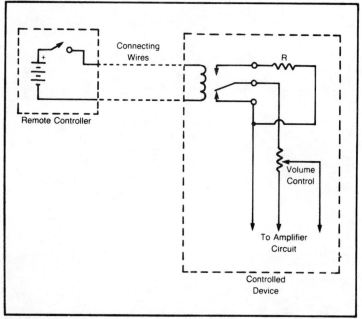

Fig. 7-8. A TV or stereo can conveniently be muted from a remote location with this circuit.

tem, so you can doze off while listening to the radio, or a tape or record. Naturally, if you're tuned to a 24-hour station, this project won't do much of anything. But for stations that shut down between midnight and dawn (or thereabouts), this device can be handy.

PROJECT 31—REMOTE CONTROL MUTE

Suppose you're watching TV or listening to the stereo when the phone or the doorbell rings. Often it would be convenient to be able to lower the volume by remote control. Figure 7-8 illustrates how this can be done. When activated, an extra resistance is switched into the circuit in series with the existing volume control potentiometer.

The amount of attenuation will depend on the value of the added resistor. As a rule of thumb, I'd say the resistor value should be about one third to one half the value of the potentiometer. For example, if the volume control is a 1 megohm potentiometer, use a 470 kΩ resistor for the added resistance.

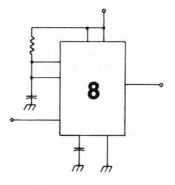

Telephone Projects

THE TELEPHONE IS A NATURAL FOR REMOTE CONTROL AND automation projects. In fact, the telephone itself is a remote control device of sorts. The very name suggests this. The word "telephone" can be freely translated as "distance-sound."

Think about what happens when you call someone. You dial a number at one location, causing a string of relays to close at another location (the telephone company's trunk lines), causing another phone to ring at still another location.

In this chapter we will carry the remote control aspects of the telephone even further. It is a very handy control device. Most of the projects in this chapter are designed to connect directly to the phone lines. Legally you are obligated to contact the local phone company before you connect anything to their lines. It is possible to disrupt phone service to hundreds of other people and/or damage expensive phone company equipment by tapping off the phone lines. None of these projects should cause any problems, but the phone company has the right to know what you are plugging into their lines.

PROJECT 32—TELEPHONE-ACTIVATED RELAY

The circuit shown in Fig. 8-1 will activate a relay when the phone rings. The relay used will depend on the device being controlled. If you have a separate unlisted number just for this purpose, you can control almost anything simply by phoning home.

That may be a bit extravagant for most of us. A more practical application would be for the relay to turn on a light when the telephone rings. This could be useful in a noisy environment, or for the hearing impaired. Another useful application would be for the relay to activate an oscillator, or other sound generating device to serve as a remote ringer. This is useful when you are outside, or if you have a large house. The parts list for this project is given in Table 8-1.

PROJECT 33—IMPROVED
TELEPHONE-ACTIVATED RELAY

The project described in the last section is certainly functional, but it has definite limitations for true remote control applications. For one thing it must be connected directly to the telephone lines. This means that you are legally required to get permission from the local telephone company. At best, this is a time-wasting nuisance.

The major limitation of the preceeding project is that it is strongly subject fo false activation whenever anyone else calls your number. You could set up a separate line just for control purpose, but this might be unduly expensive. Besides, it is no guarantee that no one else will ever ring the number. Even unlisted numbers get wrong number calls. Many commercial telephone solicitation outfits use computerized dialing systems which randomly dial valid number combinations, whether they are listed or not, so they can force their sales pitches on everyone, even those who have gotten unlisted numbers. (If I might editorialize for a moment—telephone solicitors are notoriously rude.)

All in all, the circuit of Fig. 8-1 probably isn't very practical for most serious remote control applications. It was presented here primarily as an introduction to this project. The circuit for the improved telephone activated relay is shown in Fig. 8-2. The parts list is given in Table 8-2.

No direct electrical connection is made to the telephone or its wiring. The ringing is picked up by a pair of crystal microphone elements. The microphones should be placed together near the phone. Why two microphones, instead of just one? This will be explained shortly.

When the phone rings, the sound is picked up by the microphones, triggering SCR Q7. This closes relay K2, activating a simple timer circuit made up of UJT Q8, and its associated components.

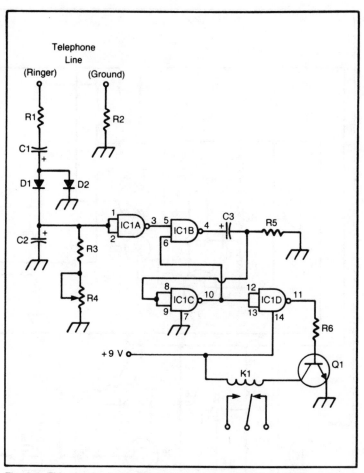

Fig. 8-1. This simple circuit will activate a relay when the telephone rings.

Table 8-1. Parts List for the Telephone-Activated Relay Circuit of Fig. 8-1.

IC1	CD4011 quad NAND gate
Q1	NPN transistor (2N2222 or similar)
D1-D3	1N4002 diode
K1	Relay selected for desired application
C1, C2	1 μF 50 V electrolytic capacitor
C3	100 μF 50 V electrolytic capacitor
R1, R2	390 kΩ resistor
R3, R5	1 MΩ resistor
R4	1 MΩ potentiometer
R6	1 kΩ resistor

117

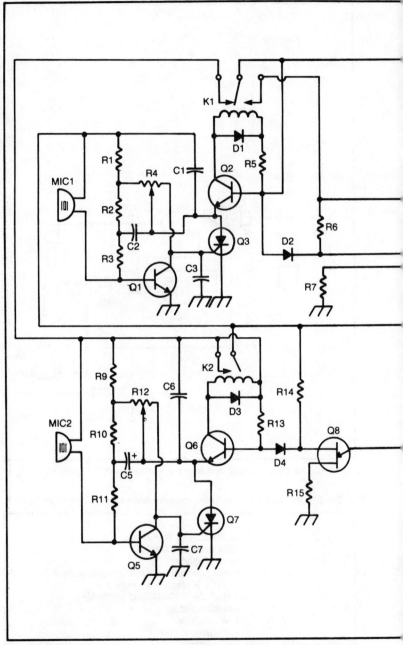

Fig. 8-2. Almost anything can be controlled with this improved telephone-activated relay circuit.

118

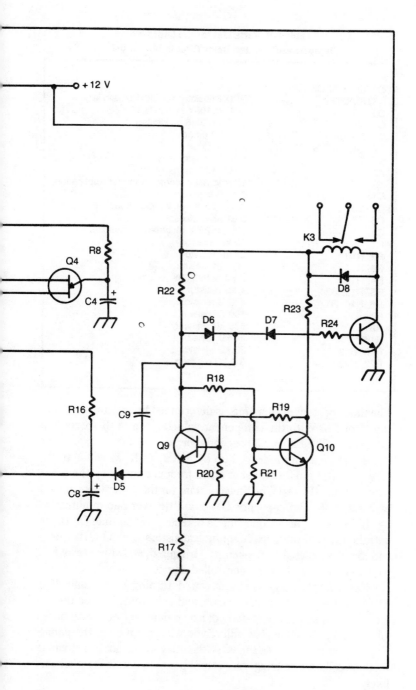

119

Q1, Q2, Q5, Q6, Q9, Q10, Q11	NPN transistor (2N3904 or similar)
Q3, Q7	SCR (C106Y or similar)
Q4, Q8	UJT (2N2646 or similar)
D1, D3, D8	1N4002 diode
D2, D4, D5, D6, D7	1N914 diode
K1	SPDT 12 Vdc relay
K2	SPST 12 Vdc relay
K3	12 Vdc relay (contacts to suit application)
C1, C6, C9	0.1 µF capacitor
C2, C5	30 µF 25 V electrolytic capacitor
C3, C7	0.01 µF capacitor
C4, C8	100 µF 25 V electrolytic capacitor
R1, R9, R20, R21	10 kΩ resistor
R2, R10	22 kΩ resistor
R3, R11	100 kΩ resistor
R4, R12	5 kΩ potentiometer
R5, R13, R24	1 kΩ resistor
R6, R14, R17	470 Ω resistor
R7, R15	100 Ω resistor
R8	680 kΩ resistor
R16	27 kΩ resistor
R18, R19	33 kΩ resistor
R22, R23	3.9 kΩ resistor

The time constant of this timer is determined by resistor R16, and capacitor C8. With the component values given in the parts list, the delay will be about 30 seconds, or so.

If a second ring is picked up by MIC1, SCR Q3 will activate relay K1. The circuit will shut down for a period set by the timer built around UJT Q4. The time constant for this timer (determined by resistor R8 and capacitor C4) is a little over one minute.

If, however, no second ring is detected by the time Q8 times out, the multivibrator made up by transistors Q9 and Q10, along with their associated components, is triggered, activating relay K3, which is connected to the controlled device.

Note that the relay will be activated, turning on the controlled device, if the telephone rings once, and only once. To use the remote control system, just dial your own number, let it ring once, and hang up. Anyone else calling you will probably let the phone ring at least two or three times, so the relay would not be activated by their calls. False triggering is still possible, but it is rather unlikely.

Once the relay is activated, it stays activated, until another single ring is detected, retriggering the Q9/Q10 multivibrator, deactivating the relay. This project can be put to work in a wide variety of practical remote control applications.

PROJECT 34—OFF-HOOK ALARM

Many families have several extension phones, all on the same number. It can be disturbing and embarassing to pick up the phone to make a call and interrupt another conversation. Or, perhaps you'd like to know when the kids are using the phone.

This project will help keep the battle of the extension phone under control. The circuit shown in Fig. 8-3 will cause the LED to light up steadily when the phone is off the hook. While this feature is probably of limited value, the LED also indicates when the phone is being dialed by blinking on and off. The LED also blinks when the phone rings.

The parts list for this simple project is shown in Table 8-3. If the LED is part of an optoisolator, the off-hook alarm can control an audible alarm, or almost anything you choose.

PROJECT 35—TELEPHONE RECORDER CONTROLLER

Some people might need a record of their phone calls. The circuit shown in Fig. 8-4 will automatically turn on a cassette recorder

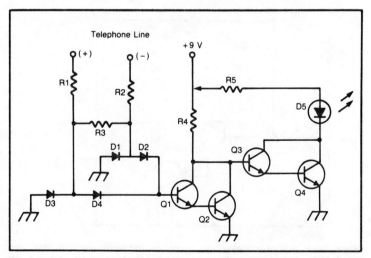

Fig. 8-3. This circuit will alert you whenever an extension phone is off the hook.

Table 8-3. Parts List for the Off-Hook Alarm Circuit of Fig. 8-3.

Q1-Q4	NPN transistor (2N3904 or similar)
D1-D4	1N914 diode
D5	LED
R1, R2, R4	10 MΩ resistor
R3	1.2 MΩ resistor
R5	1 kΩ resistor

whenever the phone is off the hook, and record all conversations.

Most standard cassette tape recorders have jacks for an external microphone, and a remote switch. This project uses both of these jacks. If the jacks are not available, the recorder must be adapted (jacks added) to be used with this circuit.

When the telephone handset is taken off the hook, the two transistors "close" the "remote switch contacts," activating the tape recorder. The audio signals through the handset are coupled

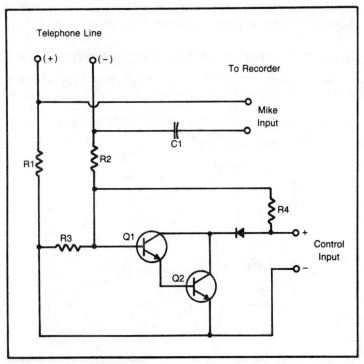

Fig. 8-4. You can automatically record your telephone conversations with this circuit.

**Table 8-4. Parts List for the Automatic
Telephone-Recorder Circuit of Fig. 8-4.**

Q1, Q2	NPN transistor (2N4954 or similar)
C1	0.022 μF capacitor
R1	1.2 kΩ resistor
R2	270 kΩ resistor
R3	68 kΩ resistor
R4	33 kΩ resistor

through a capacitor to the microphone input of the tape recorder. By leaving this system set up, all calls can be recorded.

It is a good idea to inform the other party that the conversation is being recorded. It is not legal or moral to use these (or similar) devices to "bug" a phone and record someone else's calls without their knowledge. This project is intended for personal use only. The parts list for this circuit is given in Table 8-4.

PROJECT 36—AUTODIALER

Automatic dialers are popular telephone accessories. Many commercial autodialers have been placed on the market. They are convenient, and they are fairly expensive.

A "quick and dirty" auto-dialer circuit is shown in Fig. 8-5. The parts list for this project is given in Table 8-5. This circuit uses the dial-pulse type of dialing signals, so a Touch Tone™ system is not required. Dial pulses can be recorded on a cassette tape recorder. Playing the tape back through the input of this circuit will cause the stored number to be automatically dialed.

A more versatile approach would be to use a computer to generate the dial pulses. Depending on your adeptness at programming, almost any special features you choose could be incorporated into the system.

A dial telephone works by repeatedly opening and closing the power connection to the phone. The circuit shown here uses a relay to perform this function. It is connected directly to the telephone line. If you prefer to avoid any potential legal hassles, or want a more portable system, a solenoid could be used in place of the relay to mechanically depress and release the phone's cradle button.

PROJECT 37—AUTOMATIC CALLER

The circuit shown in Fig. 8-6 is intended for use with the

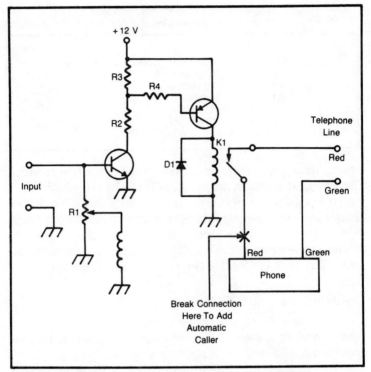

Fig. 8-5. Automatic telephone dialers are popular accessories.

preceeding project. It is inserted into the earlier circuit by breaking the connection marked with an "X" in Fig. 8-5, and wiring in this new circuitry.

Any type of NC (Normally Closed) alarm switches may be used for this circuit. A typical application would use intrusion switches for a burglar alarm. When one of the monitored switches is opened,

Table 8-5. Parts List for the Auto-dialer Circuit of Fig. 8-5.

Q1	NPN transistor (2N3904 or similar)
Q2	PNP transistor (2N3906 or similar)
D1	1N4002 diode
K1	12 Vdc relay with N.C. SPST relay
R1	500 kΩ potentiometer
R2	12 kΩ resistor
R3	1 kΩ resistor
R4	2.2 kΩ resistor
L1	Telephone pick-up coil (part of the telephone's existing circuitry)

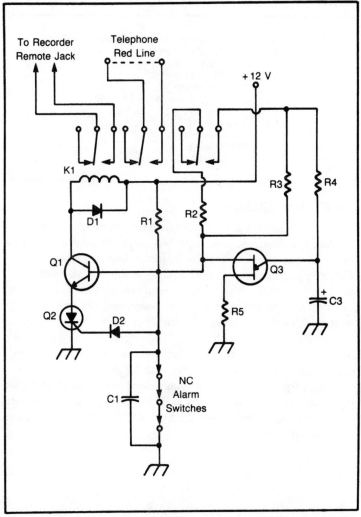

Fig. 8-6. The automatic dialer circuit of Fig. 8-5 can be adapted to automatically call for help during an emergency.

the tape recorder will be activated. A previously recorded number will be dialed. Then a previously recorded message can be played, alerting whoever answers the phone to the alarm condition. Record the spoken message two or three times. You can't predict how long it will take the other party to answer the phone, and you want to be sure they hear the entire message. The parts list for this project is given in Table 8-6.

Table 8-6. Parts List for the Automatic Caller Circuit of Fig. 8-6.

Q1	NPN transistor (2N3904 or similar)
Q2	SCR (C106Y or similar)
Q3	UJT (2N2646 or similar)
D1	1N4002 diode
C1	0.1 μF capacitor
C2	330 μF 25 V electrolytic capacitor
R1	56 kΩ resistor
R2	1 kΩ resistor
R3	470 Ω resistor
R4	68 kΩ resistor
R5	100 Ω resistor

CHAPTER SUMMARY

The telephone is an ideal candidate for remote control projects. But you must keep the legal aspects in mind. Other people rely on the same telephone lines that you're using. Anything that could possibly disrupt regular services must be avoided at all costs.

Use of the telephone lines is regulated by the FCC (Federal Communications Commission). All customer-supplied equipment must be FCC-type approved to be legally connected to the telephone lines. For these projects (the ones that connect directly to the phone lines) an approved protective coupler must be used to be legal. Check with your local phone company for details.

Don't try to bypass these regulations. Some circuit will alter the signals on the lines enough to be detected by the phone company's monitoring equipment, and you could be subject to serious legal penalties.

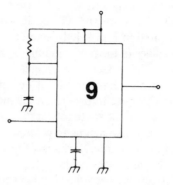

Controlling Motors

MANY REMOTE CONTROL AND AUTOMATION PROJECTS IN-
volve some sort of mechanized physical motion. In most instances, this will call for some sort of motor. Motors were discussed
briefly in Chapter 1. In this chapter we will explore the use of these
devices in a little more detail. Particular emphasis will be placed
on practical techniques for controlling motors with various electrical signals. Before getting to the practical applications, however,
let's spend a little time getting better acquainted with the motor
itself.

There are actually several different types of motors. Some motors are designed to be run off a dc voltage, while others require
an ac voltage. Dc motors include series, shunt, and compound types.
Each type of motor has its own advantages and disadvantages. In
most cases, the best choice will depend on the specific application
at hand.

DC MOTORS

Dc motors tend to be more commonly used in control applications than ac motors. They tend to be more readily available,
smaller, lighter, and less expensive than their ac counterparts.

Basically, a dc motor is made up of a moving coil called the
armature winding, and a stationary coil called the field winding.
A current flows through both coils, therefore a magnetic field is
generated around each coil. The armature rotates, so it produces

a rotating magnetic field. The fixed position of the field winding results in a stationary magnetic field. These two magnetic fields cause the motor's shaft to rotate. The basic structure of a simple dc motor is illustrated in Fig. 9-1. In some motors, a permanent magnet is used in place of the field winding to produce the stationary magnetic field. The effect is the same.

Figure 9-2 illustrates the operation of a dc motor. In A, the armature's position causes it to produce a magnetic field with the north pole at the top, and the south pole at the bottom. Unlike magnetic poles attract, and like magnetic poles repel. This forces the armature to rotate in a counterclockwise direction, due to the interaction of the two magnetic fields.

Soon the armature reaches the position shown in B. The unlike poles are now lined up. If that was all there was to the motor, it would stop rotating at this point. Certainly that wouldn't be a very useful device.

The secret to the operation of a dc motor lies in the way current is applied to the armature winding. A brush and commutator arrangement is used. It reverses the polarity of the current connections to the armature winding at the point in its rotation where the torque would drop to zero if no change was made. Now the poles of the armature's magnetic field are reversed, so the two magnetic fields are no longer lined up. Unlike magnetic poles repel each other,

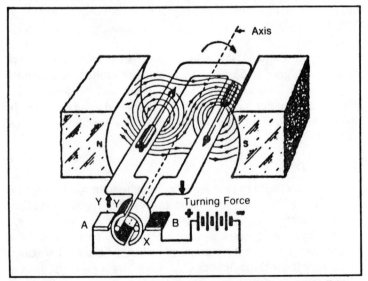

Fig. 9-1. A dc motor operates from the interaction of two magnetic fields.

128

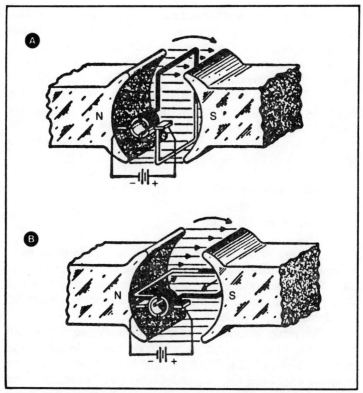

Fig. 9-2. The armature winding rotates while the field winding remains stationary.

so the armature keeps turning. Just as it reaches the point when the two fields would line up, the connections are reversed again, and we're right back where we started.

The armature is forced to keep rotating, because the two magnetic fields can never line up in a position of stability. The motor shaft is connected to the armature, so it continuously rotates too. Of course, the motor described here has been greatly simplified, but this brief outline gives you the basic idea of how a dc motor functions.

Most practical dc motors have multiple armature windings, each with its own pair of commutator segments. With just one armature winding, as in our example, the torque would be uneven, and the motion jerky. The torque would be highest when the unlike poles were coming close together, and would be significantly lower during the rest of the rotation. Multiple armature windings result in much smoother operation.

The motor we have described has just two magnetic poles from the field, so it is called a two-pole motor. While two-pole motors do exist, most practical motors have four, or more poles.

A dc motor must have current flowing through both the armature and the field windings in order to run. The way in which the two windings are connected to each other has a significant effect on the operating characteristics of the motor, in terms of speed and torque changes with varying load conditions.

There are basically three types of dc motors, distinguished by the connections between the windings. They are:

☐ the series motor
☐ the shunt motor
☐ the compound motor

In the series motor, the field and armature windings are wired in series, as illustrated in Fig. 9-3. Because of the series arrangement, all of the armature current must necessarily flow through the field winding too. The field windings of a series motor consists of comparatively few turns of heavy wire.

When power is applied to a series motor with no load, a fairly large current flows through the windings. Torque increases with both armature current and field strength. You can see that this type of motor will have a very high starting torque. The motor's shaft will rotate faster and faster, developing a high counter EMF (elec-

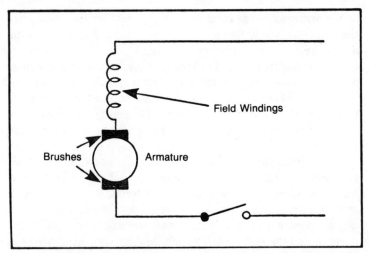

Fig. 9-3. In a series motor the field and armature windings are wired in series.

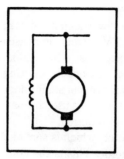

Fig. 9-4. In a shunt motor the field and armature windings are wired in parallel.

tromotive force). The counter EMF is a voltage generated in the armature winding by its rotation through the stationary magnetic field. After all, the differences between a motor and a generator are slight.

Returning to our no load series motor. As the speed increases, the field is weakened, allowing the armature to rotate even faster. A runaway feedback effect occurs. With no load, a series motor will soon destroy or damage itself by rotating at extremely high and ever increasing speeds. A series motor should never be operated without a load.

If we connect a mechanical load to the motor shaft, the series motor will have to slow down. The greater the load, the lower the speed. As the speed is reduced, the counter EMF is also reduced, while the current and torque are increased.

To summarize, a series motor has a high starting torque, and its speed is determined primarily by the mechanical load. Series motors are usually employed in applications requiring a high torque for a relatively short period of time.

The second type of dc motor is the shunt motor. As illustrated in Fig. 9-4, the armature winding is connected in parallel with the field winding. The field current in a shunt motor is considerably smaller than the field current in a series motor. The field strength can be made as large as required by increasing the number of turns of wire in the field winding. Typically, in this type of motor the field winding will be made up of a great many turns of fairly fine wire.

When power is first applied to a shunt motor, the armature current will be high, which translates to a fairly high torque. (Although, it will not be as high as the starting torque for a series motor.) As the motor comes up to speed, the counter EMF will increase until it is almost equal to the applied voltage. The speed will stop increasing at this point, and will remain relatively constant, almost independent of the mechanical load.

Applying a mechanical load will tend to slow the motor down, of course. But it will also reduce the counter EMF, which increases the torque, bringing the speed back up to close to its no-load value.

To summarize, the shunt motor has a reasonable starting torque. Its biggest advantage is its speed is nearly constant under varying load conditions. Obviously, the shunt motor is used primarily in applications where a constant speed is required.

Finally, there is the third type of dc motor, which is sort of a blend of the series motor and the shunt motor. This is the compound motor. As shown in Fig. 9-5, this type of motor has two field windings. One is in series with the armature, while the other one is in parallel with it.

The compound motor behaves much like the series motor described earlier, with one important difference. The parallel field winding prevents the speed runaway problems that can be encountered with a series motor under no load (or sometimes low load) conditions. The parallel winding provides a nearly constant field strength. The speed will not try to increase without limit.

The speed, up to some definite maximum, will be determined by the mechanical load. The compound motor is used for applications requiring a high torque over a varying load range.

Actually, there are two types of compound motors. The one just described is, by far, the more common. It is called the cumulative compound motor. The other type of compound motor is known as the differential compound motor. It behaves like a shunt motor, and offers no particular advantage in the vast majority of applications, so it is rarely used.

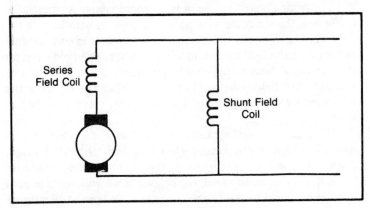

Fig. 9-5. The compound motor has two field windings.

AC MOTORS

In some applications it may be desirable to run a motor off of an ac power supply, rather than a dc power supply. There are many different types of ac motors, and we won't go into detail here.

There are eight basic types of ac motors. They are:

☐ Split-phase
☐ Capacitor-start
☐ Two-value capacitor
☐ Permanent-split capacitor
☐ Shaded pole
☐ Wound-rotor (Repulsion)
☐ Universal (or Series)
☐ Synchronous

The main differences between the various motor types lie in the amount of starting torque they develop, and their starting current requirements. The basic ac motor types are summarized in Table 9-1.

THE UNIVERSAL MOTOR

One additional type of motor should be mentioned here. The universal motor is rather unique in that it can be run off of either ac or dc power.

The operating characteristics of the universal motor are similar to those of the dc series motor. The starting torque is quite high. This type of motor is suitable for applications involving large loads and relatively short running times.

In most cases, a universal motor will run somewhat faster when it is run on dc than when it is operated on ac power. This is because in dc operation, only the winding resistance is of significance, but in ac operation, both the resistance and the reactance of the windings affect the operation.

PROJECT 38—MOTOR CONTROLLER

Now that we have some basic familiarity with the various motor types, let's consider some of the ways in which they can be controlled. In this section we will only consider switching control. Speed control will be discussed later in this chapter.

To turn a motor on and off is easy enough. For manual control you would simply use a switch to apply and/or remove power to

Table 9-1. Comparison of Various Types of Ac Motors.

Type	Horsepower ranges	Load-starting ability	Starting current	Characteristics	Electrically reversible
Split-phase	1/20 to 1/2	Easy starting loads. Develops 150 percent of full-load torque.	High; five to seven times full-load current.	Inexpensive, simple construction. Small for a given motor power. Nearly constant speed with a varying load.	Yes
Capacitor-start	1/8 to 10	Hard starting loads. Develops 350 to 400 percent of full-load torque.	Medium, three to six times full-load current.	Simple construction, long service. Good general-purpose motor suitable for most jobs. Nearly constant speed with a varying load.	Yes
Two-value capacitor	2 to 20	Hard starting loads. Develops 350 to 450 percent of full-load torque.	Medium, three to five times full-load current.	Simple construction, long service, with minimum maintenance. Requires more space to accommodate larger capacitor. Low line current. Nearly constant speed with a varying load.	Yes

Type	Horsepower range	Starting characteristics	Starting current	Comments	Reversible
Permanent-split capacitor	1/20 to 1	Easy starting loads. Develops 150 percent of full-load torque.	Low, two to four times full-load current.	Inexpensive, simple construction. Has no start winding switch. Speed can be reduced by lowering the voltage for fans and similar units.	Yes
Shaded pole	1/250 to 1/2	Easy starting loads.	Medium	Inexpensive, moderate efficiency, for light duty.	No
Wound-rotor (Repulsion)	1/6 to 10	Very hard starting loads. Develops 350 to 400 percent of full-load torque.	Low, two to four times full-load current.	Larger than equivalent size split-phase or capacitor motor. Running current varies only slightly with load.	No. reversed by brush ring re-adjustment
Universal or series	1/150 to 2	Hard starting loads. Develops 350 to 450 percent of full-load torque.	High	High speed, small size for a given horsepower. Usually directly connected to load. Speed changes with load variations.	Yes, some types
Synchronous	Very small, fractional	N/A[1]	N/A	Constant speed.	N/A

[1]N/A = not applicable.

the motor. In a remote control or automation system, it is just a matter of using the electronic equivalent of a switch. In most cases a transistor switch, or a relay would be employed. Figure 9-6 shows a typical relay based motor control circuit. Certainly there should be nothing at all surprising in this.

In many control applications we may want to reverse the direction of the motor's rotation. For example, let's consider a door opening device. Let's say that the motor shaft rotates clockwise to open the door. In order for the same motor to close the door, it will now have to rotate counterclockwise.

Reversing the direction of a dc motor is not difficult. It can be accomplished simply by reversing the direction of current flow in either the armature winding or the field winding, but not both. Reversing the direction of a dc motor with a manual DPDT switch can be accomplished with the circuitry illustrated in Fig. 9-7. A detail of the wiring of the switch is shown in Fig. 9-8. Figure 9-9 shows how the same thing can be accomplished by a pair of relays. One control signal causes the motor to run in one direction. A second control signal is used to operate the motor in the opposite direction.

While functional, this simplistic approach is far from ideal. Because two control signals are required, the control circuitry may be complicated. An extra connecting wire may be required in a remote control application.

A potentially serious problem could occur if somehow both relays were activated at the same time. This would be rather like a short circuit. The transistors and/or the motor could be damaged. Whenever multiple control signals are used, you must consider the results of two or more appearing at once. Accidents can happen. For example, consider a remote control application with two sig-

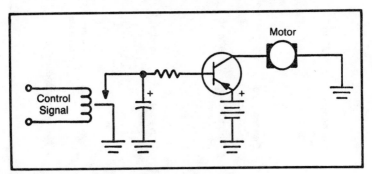

Fig. 9-6. A relay can be used to control a motor.

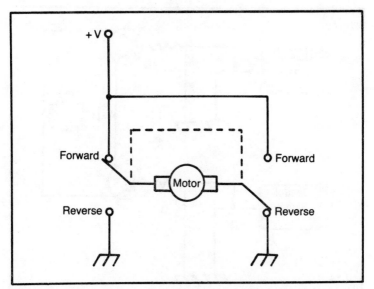

Fig. 9-7. A DPDT switch can be used to manually reverse the direction of a motor's motion.

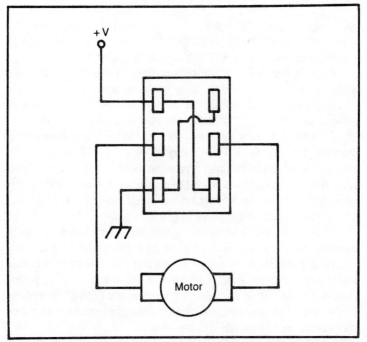

Fig. 9-8. This drawing illustrates how the switch in Fig. 9-7 should be wired.

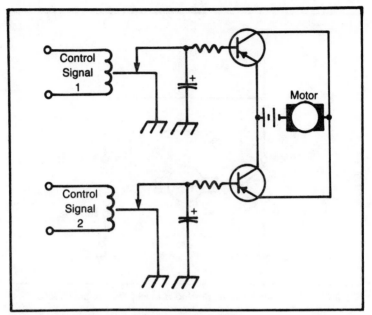

Fig. 9-9. Two relays can also be used for bidirectional motor control.

nal wires and a common wire in the connecting cable. If the two signal wires were shorted together somewhere along their length, a control signal on one will appear on the other too.

Back in Fig. 9-7 we manually controlled the direction of the motor with a DPDT switch. Why can't we use a DPDT relay to accomplish the same ends? The answer is, there is no reason at all why not. Figure 9-10 illustrates how this may be done.

A rather different approach to controlling motor direction is illustrated in Fig. 9-11. Here a digital logic signal is used to control the motor. A logic 0 (low) drives the motor in the forward direction. A logic 1 (high) reverses the motor's rotation. Switching is accomplished via four VMOŚ type FETs (field-effect transistors). The parts list for this project is given in Table 9-2.

In certain control applications, we don't want the motor shaft to rotate freely. Some limitation of its motion may be required.

As an example, let's say we have a control system that mechanically turns a potentiometer, such as a volume control. A potentiometer turns just so far, before it reaches the limit of its motion. If the motor keeps turning and tries to force the potentiometer past its normal limit, damage will result.

One potential solution to this type of problem is to use a loose

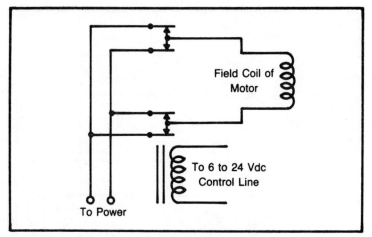

Fig. 9-10. A DPDT relay can give bidirectional control of a motor with a single control signal.

mechanical coupling between the motor and the potentiometer. When the potentiometer reaches one of its extreme positions, it will resist further movement in that direction. The loose mechanical linkage will slip, allowing the motor to continue turning without forcing the potentiometer past its limits. Unfortunately, once the coupling has slipped a few times, it may become too loose, and the linkage may become erratic. Eventually the motor won't be able to turn the potentiometer at all, because the coupling is too loose to catch at all.

A better approach is shown in Fig. 9-12. A pair of NC (Normally Closed) snap action switches are used to mark the mechanical limits of motion. The associated circuitry is illustrated in Fig. 9-13.

When the limit is reached in one direction, switch S1 will open. This allows a gate current to reach the SCR, turning it on. The relay is activated, reversing its switching contacts. The motor will now start to rotate in the opposite direction.

As soon as the motor starts moving back away from the limit position, the limit switch will be allowed to close, removing the gate signal from the SCR. This will have no effect on the SCR, which will continue to conduct until the anode/cathode is interrupted.

At the opposite limit position, switch S2 is opened. This interrupts the anode/cathode current flow through the SCR. It now shuts off, deactivating the relay. The switching contacts revert to their original position. The motor now starts turning in the original direc-

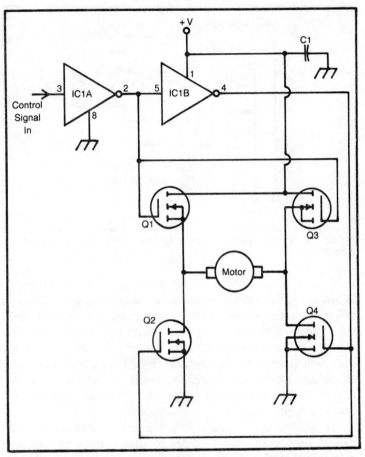

Fig. 9-11. A digital logic signal can bidirectionally control a motor with this circuit.

tion. While this system has its limitations, it would prove useful in a number of control applications.

PROJECT 39—SPEED CONTROL

In many control applications it may be important to control the

Table 9-2. Parts List for the Digital Motor Control Circuit of Fig. 9-11.

IC1	CD4049 hex inverter IC
Q1-Q4	VMOS FET (VN (VN67 or similar)
C1	0.1 μF capacitor

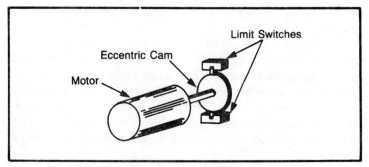

Fig. 9-12. Snap action switches can be used to limit mechanical motion.

speed as well as (or instead of) the direction of the motor's rotation. Controlling motor speed is a little more difficult than controlling direction, but it is still far from impossible. There are several possible approaches.

To a large extent the speed of a motor is determined by the applied voltage. This would suggest that you could control the speed with a simple voltage divider circuit built around a potentiometer or rheostat. In some cases this will work. In most instances, however, it will result in very unreliable operation.

One problem is that most motors draw a fairly large amount of current. The power drawn through the potentiometer could exceed the limits of standard components. The potentiometer could literally go up in smoke. High-power potentiometers and rheostats

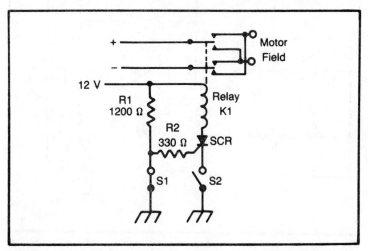

Fig. 9-13. This is the circuitry for the system illustrated in Fig. 9-12.

could be used, but they tend to be expensive and bulky. Besides, operation may still be unreliable.

The culprit is inertia. It takes more energy to start a motor moving than it takes to keep it moving. At low speed settings with a potentiometer, there may not be enough power to overcome the initial inertia. It can be done, with a little more effort. The potentiometer can be set for a relatively high speed to start the motor, then backed off to the desired low speed. This is inefficient at best, and could be difficult to accomplish conveniently in a control system.

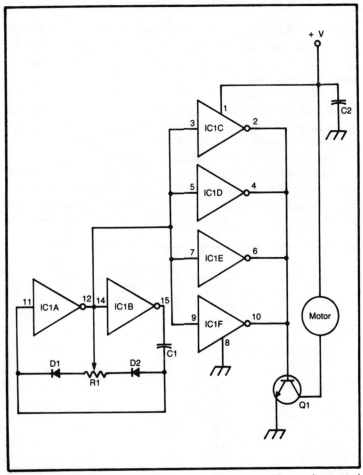

Fig. 9-14. A variable frequency square wave generator can be used to control the speed of a motor.

Table 9-3. Parts List for the Motor Speed Control Circuit of Fig. 9-14.

IC1	CD4049 hex inverter IC
Q1	NPN transistor (2N3055 or similar)
D1, D2	Diode (1N914 or similar)
R1	1 MΩ potentiometer
C1	0.022 μF capacitor
C2	0.1 μF capacitor

Instead of using voltage control to set the speed, a better approach would be to use duty cycle control. A driving oscillator is used instead of dc voltage to power the motor. The oscillator puts out a rectangle wave that switches repeatedly between V+ and ground. In other words, the V+ signal to the motor is switched on and off at a rapid rate (many times a second). The ratio between the on time and the off time is called the duty cycle. The amount of on time determines the speed of the motor.

By adjusting the frequency of the oscillator, we can control the speed. A simple circuit for accomplishing this is illustrated in Fig. 9-14. The parts list is given in Table 9-3.

By using duty cycle control, we make inertia work for us instead of against us. The motor is turned on at full speed, overcoming its starting inertia. During the off portion of the oscillator signal, the motor is turned off. But inertia works both ways. It will take some finite time before the motor comes to a complete stop. Before it gets a chance to slow down significantly, the control signal goes high again, turning on the motor full speed. The end result is a fairly smooth, constant speed that is proportional to the oscillator frequency.

In the circuit of Fig. 9-14, the oscillator frequency is set via potentiometer R1. Almost any oscillator circuit can be used in this type of application.

The 2N3055 transistor called for in the parts list should be sufficient for low-power motors. A larger, more powerful transistor may be required to drive a larger motor. The transistor must be able to handle the current drawn by the motor. Check the manufacturer's spec sheets for both the motor and the transistor.

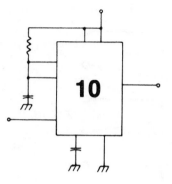

Electronic Switching

Y OU HAVE PROBABLY NOTICED BY NOW THAT CERTAIN BASIC
principles continuously crop up in control applications. Practically all remote control and automation devices involve some form
of electronic switching. This chapter will explore several important aspects of electronic switching.

RELAYS

Probably the simplest form of electronic switching is the relay. We have used these devices in many of the projects already
presented in this book.

Just what is a relay anyway? Basically, a relay consists of two
main parts, a coil, and a magnetically controlled switch. When current flows through the coil, a magnetic field builds up around it.
This magnetic field activates the switch. The magnetic field attracts
an armature in the switch. The movement of the armature makes
or breaks one or more switch contacts.

When current stops flowing through the coil, the magnetic field,
naturally, collapses. A spring pulls the armature back to its original position. The switch contacts revert to their original states.

Like manual switches, relay switch contacts come in a variety
of configurations, as illustrated in Fig. 10-1. The simplest version
has just two contacts. This is called a SPST (single pole, single
throw) switch. The contacts may be normally open (NO), or normally closed (NC). The "normal" state is the condition of the switch

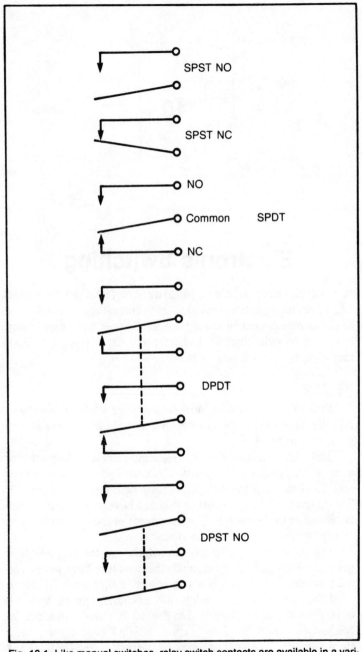

Fig. 10-1. Like manual switches, relay switch contacts are available in a variety of configurations.

contacts when the relay is not activated (no current flowing through the coil).

A SPDT (single pole, double throw) switch has three contacts. The middle contact (armature) is the common. One of the other contacts is normally open, and the other is normally closed. When the relay is activated, one contact is made, and another is broken.

The next more complex switch contact arrangement is the DPDT (double pole, double throw). The DPDT switch is essentially two independent SPDT switches that are operated in unison.

DPST (double pole, single throw) switches are also possible, but are rarely used. If you need a DPST format, use a DPDT, and leave the NC contacts open. Multiple (more than 2) poles and/or throws are also available for complex switching applications.

The coil requirements are of considerable importance. Some are designed to work on ac, others on dc. The activating voltage ranges from 1 to 250 volts. Commonly available relays generally tend to use just a few standard values, including;

☐ 6 Volts
☐ 12 Volts
☐ 24 Volts
☐ 48 Volts
☐ 117 Volts
☐ 240 Volts

Low voltage relays (under 100 volts) are usually dc types. The higher voltage ratings (117 volts and 240 volts) are usually ac models.

The applied voltage should be close to the rated value, although it doesn't need to be exact. Generally, if you are within 20% (plus or minus) of the rated value, you won't have any problems. Too high a voltage could burn out the coil, and/or damage the armature. Too low a voltage probably won't do any damage, but it could result in unreliable switching.

Whenever you have a switch in series with an inductance (coil), there is a potential for trouble. When the switch is opened (voltage removed), the magnetic field around the coil will collapse. A voltage proportional to the rate of change of current is self-induced in the coil. This voltage can be quite high, because the current drops to zero very rapidly. This high voltage could eventually damage the relay. To protect against such damage, it is a good idea to place a diode across the relay coil, as shown in Fig. 10-2.

The diode's PIV (peak inverse voltage) rating should be higher than the power supply voltage. The current handling capability should be considerably greater than the load operating current. A current handling capability of 20 to 30 times the load operating current would be appropriate.

In most of the projects in this book, I have used a 1N4002 diode, which is readily available, and its PIV and current ratings are considerably greater than required for any of the circuits.

In some applications, you will need to drive a high-current relay from a low-current source. You could cascade two relays, but generally it will be more economical to use a simple transistor amplifier, like the one shown in Fig. 10-3.

TRANSISTOR SWITCHES

One of the chief advantages of using electronic circuitry is that there are no mechanical parts. Mechanical parts wear out and perform erratically far more often than electronic components. They can jam, corrode, get dirty, break, bend, or develop any of a number of problems, especially when there are relatively small and delicate parts.

A relay, of course, is primarily a mechanical device, even though it is electrically operated. They are reasonably reliable, but are often the first part in a circuit to develop problems. In addition, while fast, a relay does take a finite amount of time to change its switch connections. When several relays are involved in a system, the cumulative time delay can add up to a significant total.

Fortunately, semiconductor devices can be used in electronic switching applications. They are small, reliable, inexpensive, and

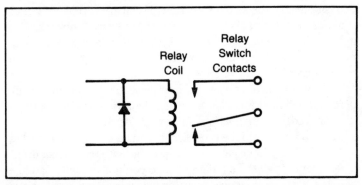

Fig. 10-2. A diode should be placed across the relay coil to protect against high voltage self-inductance spikes.

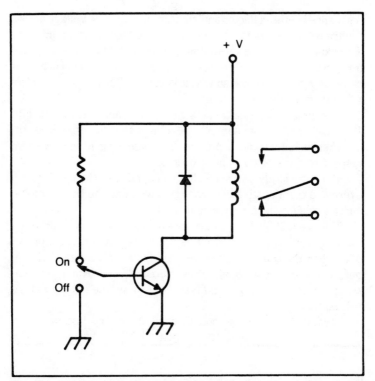

Fig. 10-3. A high-current relay can be driven from a low current source by using a simple transistor amplifier.

very fast. They also consume a relatively low amount of power, compared to relays.

Bipolar transistors make excellent electronic switches. To get a transistor to function as an electronic switch, it must be correctly biased. There are three basic biasing schemes, or modes for transistor switching circuits. They are as follows:

☐ the saturated mode
☐ the current mode
☐ the avalanche mode

We will discuss each of these modes briefly.

Saturated Mode

In the saturated mode, the transistor is turned ON by biasing it into saturation. The collector current is limited only by the resistances in the collector and emitter circuits. The voltage across the transistor (known as the saturation voltage) is at a minimum. The exact level of the saturation voltage is defined by the collector current and the load resistance. The OFF condition is achieved by biasing the transistor so that it is cut off. That is, so no collector current flows.

A simple saturation-mode switching circuit is shown in Fig. 10-4. Battery (voltage source) VBB biases the transistor into cutoff when no input signal is present. The base is made negative with respect to the emitter. The transistor is OFF.

If a sufficiently positive voltage is applied to the input, it will overcome this negative bias voltage, switching the transistor ON, and allowing collector current to flow.

Voltage will be dropped across the load resistor R_L only when there is some collector current. Since there is a collector current only when the transistor is turned on, (positive voltage at the input), there will be a voltage drop across R_L only when the transistor switch is in its ON condition. Otherwise, the output voltage will be zero.

Ideally, the transistor should switch ON and OFF instantly, with

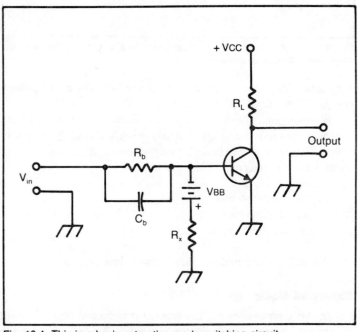

Fig. 10-4. This is a basic saturation mode switching circuit.

150

no transition time between states. This simply isn't possible with practical real-world devices. Some finite time will be required for the transistor to reverse its output state. The switching time will usually be measured in microseconds, which is close enough to instant response for the vast majority of practical applications. A transistor's switching time is considerably faster than the switching time of a relay.

Let's assume we are working with the circuit shown in Fig. 10-4. Initially, it is in its OFF state. There is no collector current, so there is no voltage across R_L.

Now, at some specific time (t_0), a positive pulse is applied to the input. Base current will start to flow right away, but there will be a brief period of time before the emitter/base voltage can climb from its initial negative value through zero, to a positive voltage. Collector current cannot even begin to flow until the emitter/base voltage is at least slightly positive. Then the collector current will require some finite time to reach its maximum level from the starting point of zero.

The turn-on time is considered to be the time from when the positive voltage is first applied to the base (t_0) and the instant when the collector current reaches 90% of its maximum value (I_1). This is called the delay time. It is almost always very small. Similarly, the transistor cannot go instantly from saturation to cutoff when the input voltage is removed.

When the positive input voltage is removed, VBB brings the voltage on the base back to a negative level. The base current momentarily goes negative, until the emitter/base voltages goes negative, and the emitter/base junction ceases to conduct. The emitter/base voltage and the collector current remain positive for a brief period after the base is brought down to a negative voltage.

The time it takes for the collector to drop to 10% of its maximum level after the positive input signal is called the storage time, and is determined by the internal capacitances formed within the transistor while it is in saturation. These capacitances are charged when the transistor is turned on, and discharge relatively slowly when the transistor is turned off. Because these internal capacitances are very small, we are generally talking about storage times in the microsecond or millisecond range.

Bridging capacitor C_b across the base resistor R_b increases the switching speed. This capacitor is not always used, because it is not essential for operation of the circuit.

To find the component values in this circuit, you must know

the saturation current $I_{c(sat)}$. This value can be easily found via Ohm's law:

$$I_{c(sat)} = \frac{V_{CC}}{R_L}$$

Resistance R_L is selected to match the output load being driven by the circuit.

Let's assume the following values are in the circuit:

$V_{CC} = 9$ volts
$V_{BB} = 1.5$ volt
$R_L = 10$ kΩ (10,000 ohms)

In this case, the saturation current works out to:

$$I_{c(sat)} = \frac{9}{10000} = 0.0009 \text{ amp} = 0.9 \text{ mA}$$

The value of resistor R_x is found using this form of Ohm's law:

$$R_x = \frac{V_{BB}}{I_{CBO}}$$

where V_{BB} is the negative base voltage, and I_{CBO} is the collector-to-base leakage current when the transistor is operating at its maximum temperature. This value can be obtained from the manufacturer's specification sheet for the transistor used. If we assume I_{CBO} is 2 μA (0.000002 amp), R_x should have a value of:

$$R_x = \frac{1.5}{0.000002} = 750,000 \text{ ohms} = 75 \text{ kΩ}$$

Next, we need to look at a characteristic curve graph for the transistor (included in the specification sheet). A typical characteristic curve graph is shown in Fig. 10-5.

Plot the load line for the collector circuit (the solid line marked "Load" in the graph). An estimated value for the base current (I_{BS}) is indicated by the point where the load line crosses the transis-

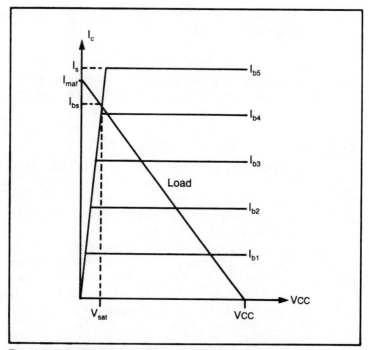

Fig. 10-5. A characteristic curve graph illustrates a transistor's operating characteristics under various conditions.

tor's saturation resistance curve. In our example, this is just a little greater than I_{b4}.

We can now find the value of the base resistor (R_b):

$$R_b = \frac{V_{IN(max)}}{I_{BS} - I_{CBO}}$$

where $V_{IN(max)}$ is the maximum input voltage.

Let's say that I_{BS} works out to 0.225 mA (0.000225 amp), and the maximum input voltage is 2.50 volts. In this case R_b should have a value approximately equal to:

$$R_b = \frac{2.50}{0.000225 - 0.000002}$$

$$= \frac{2.5}{0.000223}$$

153

$$= 11211 \text{ ohms}$$
$$\approx 12,000 \text{ ohms} = 12 \text{ k}\Omega$$

If capacitor C_b is used, its value could be derived mathematically, but it is usually easier just to breadboard the circuit, and experiment with different capacitance values until the best switching speed is obtained.

Current Mode

Higher switching speeds can be obtained if the transistor is not put into saturation when it is turned on. In the current mode, the transistor is biased so that it operates close to, but not quite in saturation. The collector-emitter voltage is therefore somewhat greater than the saturation voltage of the device.

As in the saturated mode, the transistor switch is turned off by biasing it so the semiconductor is in the cut-off (nonconducting) state.

A typical current-mode switching circuit is illustrated in Fig. 10-6. Notice that it is very similar to the saturated mode circuit of Fig. 10-4.

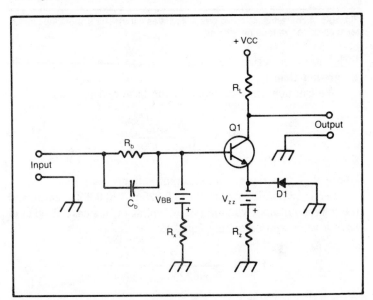

Fig. 10-6. A current-mode switching circuit is similar to, but faster than a saturated-mode switching circuit.

The battery (VBB) and resistor (R_x) combination in the base circuit holds the transistor cut off when there is no input signal. This works essentially the same as the saturated-mode circuit described earlier.

The emitter voltage source (VEE) keeps diode D1 turned on (conducting) at all times. Assuming a silicon diode is used, there will be approximately 0.7 volt across this component. If the base of the transistor is at ground potential (0 volts), only the 0.7 volt across the diode will be between the emitter and the base. This would keep the transistor conducting with 0 volts at the base.

The base bias voltage (VBB) has to be cancelled out by an input signal with the opposite polarity. When V_{in} is equal to or greater than VBB, the transistor is switched on. When V_{in} is less than VBB, the transistor is cut off.

If VEE was not included in the circuit, we would have practically the same situation as with the saturated mode circuit of Fig. 10-4. When the transistor is turned on by a positive pulse at the input, the collector will be equal to the beta of the transistor multiplied by the base current. If the base current is large enough, the transistor will be driven into saturation.

The three added components in the emitter circuit (VEE, R_e, and D1) limit the input current, and therefore, the collector current. The maximum current through the transistor is less than the saturation value. The maximum current flow through this circuit's transistor is determined by the component values in the emitter circuit.

The diode's polarity prevents any current from the emitter from flowing through it, but the 0.7 volt across the diode does limit the current flow through R_e, which is the maximum current that can flow through either the emitter or the collector in this circuit. The transistor will not be driven into saturation as the saturation current value is greater than the current through R_e. In practical circuits, the current through the load resistor (R_L) should be limited to a maximum level equal to the current through the emitter resistor (R_e).

In our saturated-mode example in the last section, we found that the saturated collector current (the transistor's ON current) was 0.9 mA. For a current-mode circuit, we want the emitter limiting current $(I_{e1} = VEE/R_e)$ to be less than this value. Let's assume we want a value of 0.7 mA (0.0007 amp). If VEE is 1.5 volt, the emitter resistor should have a value of about:

$$R_e = \frac{V_{EE}}{I_{el}} = \frac{1.5}{0.0007} = 2143 \text{ ohms}$$

If we use a standard 2.2 kΩ (2200 ohm) resistor, the maximum collector current/emitter current will be approximately:

$$I_{cmax} = \frac{1.5}{2200} = 0.00068 = 0.68 \text{ mA}$$

The transistor will not be put into saturation when it is turned on.

Because the transistor does not have to work quite so hard (conduct as much current) in its ON state, it can switch between states considerably faster than in a comparable saturated-mode switching circuit.

Avalanche Mode

The third switching mode is also the fastest. This is the avalanche mode. The ON and OFF states of the transistor switch are kept within the breakdown portion of the transistor's operating curve. Faster switching can be obtained with special devices such as hot-carrier, pin, snap-off, or tunnel diodes.

Saturated-mode and current-mode switching circuits require a specific base voltage to be maintained to hold the transistor OFF (or ON). In an avalanche mode circuit, however, a brief pulse is all that is needed to hold the transistor in either ON or OFF state. A continuous input voltage signal is not required.

OTHER SEMICONDUCTOR SWITCHING DEVICES

In the last section we considered switching circuits built around bipolar transistors. Other semiconductor devices, such as FETs, UJTs, PUTs, SCRs, and triacs can also be employed in electronic switching applications.

FET Switches

The FET (field-effect transistor) is a semiconductor device with operating characteristics similar to those of a vacuum tube. FETs have better on-to-off current ratios than bipolar transistors. However, FET switches operate somewhat slower than circuits built around bipolar devices. This is due to the large internal capacitances

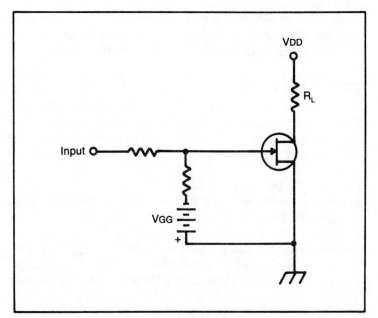

Fig. 10-7. FETs can also be used for switching applications.

of a FET. A switching circuit built around a FET is illustrated in Fig. 10-7.

UJT Switches

Another variation on the transistor is the UJT, or Unijunction transistor. It too can be used in switching applications. An ordinary (bipolar) transistor has two PN junctions. A unijunction transistor, on the other hand, has just one. Its three leads include an emitter, and two base connections. A UJT is quite simple, as shown in Fig. 10-8.

An alternate form of the UJT is the PUT (programmable

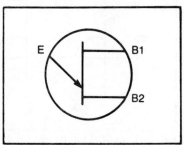

Fig. 10-8. Some switching circuits are built around UJTs.

Unijunction transistor). It is very similar to the UJT, except more of its operating characteristics are determined by the external circuitry, offering greater flexibility to the circuit designer.

SCR Switches

Many switching circuits use the SCR (silicon controlled rectifier). This device is essentially a gated diode. That is, a diode that can be electrically turned on and off. Like an ordinary diode, the SCR has an anode and a cathode. It also has a third lead called the gate.

The SCR will not conduct until a triggering pulse is applied to the gate. Current will now start flowing from the anode to the cathode. Current will continue to flow, even after the gate signal is removed. Once the SCR has been turned on, the only way it can be turned off is to break the anode/cathode current path, or to reverse the direction of the current flow. The SCR, like the diode, conducts in only one direction. It will block current of the opposite polarity.

In some circuits this mono-polarity can be very useful. For example, in many light dimmers, the SCR is used to cut-off part of each ac cycle, as shown in Fig. 10-9. When the signal exceeds a specific switching level, the gate is activated, and the SCR starts to conduct. When the ac cycle goes into its negative portion, the SCR is cut off. This whole process limits how much of the ac power will reach the load.

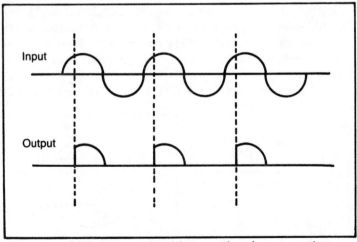

Fig. 10-9. An SCR can be used to delete a portion of an ac waveform.

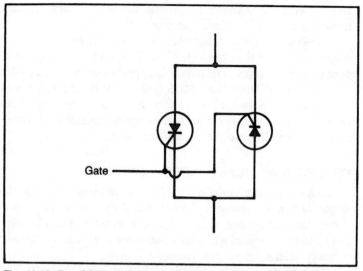

Fig. 10-10. Two SCRs can be connected like this for bipolar operation.

In other applications, the mono-polarity of the SCR could be problematic. If we need to conduct current in both directions, we can place two SCRs in reverse polarity, as illustrated in Fig. 10-10. An even more convenient solution is to use a triac. This device is essentially a pair of back to back SCRs in a single housing. The schematic symbol for a triac is shown in Fig. 10-11.

DC CONTROLLED SWITCHES

An extremely handy device has appeared on the market in the

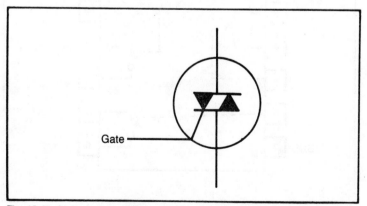

Fig. 10-11. A triac is essentially a pair of back-to-back SCRs in a single housing.

last few years. It is known by various names, including "dc controlled switch," and "bipolar analog switch."

These are electrically operated switches in IC form. The most common device of this type is the CD4066. It contains four independent switching stages. The pinout diagram is shown in Fig. 10-12.

While the CD4066 is a CMOS type digital IC, it may be used with either digital or analog circuitry. A digital control signal can be used to operate a switch carrying an analog signal in either direction. The switches are not polarity sensitive.

PROJECTS 40 AND 41—TOUCH SWITCHES

One of the most unexpected switching devices is a touch of a finger, or foot, or whatever. Touch control circuits can be used to control almost anything, with just the lightest touch. A touch switch can be easily operated when your hands are full, or it can be used in many hidden sensor applications.

A simple touch switch circuit is illustrated in Fig. 10-13. The parts list is given in Table 10-1. There is a lot of flexibility in this circuit. Nothing is terribly critical. Almost any N-channel FET and NPN transistor may be used. The transistor must be able to com-

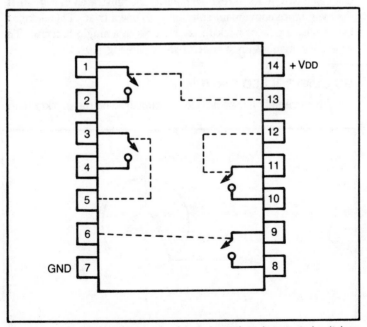

Fig. 10-12. The CD4066 IC contains four independent dc-operated switches.

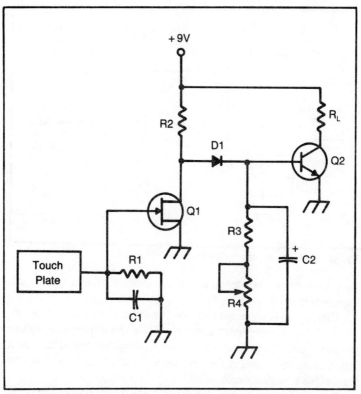

Fig. 10-13. Almost anything can be controlled by a simple touch with this circuit.

fortably handle the current drawn by the load.

The touch plate is an exposed metallic contact. Obviously it must be 100% isolated from any ac power source for safety. Only low-power dc voltages flow through the touch switch circuit itself.

Table 10-1. Parts List for the First Touch Switch Circuit (Fig. 10-13).

Q1	N channel FET (see text)	
Q2	NPN transistor (see text)	
D1	1N914 diode	
C1	100 pF capacitor	
C2	15 μF 25 V electrolytic capacitor	
R1	10 MΩ resistor	
R2	2.7 kΩ resistor	
R3	22 kΩ resistor	
R4	50 kΩ potentiometer	
R_L	Load resistance	

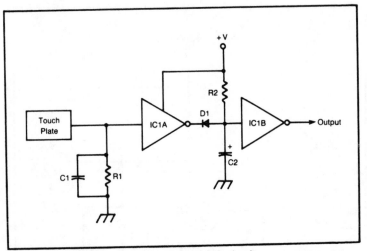

Fig. 10-14. This is an alternative touch switch circuit.

Potentiometer R4 is used to adjust the shut-off time of the circuit. Experiment with settings.

I strongly recommend that you bread-board this circuit before constructing a permanent version. While the component values are not especially critical, sometimes this type of circuit may be a little fussy, and it might require some minor changes or fine tuning before it will operate reliably.

A second touch switch circuit is shown in Fig. 10-14. The parts list for this project is given in Table 10-2.

How do these circuits work? Sixty-hertz power signals are almost always all around us. Low level 60-hertz signals are picked up by the body, and can be transmitted through a fingertip (or other body part) to a small touchplate. In some cases, a simple bare end of wire will do, but usually a larger plate will be more convenient, and possibly more reliable. I often use a small piece of copper clad circuit board (the type used for home-made PC boards) but almost anything conductive will do the trick.

Table 10-2. Parts List for the Second Touch Switch Circuit (Fig. 10-14).

IC1	CD4049 hex inverter
D1	1N914 diode
C1	100 pF capacitor
C2	1 μF capacitor
R1	10 MΩ resistor
R2	100 kΩ resistor

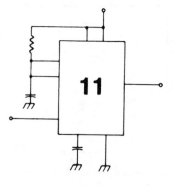

Timers

V IRTUALLY ALL AUTOMATION APPLICATIONS REQUIRE SOME sort of timer. Sometimes a 24-hour clock will be used to turn something on or off at a specific time. In other cases, some action will be periodically repeated at regular intervals. In still other applications, a timer will be used to introduce a delay between events.

There are many different possible approaches to timer circuitry. IC timer devices are widely available, inexpensive and easy to use, so there is little point in using discrete components for timing applications.

In this chapter, we will look at some of the most popular timer ICs and some of the ways they can be employed in automation applications.

THE 555 TIMER

Without the slightest doubt, the most popular timer device is the 555 IC. The pinout diagram for this device is shown in Fig. 11-1. Entire books have been written about just this one device and its many applications.

Simple timers can be built from discrete components, such as bipolar and unijunction transistors, but such circuits have some important limitations. For one thing, they tend to be very power supply dependent. If the supply voltage changes for any reason, the timing period can be altered, often by a significant amount.

The 555 timer IC employs a rather tidy solution to this poten-

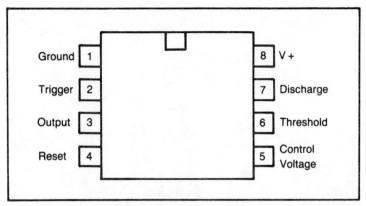

Fig. 11-1. The 555 is unquestionably the most popular timer IC around today.

tial problem. The timing period is not dependent on the absolute voltage. Instead, the 555 operates by using the ratio of the supply voltage and certain IC terminal voltages. If the supply voltage changes, the terminal voltages will also change by a like amount, holding the ratio constant.

The 555 timer IC is very tolerant when it comes to the power supply. It will work just fine with supply voltages ranging from +4.5 volts to +15 volts dc. In addition, although it is principally a linear device, the 555 can easily be directly interfaced to TTL or CMOS digital circuits.

Some of the pin labels may not be familiar to you, so let's take a closer, pin-by-pin look at the 555 timer.

Pin 1—Ground. This one is clear enough. It is the ground (common) connection for the supply and signal voltages.

Pin 2—Trigger. This pin is used to initiate a timing cycle. The 555 is triggered by dropping pin 2 below 1/3 V+. Ordinarily, this pin is held at a level above this point. The triggering voltage is typically about one half the voltage applied to pin 5. Triggering is level sensitive, so slow changing waveforms (such as sine waves) can be used, as well as more traditional and direct switching waveforms, (such as rectangle waves). If the trigger input is held below 1/3 V+ for longer than the timing period, the trigger will be immediately retriggered. This may or may not be desirable, depending on the application. Generally, the triggering signal should be at least 1 μs (0.000001 second) long for reliable triggering.

Pin 3—Output. This pin is also pretty self explanatory. This is where the timing pulses generated by the 555's internal circuitry may be tapped off. Note that the output of a timer is like a digital signal. It may take on either of two states: a low level (near ground) and a high level (near V +). There are no intermediate output levels.

Pin 4—Reset. This pin is used to reset the internal latch, and drive the output back to its normal low state. The reset threshold level is 0.7 volt, and a sink current of 0.1 mA is required for resetting the timer. These values are independent of the supply voltage. The reset pin serves an overriding function. It can force the timer to the reset condition, regardless of the signals at any of the other input pins. It is used to tell the timer that the timing period is over.

Pin 5—Control Voltage. This pin allows an external voltage to control the switching levels of the internal comparators. This permits a great deal of flexibility in using the timer. Voltage-controlled oscillators and timers, and similar applications take advantage of this pin.

Pin 6—Threshold. This pin is one of the inputs to the upper internal comparator. It is used to reset the internal latch (which drives the output low). Resetting with pin 6 is accomplished by raising the voltage on this pin to a level of about 2/3 V + . This function is level sensitive, permitting the use of slowly changing waveforms.

Pin 7—Discharge. This is the collector of an internal discharge transistor. The transistor is on when the output is low, and cut off when the output is high. This transistor switch clamps the appropriate nodes of the timing network to ground.

Pin 8—V + . This is the positive supply voltage terminal.

Virtually all timer applications are variations on multivibrators. A multivibrator is a circuit with two possible output states. The output is either at a low level, or a high level. There are no intermediate output levels. There are three types of multivibrator circuits.

A *monostable multivibrator* has one stable output state. When triggered, the output will go to the other output state for a specific length of time, and then revert back to the original stable state. The action of a monostable multivibrator is illustrated in Fig. 11-2.

A *bistable multivibrator* has two stable output states. Either output state may be held indefinitely, until a trigger pulse is received, at which point the output will reverse states. In a sense, a bistable multivibrator "remembers" its previous output state. The action of a bistable multivibrator is illustrated in Fig. 11-3.

An *astable multivibrator* has no stable output states at all. It continuously switches back and forth between output states with no

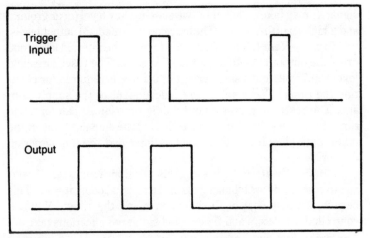

Fig. 11-2. The monostable multivibrator briefly reverses its output state when a trigger pulse is received.

trigger pulse input at all. An astable multivibrator is essentially a rectangle wave (or square wave) generator, as shown in Fig. 11-4.

For our purposes here, we are concerned with monostable and astable multivibrators. Timer ICs like the 555 can be used in both of these applications.

The basic circuit for a monostable multivibrator built around a 555 timer IC is shown in Fig. 11-5. This is its most basic mode of operation. Notice that there are only three external components: two capacitors and one resistor.

Strictly speaking, capacitor C2 isn't absolutely necessary in

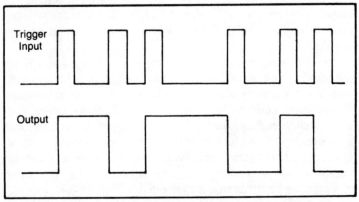

Fig. 11-3. A bistable multivibrator "remembers" its previous state, reversing output states each time a trigger pulse is received.

166

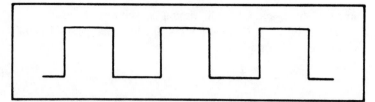

Fig. 11-4. An astable multivibrator is free running, and does not require a trigger signal to reverse output states.

many applications. Its purpose is to improve noise immunity. The 555 does pretty well in this respect on its own. Still, it is a good idea to include this capacitor, just in case. After all, it doesn't cost much, and doesn't take up much room. Typically the value of this capacitor should be between about 0.0005 μF and 0.05 μF.

The other two components, R1 and C1, define the timing period of the circuit. The formula couldn't be much simpler:

$$T = 1.1 \; R1C1$$

where T is the timing period in seconds, R1 is the timing resis-

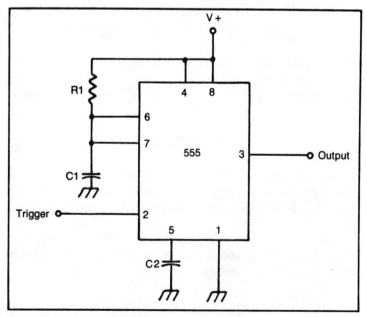

Fig. 11-5. A simple monostable multivibrator circuit can be built around the 555 timer.

tance in ohms, and C1 is the timing capacitance in farads.

For example, if R1 is 470 kΩ (470,000 ohms), and C1 is 0.22 μF (0.00000022 farad), the timing period will be:

$$
\begin{aligned}
T &= 1.1 \times 470000 \times 0.00000022 \\
&= 0.11374 \text{ second}
\end{aligned}
$$

For reliable operation, the timing resistance should be between approximately 10 kΩ (10,000 ohms) and 14 MΩ (14,000,000 ohms), and C1 should be between 100 pF (0.0000000001 farad) and 1000 μF (0.001 farad). This means that the timing period may range anywhere from a minimum of:

$$
\begin{aligned}
T &= 1.1 \times 10000 \times 0.0000000001 \\
&= 0.0011 \text{ ms} = 1.1 \ \mu s
\end{aligned}
$$

to a maximum of:

$$
\begin{aligned}
T &= 1.1 \times 14000000 \times 0.001 \\
&= 15,400 \text{ seconds} \\
&= 256.6667 \text{ minutes} \\
&= 4 \text{ hours, 16 minutes, and 40 seconds}
\end{aligned}
$$

That is quite an impressive range, isn't it?

In most practical applications, the designer will be trying to achieve a timing period of a specific length. The timing equation can be rearranged like this:

$$
R1 = T/1.1 \ C1
$$

A likely value is arbitrarily selected for C1, and this equation is used to solve for R1. If the resulting resistance value is awkward, or outside the acceptable range, you can select a new value for C1 and try again.

Let's say we need a timing period of 1 second. We will use a value of 0.1 μF (0.0000001 farad) for C1. This means we will need a timing resistance equal to:

$$
\begin{aligned}
R1 &= 1/(1.1 \times 0.0000001) \\
&= 9,090,909 \text{ ohms}
\end{aligned}
$$

9.1 Meg (9,100,000 ohms) is nominally a standard resistance value, and it is very close to the calculated value. But, in actuality, a resistor with this value would be pretty difficult to find. We'd probably do better with a smaller resistance. We therefore need to try another, larger value for C1. This time we will try a 22 μF (0.000022 farad) capacitor:

$$R1 = 1/(1.1 \times 0.000022)$$
$$= 41,322 \text{ ohms}$$

A 42 kΩ resistor would probably be close enough. Or, we could use a more readily available 39 kΩ resistor, and a 2.2 kΩ resistor in series, giving a total nominal resistance of 41,200 ohms.

There is some leeway in the values, because the component tolerances imply that they probably won't be exactly at their nominal values anyway. For precision applications, high quality (low tolerance) components should be used, of course. In addition, a variable resistance (potentiometer) can be used to fine tune for the exact timing period desired. A ten-turn potentiometer will offer the most precise control.

Now, let's examine how this monostable circuit actually works. As long as a voltage greater than 1/3 V + is applied to the trigger input (pin 2), the timer remains in its standby mode. The output is low, at approximately ground potential (0 volts).

If a voltage less than 1/3 V + (a negative going pulse) is applied to the trigger input, the timer is turned on, and begins its timing cycle. The output snaps high, to a level just slightly below V +. The capacitor starts to charge up. At some point, the voltage across C1 will exceed 2/3 V +. This voltage is fed to the threshold input (pin 6). As soon as this voltage exceeds 2/3 V +, the timer realizes that the timing period is over, and it returns to the standby mode. The output snaps back to its low (ground) level. Capacitor C1 discharges through pin 7 of the IC.

The charging rate of the capacitor is determined by the RC time constant of R1 and C1. Obviously, the longer the time constant is, the longer it will take for the capacitor to build up a charge of 2/3 V +, and the longer the timing period of the circuit will be.

Figure 11-6 shows a timing diagram summarizing the key signals within this circuit. Notice that all operating voltages are based on the value of the supply voltage (V +). If the supply voltage should

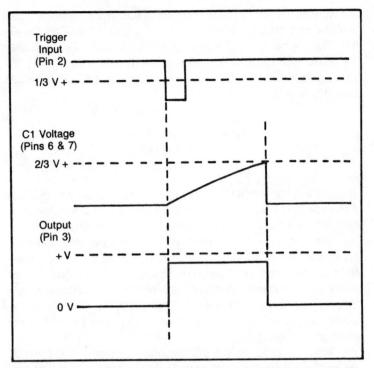

Fig. 11-6. The key signals from the circuit of Fig. 11-5 are summarized in this timing diagram.

change for any reason, the operating voltages will all change by a similar amount, so circuit operation will be virtually unaffected.

Notice also that the length of the triggering input pulse has no effect on the length of the output timing period. (Unless the triggering pulse is longer than the timing period.) Monostable multivibrators are sometimes called pulse stretchers, since the output pulse is longer than the input pulse.

The other basic timer application is the astable multivibrator. The basic 555 astable multivibrator circuit is illustrated in Fig. 11-7. Notice how similar it is to the monostable circuit presented earlier in this section.

The main differences are that there are two timing resistors (R1 and R2) in this circuit, and the trigger input (pin 2) is shorted to the threshold input (pin 6). No external input signal is used in the basic astable multivibrator. It is free-running.

When power is initially applied to this circuit, the voltage across timing capacitor C1 will, naturally, be low. As a result of this, the timer is triggered (through pin 2). The output goes to its high state, and the internal discharge transistor (at pin 7) is turned off. A complete circuit path through C1, R1, and R2 is formed, charging the capacitor. When the charge on the capacitor exceeds 2/3 V +, the upper threshold is reached. This voltage on pin 6 forces the output back to its low state.

Timing capacitor C1 now starts to discharge through R2 (but not R1). When the voltage across the capacitor drops below 1/3 V +, the timer is automatically retriggered, and a new cycle begins.

The timing signals within this circuit are illustrated in Fig. 11-8. Notice that since both R1 and R2 affect the charging time (high output—T1), and only R2 affects the discharging time (low output—T2), the low output time will always be at least slightly less than the high output time. A true 50% duty cycle square wave is not possible with this circuit, although you can come pretty close if the value of R1 is relatively small with respect to R2.

To predict the action of this circuit, we need several simple formulae.

The charging time (high output time) equals:

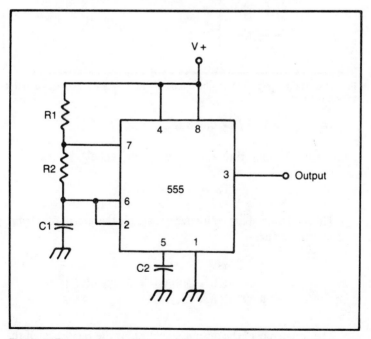

Fig. 11-7. The other basic application for the 555 timer IC is the astable multivibrator.

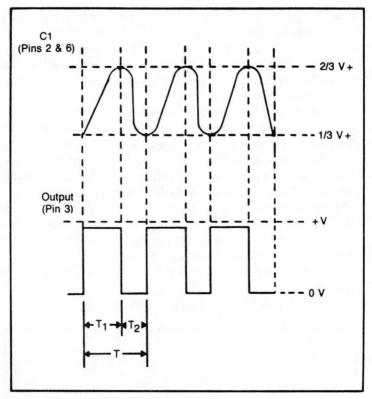

Fig. 11-8. The key signals from the circuit of Fig. 11-7 are summarized in this timing diagram.

$$T1 = 0.693 (R1 + R2)C1$$

and the discharging time (low output time) equals:

$$T2 = 0.693 \ R2C1$$

The total time of the entire cycle is simply the sum of the charge and discharge times:

$$\begin{aligned} T &= T1 + T2 \\ &= 0.693 (R1 + R2) \ C1 + 0.693 \ R2 \ C1 \\ &= 0.693 (R1 + 2R2) \ C1 \end{aligned}$$

The frequency of the output waveform is the reciprocal of the time of the entire cycle. That is:

$$F = \frac{1}{T}$$

With a little bit of algebraic rearranging, the frequency formula becomes:

$$F = \frac{1.44}{(R1 + 2R2)C1}$$

The same limitations on the component values hold, as for the monostable multivibrator. The combined sum of R1 and R2 should be between 10 kΩ and 14 MΩ. The timing capacitor (C1) should have a value between about 100 pF and approximately 1000 μF.

Let's work through a few typical examples. To begin with, let's assume we have the following component values:

$$
\begin{aligned}
R1 &= 47 \text{ k}\Omega \ (47,000 \text{ ohms}) \\
R2 &= 47 \text{ k}\Omega \ (47,000 \text{ ohms}) \\
C1 &= 0.1 \ \mu\text{F} \ (0.0000001 \text{ farad})
\end{aligned}
$$

In this case, the output will be high for a time equal to:

$$
\begin{aligned}
T1 &= 0.693 \ (R1 + R2)C1 \\
&= 0.693 \times (47,000 + 47,000) \times 0.0000001 \\
&= 6.6 \text{ ms}
\end{aligned}
$$

The low output time will be equal to:

$$
\begin{aligned}
T2 &= 0.693 \ R2C1 \\
&= 0.693 \times 47,000 \times 0.0000001 \\
&= 3.3 \text{ ms}
\end{aligned}
$$

This means that the entire output cycle will last approximately:

$$
\begin{aligned}
T &= T1 + T2 \\
&= 0.0065 + 0.0033 \\
&= 9.8 \text{ ms}
\end{aligned}
$$

Taking the reciprocal of this, we get an approximate output frequency of:

$$F = \frac{1}{T}$$

$$= \frac{1}{0.0098}$$

$$\approx 102 \text{ Hz.}$$

We can doublecheck our work, by utilizing the alternate frequency equation:

$$F = \frac{1.44}{(R1 + 2R2)C1}$$

$$= \frac{1.44}{(47000 + 2 \times 47000) \times 0.0000001}$$

$$= 102 \text{ Hz}$$

Notice that using identical values for R1 and R2 certainly does not give us a 1:2 duty cycle waveform.

Let's try a second example. This time we will assume the following component values:

$$R1 = 22 \text{ k}\Omega \text{ (22,000 ohms)}$$
$$R2 = 820 \text{ k}\Omega \text{ (820,000 ohms)}$$
$$C1 = 0.47 \text{ }\mu\text{F (0.00000047 farad)}$$

The cycle times in this example work out to:

T1 =	0.2742 second	=	274.2 ms
T2 =	0.2671 second	=	267.1 ms
T =	0.5413 second	=	541.3 ms

Notice that since R2 is so much larger than R1, the result is very close to a 1:2 (50%) duty cycle square wave.

Finally, we can solve for the output frequency of our sample circuit:

$$F = \frac{1.44}{(22000 + 2 \times 820000) \times 0.00000047}$$

$$= \frac{1.44}{(1662000) \times 0.00000047}$$

$$= \frac{1.44}{0.78114}$$

$$\approx 1.84 \text{ Hz}.$$

In many practical applications, we will only be interested in the output frequency, and we don't have to bother with calculating the timing periods at all. Large component values result in low output frequencies. For instance:

R1 = 3.3 MΩ (3,300,000 ohms)

R2 = 10 MΩ (10,000,000 ohms)

C1 = 1000 μF (0.001 farad)

$$F = \frac{1.44}{(3300000 + 2 \times 10000000) \times 0.001}$$

= 0.000062 Hz = 0.062 MHz

This is about one complete cycle every four and a half hours. This is close to the lower limit for the basic 555 astable multivibrator circuit.

On the other hand, small component values result in high output frequencies. As an example:

R1 = 6.8 k (6800 ohms)
R2 = 3.9 k (3900 ohms)
C1 = 100 pF (0.0000000001 farad)

$$F = \frac{1.44}{(6800 + 2 \times 3900) \times 0.0000000001}$$

= 986,301 Hz
$\approx$ 986 kHz

As you can see, this circuit is capable of a very wide range of output frequencies.

For stable operation, however, it is not recommended that this circuit be used at frequencies above about 100 kHz. This is due to internal storage times within the 555 chip itself.

Duty cycles of near 50% to 99% can be set up with the proper selection of values for R1 and R2. R1 may be as small as 100 ohms, or R2/100, whichever is larger.

MULTIPLE 555 ICs

The 555 timer is so versatile, it is often used several times in a single circuit. Individual 555 timer IC packages can be used, but a more elegant solution is available.

Multiple timers in a single IC package permit convenient and compact construction of complex circuits. Figure 11-9 shows the pinout diagram for the 556 IC. This is a dual timer chip. It contains two independent 555 type timers in a single package.

The 558 is a quad timer IC. It is sometimes known as the 5558. As the pinout diagram in Fig. 11-10 indicates, the 558 contains four timers that are each similar to the 555, although the available connections are somewhat simplified.

PRECISION TIMERS

The 555 is unquestionably the most popular IC timer around. But it is far from the only one available. Nor is it the best choice for all applications. The 555 is certainly cheap and convenient, but

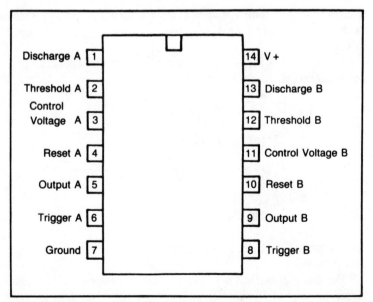

Fig. 11-9. The 556 dual timer IC contains two 555 timers in a single package.

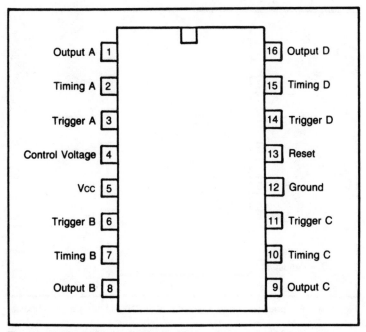

Fig. 11-10. The 558 is a quad timer IC.

in some applications, greater precision may be required.

The 322, shown in Fig. 11-11 is a popular precision timer IC. Closely related to the 322 is its "little brother," the 3905, which is illustrated in Fig. 11-12. The internal circuitry of these two devices is essentially the same, so we will just concentrate on the 322 here.

In many ways these chips offer a step up from the standard 555 timer. The most important advantages of the 322 include:

☐ A wider range of acceptable supply voltages.
☐ Greater immunity to supply voltage variations.
☐ A wider range of possible timing periods.
☐ Simpler calculations.
☐ Higher and more flexible voltage output stage.
☐ Improved timing period accuracy.

There is one major disadvantage to the 322 (aside from the higher cost). This device is not really suitable for astable operation. It is only intended for use in monostable multivibrator circuits.

The timing period calculation is simplified for the 322 (com-

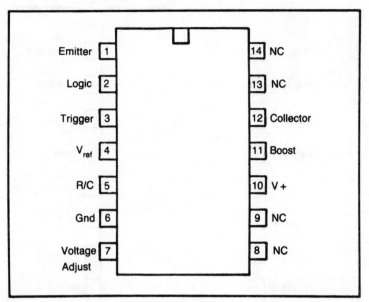

Fig. 11-11. For precision timer applications, the 322 is often a good choice.

pared to the 555) by the fact that the timing voltage reference is 0.632 times the supply voltage. This eliminates the constant in the timing equation. The formula for the timing period of the 322 is simply:

$$T = R1C1$$

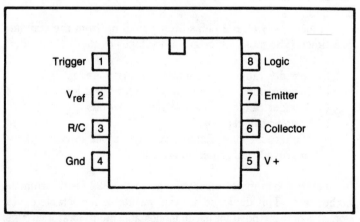

Fig. 11-12. The 3905 precision timer IC is basically a simplified version of the 322.

The timing voltage for the 322 is derived from an internal voltage regulator stage, which provides a precise 3.15 volts to the divider network. This makes the circuit even less sensitive to any variations and noise in the power supply lines than the 555.

The 322 is more versatile than the 555. The output stage may be wired in either a common-collector or a common-emitter configuration, depending on the requirements of the specific application at hand.

Additional flexibility is offered by the logic pin. In the 555 the output is normally low, and goes high only during the timing cycle. On the 322, holding the logic pin high will give the same response. A low signal on the logic pin will reverse this action. The output will normally be high, and go low only during the timing cycle. This eliminates the need for a separate inverter stage in many circuits.

Let's take a brief look at each of the pins on the 322 precision timer IC.

Pin 1—Emitter (Pin 7 on the 3905). This is an output pin. It is connected to the emitter of the internal NPN transistor. If the output is being taken off of this pin, the collector pin (12) is connected to $V+$, or some other positive voltage.

Pin 2—Logic (Pin 8 on the 3905). This pin is a logic input. It determines the normal output condition. If the logic pin is held low, the output is normally high. If the logic pin is held high, the output is normally low.

Pin 3—Trigger (Pin 1 on the 3905). This is the input pin for the trigger pulse that initiates the timing cycle. It is similar to the trigger input on the 555. The timing cycle will not be retriggered if the trigger pulse is longer than the period of the timer. The output will time out and return to its normal state, however, the timing capacitor will not be discharged until the trigger pulse is removed. The trigger input is normally held low. The timer is triggered when this input goes high (positive).

Pin 4—V_{ref} (Pin 2 on the 3905). This is a reference voltage output. It is the output of the internal 3.15 volt regulator. An external load of up to 5 mA can be applied to this output. The timing resistor (R_t) is normally connected between this pin and the R/C pin (pin 5). This reference voltage is very precise. Drift is typically 0.01% per degree centigrade.

Pin 5—R/C (Pin 3 on the 3905). This is the common connection point for the timing resistor (R_t) and the timing capacitor (C_t).

Pin 6—Gnd (Pin 4 on the 3905). This is the ground connection pin for the IC.

Pin 7—Voltage Adjust (not used on the 3905). This pin allows the designer to access the comparator reference point for charging and discharging the timing capacitor. The normal comparator reference point is 2 volts. If this pin is not used, noise immunity of the circuit can be improved by bypassing it to ground with a capacitor in the 0.01 μF to 0.1 μF range.

Pin 8—No Connection.

Pin 9—No Connection.

Pin 10—V+ (Pin 5 on the 3905). This is the positive supply voltage pin.

Pin 11—Boost (not used on the 3905). Connecting this pin to V+ increases the switching speed of the internal comparator. It is generally used to improve the timing accuracy for periods less than about 1 ms (0.001 second).

Pin 12—Collector (Pin 6 on the 3905). This is an alternate output pin. It is the collector of the internal NPN output transistor. If this output is used, the emitter output (pin 1) will generally be grounded. An output from this pin is taken across a load to V+.

Pin 13—No Connection.

Pin 14—No Connection.

A basic monostable multivibrator circuit using the 322 precision timer IC is illustrated in Fig. 11-13. The logic input is shown as switchable here. Normally it will be permanently connected to either ground or V_{ref} depending on the desired output pattern.

The value of resistor R1 should be between about 10 kΩ (10,000 ohms) and 100 MΩ (100,000,000 ohms). Capacitor C1 should be between about 100 pF (0.0000001 farad) and 1000 μF (0.00 farad).

The timing equation is simply:

$$T = R1C1$$

This means the timing period can range from:

$$
\begin{aligned}
T &= 10000 \times 0.0000000001 \\
&= 0.001 \text{ ms} \\
&= 1 \ \mu s
\end{aligned}
$$

to:

$$T = 100000000 \times 0.001$$

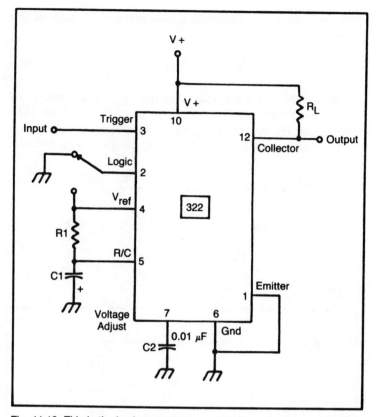

Fig. 11-13. This is the basic monostable multivibrator circuit using the 322.

    = 10,000 seconds
    = 2 hours, 46 minutes, 40 seconds

Certainly an impressive range!

THE 2240 PROGRAMMABLE TIMER

A particularly exciting and versatile timing device is the 2240 programmable timer. The pinout for this IC is shown in Fig. 11-14.

One of the first things you'll notice in this pinout diagram is that there are 8 timing outputs. These outputs are actually part of an eight-bit binary counter. By combining these outputs in the proper combinations, we can create timing periods of from 1 to 255 times the basic timing cycle period (T). The basic timing cycle period is calculated with the same simple equation we used for the

322 precision timer discussed in the preceding section of this chapter:

$$T = R_tC_t$$

This is the timing period at the output of pin 1. The remaining outputs are binary multiples of the basic timing cycle period (T). To see how this works, let's try an example.

We will assume we are using the following component values:

$$R_t = 39 \text{ k}\Omega \text{ (39,000 ohms)}$$
$$C_t = 0.5 \text{ }\mu\text{F (0.0000005 farad)}$$

In this case, the basic timing cycle period would be equal to:

$$T = 39000 \times 0.0000005$$
$$= 0.0195 \text{ second}$$
$$= 19.5 \text{ ms}$$

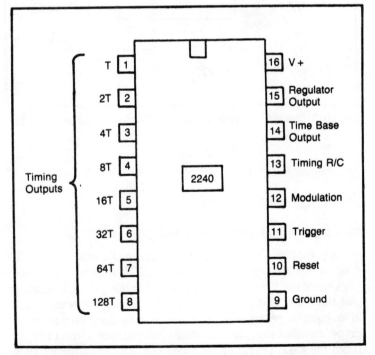

Fig. 11-14. One of the most versatile timing devices is the 2240 programmable timer IC.

When the circuit is triggered (pin 11) at output pin 1 we will have a 0.0195 second pulse. Each of the other output pins will put out pulses of the following lengths:

Pin 2	2T	=	2	× 0.0195	=	0.039 second
Pin 3	4T	=	4	× 0.0195	=	0.078 second
Pin 4	8T	=	8	× 0.0195	=	0.156 second
Pin 5	16T	=	16	× 0.0195	=	0.312 second
Pin 6	32T	=	32	× 0.0195	=	0.624 second
Pin 7	64T	=	64	× 0.0195	=	1.248 second
Pin 8	128T	=	128	× 0.0195	=	2.496 second

All with a single circuit!

We can also combine output pins to create different multiples of the basic timing cycle. For example, if we ADD together pins 1, 2, 4, and 7, the output pulse will be:

$$T + 2T + 8T + 64T$$

$$= 75T$$
$$= 75 \times 0.0195$$
$$= 1.4625 \text{ second}$$

The maximum, of course, would be the sum of all 8 output pins.

$$T + 2T + 4T + 8T + 16T + 32T + 64T + 128T$$

$$= 255T$$
$$= 4.9725 \text{ seconds}$$

We can select output pulses ranging from just under 20 ms to almost 5 seconds with just a single set of component values!

Let's consider the remaining pins on the 2240.

Pin 9—Ground. This is the common connection point.

Pin 10—Reset. This pin is similar in function to the Reset pin on the 555.

Pin 11—Trigger. This is the input used to initiate the timing cycle.

Pin 12—Modulation. This input pin allows the designer access to the comparator reference voltage (normally 0.731 times V+). This pin permits simple voltage control of the timing period.

Pin 13—Timing R/C. This is the common connection point

for the timing resistor and capacitor, which determines the length of the timing period.

Pin 14—Time Base Output. The output of the internal time base oscillator is made available at this pin. This pin is normally high, but goes low during the timing period cycle.

Pin 15—Regulator Output. This pin is the output of the internal voltage regulator stage. This voltage is somewhat dependent on the supply voltage. If the supply voltage is 5 volts, the regulator voltage will be about 4.4 volts. For a supply voltage of 15 volts, the regulator puts out 6.3 volts. If, for some reason, the supply voltage is 4.5 volts, or less, pin 15 should be shorted to the V + terminal (pin 16).

Pin 16—V +. This is the pin for applying the positive supply voltage to the chip. The 2240 can be operated over a wide range of supply voltages. The acceptable supply voltage range extends from + 4 volts to + 15 volts.

Like the 555 timer, the 2240 programmable timer can be used in either the monostable or the astable mode. Figure 11-15 shows the basic 2240 monostable multivibrator circuit. This circuit is programmable. Different output times can be obtained without changing any component values, just by selecting the proper output(s). The selection can be made via switches, jumper wires, or any similar method, to suit your individual application. The circuit output is taken off across the load resistor, R1. This load resistor will typically have a value of about 10 kΩ (10,000 ohms).

The time base is established by the values of R2 and C1. This formula couldn't possibly be any simpler:

$$T = R2C1$$

A broad range of component values may be used with the 2240. Resistor R2's value should be between 1 kΩ (1000 ohms) and 10 MΩ (10,000,000 ohms), and capacitor C1 should have a value between 0.01 μF (0.00000001 farad) and 1000 μF (0.001 farad). In addition, the internal circuitry within the chip places a minimum timing period of 10 μs (0.00001 second) on the device.

The maximum timing period is obtained when R2 equals 10 Megohms, and C1 is 1000 μF:

$$T = 10000000 \times 0.001$$
$$= 10,000 \text{ seconds}$$
$$= 2 \text{ hours, 46 minutes, 40 seconds}$$

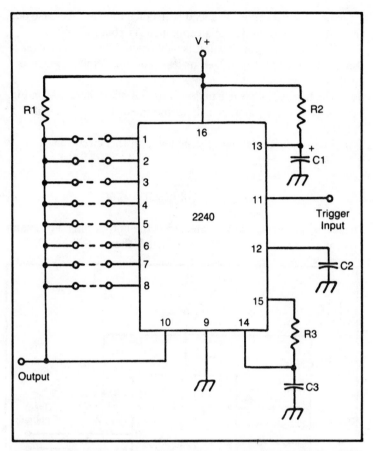

Fig. 11-15. This is the basic programmable monostable multivibrator circuit using the 2240.

The programmable outputs can be selected to give an output pulse equal to up to 255 times the time base period:

$$255T$$
$$= 255 \times 10000$$
$$= 708 \text{ hours, } 20 \text{ minutes}$$
$$= 29 \text{ days, } 12 \text{ hours, } 20 \text{ minutes}$$

That's almost an entire month! The 2240's range should be more than sufficient for the vast majority of practical applications.

Capacitor C2 is used to improve noise immunity. It typically has a value of about 0.01 μF.

185

Resistor R3 serves as a load resistance for the time-base output. A typical value for this component is about 22 kΩ.

Capacitor C3 is optional. It is only needed if the timing capacitor (C1) has a value of 0.1 μF or less, and the supply voltage is 7 volts or more.

The basic 2240 astable multivibrator circuit is illustrated in Fig. 11-16. Notice how similar it is to the monostable circuit of Fig. 11-15.

The fundamental output frequency in this circuit is:

$$F = \frac{1}{2n\text{R2C1}}$$

where n is the count value selected at the output pins. For example, if pins 3 (4T) and 5 (16T) are used, then n will be 20.

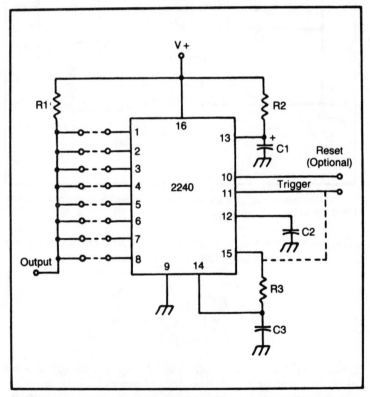

Fig. 11-16. The 2240 can also be used to build a programmable astable multivibrator circuit.

This is a triggered astable multivibrator circuit. It will not self-start when power is applied, because the internal logic within the 2240 chip will revert to the reset state. A brief pulse applied to the trigger input (pin 11) will get the oscillations started. The oscillations can be halted at any time, by applying a pulse to the reset pin (10). This control over the oscillations can be very handy in a number of control applications.

If the triggering feature is not desired, the circuit can be forced to self-start by tying the trigger pin (11) to the regulator output pin (15).

CASCADING TIMERS

In many applications, we will need multiple timer circuits. This is often the case when long time delays are required, or when multiple events are to occur at varying times.

Timers may be cascaded in parallel, or in series. Parallel cascaded timers, as shown in Fig. 11-17, generate multiple outputs that begin together, but may end at different times. A typical timing diagram for this system is shown in Fig. 11-18.

Series cascaded timers, as illustrated in Fig. 11-19, also generate multiple outputs that may be of unequal lengths, but they are

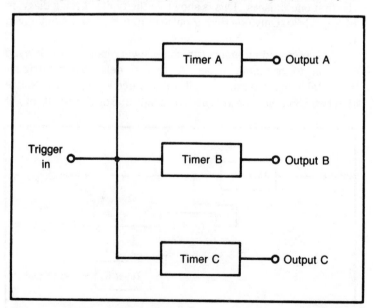

Fig. 11-17. Parallel cascaded timers generate multiple outputs that begin together but may end at different times.

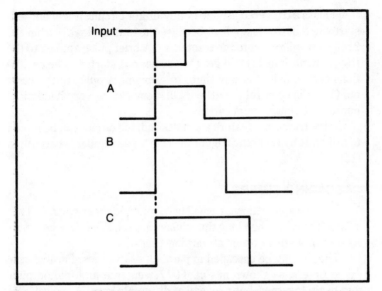

Fig. 11-18. This is the timing diagram for a typical parallel cascaded timer system.

sequential, rather than simultaneous. The second one begins after the first one finishes. This is shown in the typical timing diagram of Fig. 11-20. Only one timing pulse output is active at any given time.

Series cascading timers can come in very handy for a delayed reaction to an input pulse. A typical delayed-action-trigger monostable-multivibrator circuit is illustrated in Fig. 11-21. Notice that two 555 timer ICs are used. (A single 556 dual timer IC might

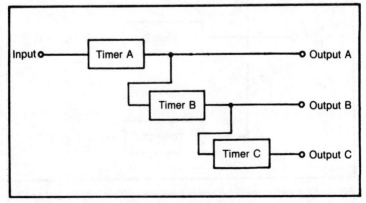

Fig. 11-19. Series cascaded timers generate multiple outputs in sequence.

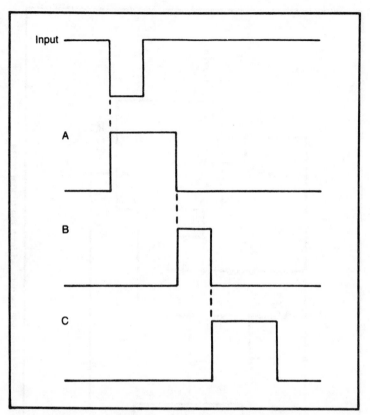

Fig. 11-20. This is the timing diagram for a typical series cascaded timer system.

be substituted, of course.) IC1, and its associated components control the delay time between reception of the input pulse, and the beginning of the output pulse. IC2, and its associated components control the length of the output pulse. A typical timing chart for this circuit is shown in Fig. 11-22.

The delay time is set by the values of R1 and C1:

$$T_d = 1.1R1C1$$

and the output pulse is determined by the values of R3 and C4:

$$T_o = 1.1R3C4$$

Do these equations look familiar? They certainly should. They're just the standard 555 monostable timing equations dis-

189

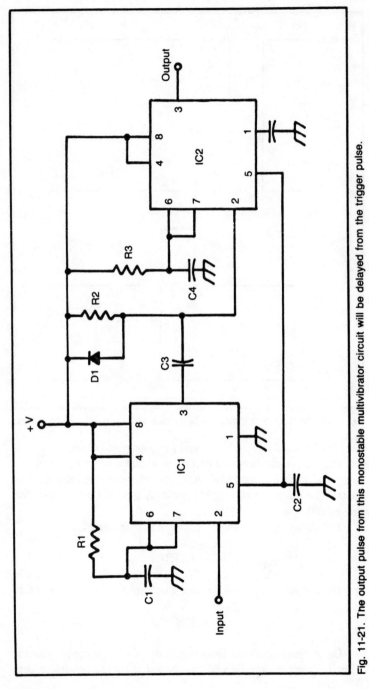

Fig. 11-21. The output pulse from this monostable multivibrator circuit will be delayed from the trigger pulse.

190

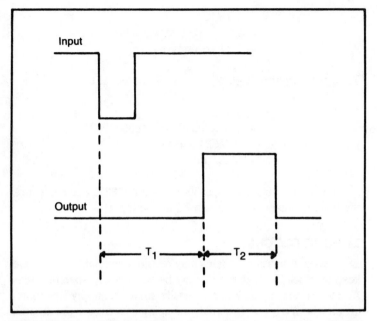

Fig. 11-22. This is the timing diagram for the delayed monostable multivibrator circuit of Fig. 11-21.

cussed earlier in this chapter.

We will look at just one example of this circuit in use. We will assume the following component values:

R1	470 kΩ	(470,000 ohms)
R2*	10 kΩ	(10,000 ohms)
R3	220 kΩ	(220,000 ohms)
C1	10 μF	(0.00001 farad)
C2*	0.01 μF	(0.00000001 farad)
C3*	0.001 μF	(0.000000001 farad)
C4	0.22 μF	(0.00000022 farad)
C5*	0.01 μF	(0.00000001 farad)
D1*	1N914	

The components marked with an asterisk (*) do not affect the output signal, and have more or less standardized values. Only R1, R3, C1, and C4 need to be selected by the designer for the specific application at hand.

Ordinarily, the output of this circuit is low. When an input pulse is received, the output will remain low for a delay period equal to:

$$T_d = 1.1R1C1$$
$$= 1.1 \times 470000 \times 0.00001$$
$$= 5.17 \text{ seconds}$$

Then the output will go high for a period equal to:

$$T_o = 1.1R3C4$$
$$= 1.1 \times 220000 \times 0.00000022$$
$$= 0.05324 \text{ second}$$
$$= 53.24 \text{ ms}$$

The output drops back to its low state 5.22324 seconds after the trigger pulse was first sensed at the input.

24-HOUR CLOCKS

Some automation systems may require a regular 24-hour time-keeping clock, so that events may be triggered at specific times. An electric alarm clock can be easily adapted, simply by tapping off the alarm triggering signal, and using it to trigger the automation circuitry. A more inexpensive, compact, and possibly versatile approach might be to use one of the many digital clock ICs on the market. Great bargains are offered by surplus dealers.

Because there are so many clock ICs around, including many discontinued surplus devices, there wouldn't be much point in going into detail about any specific device here. Most clock ICs are very easy to use, as long as you have the manufacturer's specifications sheet at hand.

For less exacting applications, you could set up an astable multivibrator circuit with a cycle period of 24-hours per cycle. You may need to cascade several timer stages to achieve this much delay. The 2240 programmable timer IC can generate cycles this long directly by using its upper outputs.

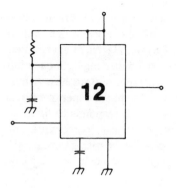

Wireless Control

S O FAR IN THIS BOOK, WE HAVE ASSUMED THAT ALL REMOTE
control signals are transmitted over connecting wires and cables between the controller and the controlled device. This is certainly the simplest and most direct method of communication within
the control system. In many applications it will be the best choice,
if only for economic reasons. In other applications, however, a connecting cable might be inconvenient, or even impossible. Fortunately, other alternatives exist. This chapter will explore several
popular means of wireless control, including:

- ☐ Light beam control.
- ☐ Tone control.
- ☐ Carrier-current control.
- ☐ Radio control.

As may well be expected, each of these offers its own set of
advantages and disadvantages. There are a number of possible variations within each of these categories.

LIGHT-BEAM CONTROL

Any form of energy can be converted into another form of
energy. In our control system we generally want to start out with
electrical energy at the controller, and end up with electrical energy

at the controlled device. This energy can be converted to another form for transmission.

Light is a form of energy that is relatively easy to convert back and forth from electrical energy. A light bulb or an LED will emit light proportional to the electrical energy being fed to it.

When it comes to converting light back into electrical energy, there are several different approaches. A number of photosensitive devices are available to the experimenter. A photosensitive device is simply one which responds to light.

Photosensitive electrical components are often called photocells, but this usage can be rather confusing. Properly speaking, a photocell is a photovoltaic cell, or solar cell.

Photovoltaic Cells

Photovoltaic cells are basically just a simple PN junction, usually made of silicon. They are essentially similar in construction to standard diodes, but the silicon is exposed to light. Silicon is a photosensitive material. This is why ordinary semiconductor devices are enclosed in a light-tight housing.

Usually the silicon of a photovoltaic cell is spread out into a relatively large, thin plate for the largest possible contact area (exposure to the light source). The schematic symbol for a photovoltaic cell is shown in Fig. 12-1. Notice that it is very similar to the symbol for an ordinary battery (dc voltage source).

When the silicon surface is shielded from light, no current will flow through the cell. But when it is exposed to a bright light, a small voltage is generated within the cell, due to the photoelectric effect.

If an illuminated photovoltaic cell is hooked up to a load, cur-

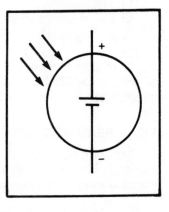

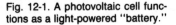
Fig. 12-1. A photovoltaic cell functions as a light-powered "battery."

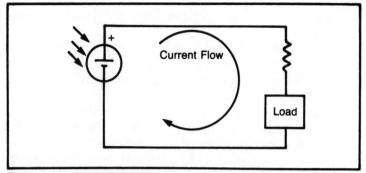

Fig. 12-2. If an illuminated photovoltaic cell is connected to a load, current will flow through the circuit.

rent will flow through the circuit, as illustrated in Fig. 12-2. Just how much current will flow is dependent on the amount of light striking the photosensitive surface of the cell. The brighter the light, the higher the current available from the cell.

The photovoltaic's output voltage, on the other hand, is relatively independent of the light level. The voltage produced by most commercially available photovoltaic cells is approximately half a volt.

The most obvious use for a photovoltaic cell is as a substitute for an ordinary dry cell. Of course, the half volt output of a single cell is too low for most practical applications, so a number of photovoltaic cells are usually added together in series to form a battery, just as with ordinary dry cells. If the circuit you want to power from photovoltaic cells requires more power than your photocells can provide, more cells can be added in a parallel battery configuration.

You can power almost any dc circuit with a combination of series and/or parallel connected photovoltaic cells. This is a simple form of solar power, and the combination of cells is called a solar battery, even though it will work just as well under artificial light.

There's one important factor that should be kept in mind—the more cells there are in a solar battery, the larger the total surface area must be, and the harder it will be to arrange the cells so they will all be lighted evenly. This means that generally solar batteries are best suited for fairly low power circuits. This is why solar power will probably never be a significant primary power source, despite its definite advantages as a secondary power source.

Bear in mind that photovoltaic cells, like any other dc voltage source, have a definite polarity. That is, one lead is always positive, and the other is always negative. The connections should never be reversed.

In a control system, a photovoltaic cell can be used to trigger a relay, as illustrated in Fig. 12-3. Note that the controlled circuit requires a separate power supply. The photocell only opens and closes the relay contacts.

Because the output of a photovoltaic cell is fairly small, it can only be used to drive a relatively light duty relay. If the device you want to control requires a heavier relay, there are two ways to solve the problem. One method is to use the light duty relay to control the heavy duty relay, as shown in Fig. 12-4. Alternatively, the output of the photovoltaic cell can be amplified with a transistor, as illustrated in Fig. 12-5. The potentiometer is used to adjust sensitivity (how much light will be required to trigger the relays).

Notice that both of these methods require an extra voltage source, in addition to the photovoltaic cell and the controlled circuit's power supply. All of these relay circuits respond only to the presence or absence of a given amount of light. Because a photovoltaic cell's voltage output is relatively constant, this device cannot be used to monitor varying light levels.

Photoresistors

Another popular light-sensitive device is the photoresistor, or light dependent resistor (LDR). As the name implies, a photoresistor changes its resistance value in step with the level of illumination on its surface. Photoresistors generate no voltage themselves.

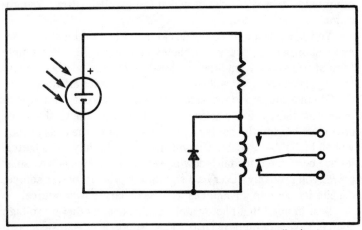

Fig. 12-3. A photovoltaic cell can be used to trigger a small relay.

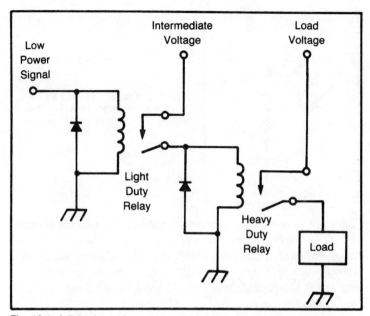

Fig. 12-4. A light-duty relay can control a larger heavy-duty relay.

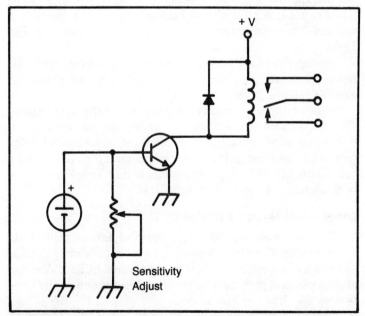

Fig. 12-5. A larger relay can be driven by amplifying the output of a photovoltaic cell with a transistor.

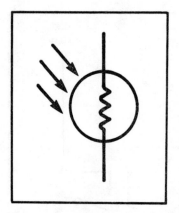

Fig. 12-6. The resistance of a photoresistor is dependent on the amount of illumination on its surface.

They are usually made of cadmium sulfide, or cadmium selenide.

These devices can generally cover quite a broad resistance range—often on the order of 10,000 to 1. Maximum resistance (typically about 1 Megohm—1,000,000 ohms) is usually achieved when the cell is completely darkened. As the light level increases, the resistance decreases.

Photoresistors are junctionless devices just like regular resistors and they have no fixed polarity. In other words, they can be hooked up in either direction without affecting circuit operation in any way. The schematic symbol for a photoresistor is shown in Fig. 12-6.

Photoresistors are perfect for a wide range of electronic control applications. They can easily be used to replace almost any variable resistor in virtually any circuit.

Photoresistors can also be used in many of the same applications as photovoltaic cells, usually with just the addition of a battery and another resistor. They offer the advantage of being sensitive to different light levels. For example, Fig. 12-7 shows a light-controlled relay. A potentiometer can be added so that the relay switches at any desired light level.

Other Photosensitive Devices

There are numerous other light sensitive devices available today. Generally these are photosensitive versions of more familiar semiconductor devices, such as light-activated SCRs (LASCRs), photodiodes, and phototransistors. The schematic symbols for these devices are shown in Fig. 12-8.

Phototransistors are especially useful in a number of applications because they can be used as amplifiers whose effective gain

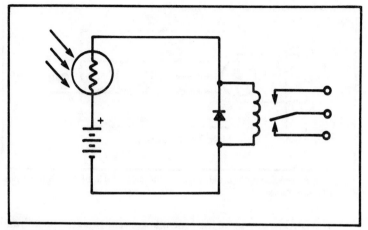

Fig. 12-7. A relay can be triggered with a photoresistor.

is controlled by light intensity. Usually, on phototransistors, the actual base lead is left unconnected in the circuit. The base-collector current is produced by the photoelectric effect.

Many circuits that use bipolar transistors could be rebuilt with phototransistors, resulting in some very unique effects. Of course, the base lead could be used too, so the output would depend on both the signal on the base lead and the light intensity.

An optoisolator is another extremely useful device. As the name implies, it isolates two interconnected circuits, so that their only connection is optical (light). Most practical optoisolators consist of an LED and a photoresistor, photodiode, or phototransistor encapsulated in a single light-tight package. The schematic symbol for a typical optoisolator is shown in Fig. 12-9.

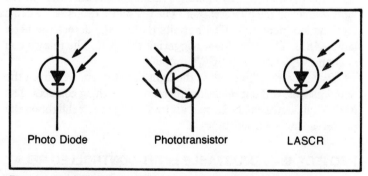

Fig. 12-8. Light-controlled versions of several standard semiconductor devices are available, including photodiodes, phototransistors, and LASCRs.

199

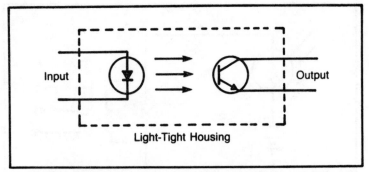

Fig. 12-9. An optoisolator contains a light source and a light detector in a single light-tight housing.

The LED is wired into the controlling circuit, and the phototransistor (or other photosensitive device) is wired into the circuit to be controlled. This provides a convenient means of control with virtually no undesirable crosstalk between the two circuits. Essentially the same effects can be achieved with a separate LED and phototransistor (or photoresistor), but they must be carefully shielded from all external light to prevent any uncontrolled interference.

PROJECT 42—LATCHING LIGHT-CONTROLLED RELAY

Now that we have gained some familiarity with light sensitive devices, we can put some of them to work in a few practical control projects. A practical light-controlled relay circuit is illustrated in Fig. 12-10. The parts list is given in Table 12-1.

A latching relay should be used in this project. The relay is activated by momentarily shining a flashlight (or other convenient light source) on the photoresistor. The resistance drops as the cell's illumination increases. This permits the voltage across the neon lamp (NE1). The lamp fires, triggering the SCR. The relay's coil is connected across the SCR's output.

By using a latching relay, the light may be removed from the photoresistor, without releasing the relay's switching contacts. The controlled device can be turned off by shining the flashlight on the photoresistor a second time.

PROJECT 43—ADJUSTABLE LIGHT-CONTROLLED RELAY

One problem with the last project is that the light level required to trigger the relay is fixed. There is no way for the user to adjust it.

200

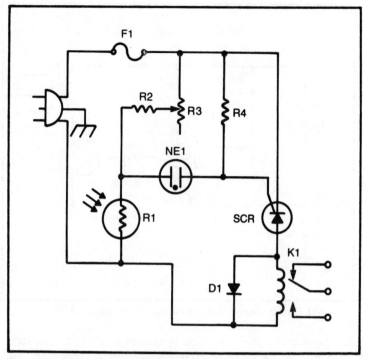

Fig. 12-10. This is a practical light-controlled relay circuit.

The circuit shown in Fig. 12-11 offers the advantage of being adjustable. The parts list for this project is given in Table 12-2. The op amp is set up as a comparator. The voltage dropped across the photoresistor is compared to the voltage dropped across the upper half of the potentiometer. When the comparator switches over, it triggers the relay. Once again, a latching relay would prob-

**Table 12-1. Parts List for the Latching
Light-Controlled Relay Circuit of Fig. 12-10.**

SCR	200-V 4-A SCR
D1	1N4002
K1	120 Vac Latching Relay (see text)
NE1	Neon lamp
F1	4.5-A fuse and holder
R1	Photoresistor
R2	22 kΩ resistor
R3	1 MΩ trimpot
R4	100 Ω resistor

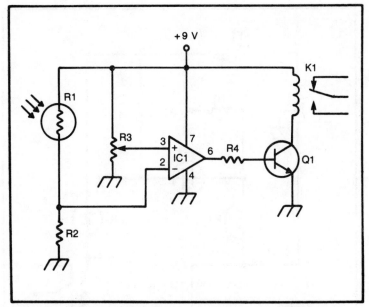

Fig. 12-11. This light-controlled relay circuit is fully adjustable.

ably be your best choice for most applications. One light pulse turns the controlled device on. A second light pulse will turn it off. The transistor is used to amplify the comparator's output signal. A low power relay is not needed.

PROJECT 44—ANOTHER LIGHT-CONTROLLED RELAY

One more approach to light control of a relay is illustrated in Fig. 12-12. The parts list is given in Table 12-3. When the light level shining on the photoresistor exceeds a specific level, the 555 timer is triggered, activating the relay.

**Table 12-2. Parts List for the Adjustable
Light-Controlled Relay Circuit of Fig. 12-11.**

IC1	Op amp (741 or similar)
Q1	NPN transistor (2N2222 or similar)
K1	9-V relay (contacts to suit application)
R1	Photoresistor
R2, R4	100 kΩ resistor
R3	250 kΩ potentiometer

202

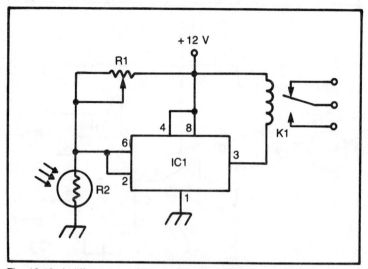

Fig. 12-12. A different approach to a light-controlled relay is shown here.

PROJECT 45—LIGHT INTERRUPTION DETECTOR

The circuits discussed so far in this chapter are activated by the presence of light. The circuit shown in Fig. 12-13 is used to detect the absence of light. The parts list for this project is given in Table 12-4.

A light source is positioned so that it shines continuously on the phototransistor. If an object passes between the light source and the phototransistor, the light beam will be cut off or interrupted. The output of this circuit will put out a pulse.

The output pulse could be used to trigger a relay or other switching circuit. Another application would be to use this circuit to drive a digital counter. The number of times the light beam is interrupted can be counted, either to keep a running total, or to trigger some event when a given number has been passed.

Still another possibility would be to incorporate a timer into

**Table 12-3. Parts List for the Third
Light-Controlled Relay Circuit of Fig. 12-12.**

IC1	555 timer
K1	12-V relay (contacts to suit application)
R1	10 kΩ potentiometer
R2	Photoresistor

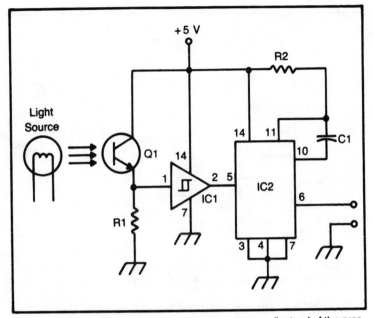

Fig. 12-13. Sometimes a circuit that detects the absence (instead of the presence) of light can be useful.

the system. Whether or not the light beam is interrupted X number of times within a given period will determine the event controlled by the output. Many other potential applications could be devised for this circuit. As always, use your imagination.

PROJECT 46—LIGHT-BEAM TRANSMITTER

More advanced applications can be served by modulating the light beam. Modulation is simply the process of imposing an audio (usually) signal onto the carrier (light beam). The light beam will

Table 12-4. Parts List for the
Light-Interruption Detector Circuit of Fig. 12-13.

IC1	7414
IC2	74121
Q1	Phototransistor (TL81 or similar)
C1	0.01 μF capacitor
R1	100 Ω resistor
R2	15 kΩ resistor

dim and brighten in step with the amplitude fluctuations of the program signal.

You might expect this type of application to require some very complex circuitry, but that isn't necessarily so. The circuit illustrated in Fig. 12-14 is quite simple, including just a handful of components, but it will do an acceptable job as a light beam modulator/transmitter.

With no input signal, potentiometer R1 is adjusted until the LED is glowing at half brightness. Now, when an audio signal is applied to the input, the LED's brightness will vary above and below the midpoint (zero level).

Resistor R4 limits the current flow through the LED. You may want to experiment with different values to optimize the performance for the specific transistor and LED you are using.

The modulated signal may be monitored with an ac voltmeter, or an oscilloscope at the junction of the LED and resistor R5. The parts list for this project is given in Table 12-5.

PROJECT 47—LIGHT-BEAM RECEIVER

Of course the transmitter in Project 46 won't be of very much

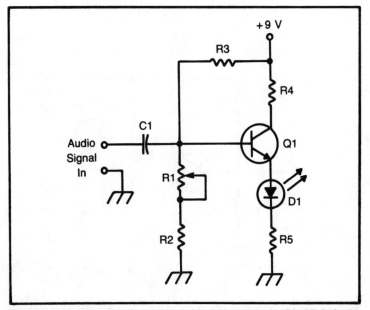

Fig. 12-14. More complex control signals can be sent out with a light beam modulator/transmitter.

Table 12-5. Parts List for the Light-Beam Transmitter Circuit of Fig. 12-14.

Q1	NPN transistor (2N2222 or similar)
D1	LED
C1	0.01 μF capacitor
R1	10 kΩ potentiometer
R2	1.2 kΩ resistor
R3	47 kΩ resistor
R4	2.2 kΩ resistor (see text)
R5	15 Ω

use without a suitable receiver. A light beam receiver/demodulator circuit is shown in Fig. 12-15. The parts list is given in Table 12-6. It is designed to complement the transmitter circuit of Fig. 12-14.

The two circuits must be positioned so that the light from the LED in the transmitter reaches the solar cell of the receiver. The range of these circuits is rather limited, but will be adequate for many remote control applications. The range will be better in a darkened environment. Obviously, any external light source will interfere with the light from the LED. A shield over the photosen-

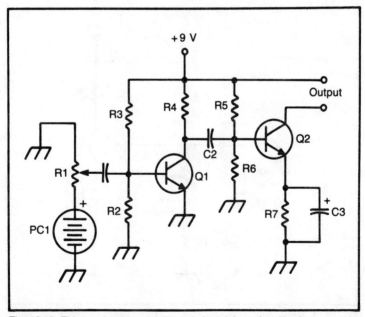

Fig. 12-15. This receiver circuit is intended to pick up the signals sent out by the transmitter of Fig. 12-14.

Table 12-6. Parts List for the Light-Beam Receiver Circuit of Fig. 12-15.

Q1, Q2	NPN transistor (2N4123 or similar)
PC1	Photocell
C1, C2	0.1 μF capacitor
C3	100 μF 35 V electrolytic capacitor
R1	1 kΩ potentiometer
R2, R4, R5	10 kΩ resistor
R3	100 kΩ resistor
R6, R7	1 kΩ resistor

sor will help some. An infrared emitter and sensor will do somewhat better than if visible light is used.

If the wireless function is not absolutely essential, a fiberoptic connection could be used, greatly increasing the range, and permitting the signal to travel around corners. Fiberoptics will be discussed a little later in this chapter. Potentiometer R1 in the receiver circuit is a gain control.

The output impedance from this circuit is in the moderate range—about 1000 ohms to 3000 ohms. If the device being driven has a different input impedance, you should use a transformer or some other impedance matching circuit.

PROJECT 48—INFRARED TRANSMITTER

Using a light beam transmitter/receiver system like in the last two projects has certain limitations. Primarily, there can be interference problems from external light sources. Also, in some applications, a visible beam of light may be undesirable.

One solution is to use an infrared light beam, which is invisible to the human eye. An infrared transmitter circuit is illustrated in Fig. 12-16. The parts list is given in Table 12-7.

This transmitter circuit operates at approximately 25 kHz. The multiple infrared LEDs in series increase the range of the system.

PROJECT 49—INFRARED RECEIVER

A compatible infrared receiver to go with the last project is shown in Fig. 12-17, with the parts list given in Table 12-8.

By properly arranging the array of infrared sensors, the system range can be as high as 30 feet. This should be adequate for most remote control applications. Of course, this system can only function along the line of sight. If anything blocks the infrared beam, there will be nothing for the receiver to detect.

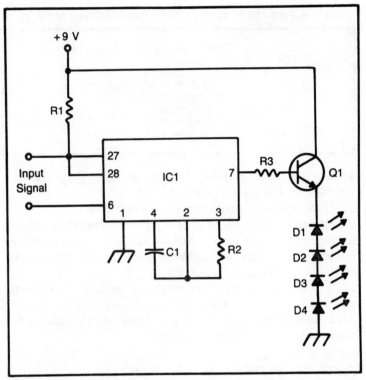

Fig. 12-16. An infrared beam is invisible to the human eye, but can be transmitted like a regular light beam.

PROJECT 50—MULTIFUNCTION INFRARED TRANSMITTER

All of the light control projects we have discussed so far in this chapter suffer from one important limitation. Each circuit can control only a single function. Of course, this is just fine for turning a single device on and off. However, many practical remote con-

Table 12-7. Parts List for the Infrared Transmitter Circuit of Fig. 12-16.

IC1	ED-15
Q1	NPN transistor (2N4401 or similar)
D1-D4	Infrared LED (Monsanto MV5000 or similar)
C1	250 pF capacitor
R1	820 Ω resistor
R2	91 kΩ resistor
R3	3.3 kΩ resistor

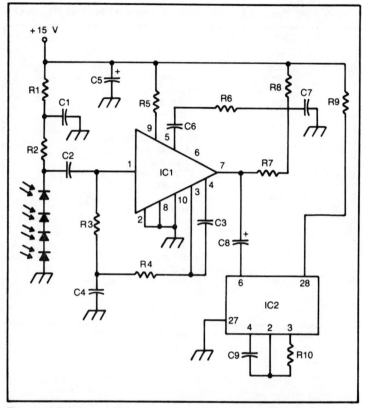

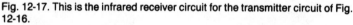

Fig. 12-17. This is the infrared receiver circuit for the transmitter circuit of Fig. 12-16.

trol applications are more complex. For example, a TV remote control should allow you to turn the set on and off, adjust the volume, and change the channel. Obviously, multiple channel signals are required.

You could build several separate single channel control devices, but this would rapidly become unwieldy and expensive. We need a true multifunction transmitter/receiver combination.

In most cases, a digital circuit would be your best choice, because of the convenience of digital gating for separating the encoded signals. A multifunction infrared transmitter circuit is illustrated in Fig. 12-18, with the parts list given in Table 12-9.

Sixteen NO (Normally Open) SPST switches arranged in an X/Y matrix are used to manually enter data. A sixteen-key keypad would probably be the most convenient choice. Up to fifteen func-

Table 12-8. Parts List for the Infrared Receiver Circuit of Fig. 12-17.

IC1	CA3035
IC2	ED-15
D1-D4	Infrared sensor (BP104 or similar)
C1	0.01 μF capacitor
C2	4700 pF capacitor
C3	0.033 μF capacitor
C4	0.025 μF capacitor
C5	10 μF 35 V electrolytic capacitor
C6	0.0025 μF capacitor
C7	0.05 μF capacitor
C8	2.2 μF 35 V electrolytic capacitor
C9	270 pF capacitor
R1	100 kΩ resistor
R2, R6	10 kΩ resistor
R3	33 kΩ resistor
R4	150 kΩ resistor
R5	1 kΩ resistor
R7	100 Ω resistor
R8	4.7 kΩ resistor
R9	2.7 kΩ resistor
R10	91 kΩ resistor

tions can be controlled from these switches. (The "O" key is ignored.)

IC1 is an encoder which converts the appropriate switch number into a four bit digital value:

0	0000
1	0001
2	0010
3	0011
4	0100
5	0101
6	0110
7	0111
8	1000
9	1001
A (10)	1010
B (11)	1011
C (12)	1100
D (13)	1101
E (14)	1110
F (15)	1111

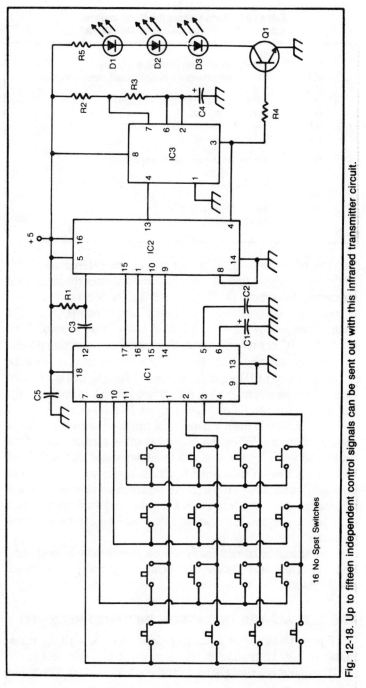

Fig. 12-18. Up to fifteen independent control signals can be sent out with this infrared transmitter circuit.

16 No Spst Switches

211

Table 12-9. Parts List for the Multifunction
Infrared Transmitter Circuit of Fig. 12-18.

IC1	74922 sixteen key keyboard encoder
IC2	74193 synchronous up/down dual clock counter
IC3	555 timer
Q1	NPN transistor (2N2222 or similar)
D1-D3	Infrared LED (XC880 or similar)
C1	1 μF 25 V electrolytic capacitor
C2, C5	0.1 μF capacitor
C3	0.001 μF capacitor
C4	2.2 μF 25 V electrolytic capacitor
R1	12 kΩ resistor
R2	1 kΩ resistor
R3	1.8 kΩ resistor
R4	2.2 kΩ resistor
R5	100 Ω resistor

This binary value is fed to the DATA inputs of the counter (IC2).
The BORROW output (pin 13) goes high and activates the multivibrator circuit built around the 555 timer (IC3). The 555's output is connected to the COUNT DOWN input (pin 4) of the counter (IC2). The
counter counts down from the loaded DATA value to zero. (That
is why the "0" key doesn't work—there aren't any counting pulses.)

On each counting pulse the transistor is turned on, causing the
infrared LEDs (LED1 - LED3) to flash. Multiple LEDs are used
to increase the output level of the infrared signal, maximizing the
transmission range. The range is about 15 feet, or so.

The LEDs will flash a number of times equal to the value of
the closed switch. When the counter reaches zero, it cuts off the
timer, and waits for the next key to be depressed. All of this will
happen much faster than you'd be able to notice, even if you could
see the infrared pulses. Even the highest number of pulses (15) will
be completed in a tiny fraction of a second. You won't have to wait
at all before pressing the next key. Your reflexes can't outrace the
counter.

You should be careful not to depress two or more keys at once,
however. This could confuse the circuit, and the output will be unpredictable.

PROJECT 51—MULTIFUNCTION INFRARED RECEIVER

Figure 12-19 shows a receiver circuit for use with the transmitter of Fig. 12-18. The parts list is given in Table 12-10.

The phototransistor (Q1) detects the infrared pulses. The pulses

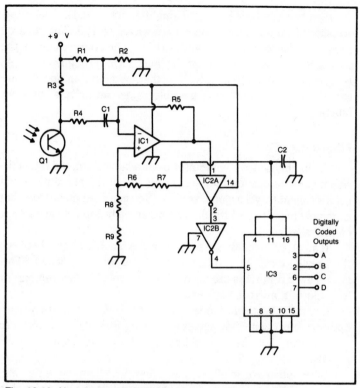

Fig. 12-19. Here is a receiver for the transmitter circuit of Fig. 12-18.

Table 12-10. Parts List for the Multifunction
Infrared Receiver Circuit of Fig. 12-19.

IC1	Op amp (748 or similar)
IC2	7414 hex inverter
IC3	74193 synchronous up/down dual clock counter
Q1	Phototransistor (TIL414 or similar)
C1	2500 pF capacitor
C2	0.1 μF capacitor
R1	12 kΩ resistor
R2, R6	5.1 kΩ resistor
R3	33 kΩ resistor
R4	1 kΩ resistor
R5	1 MΩ resistor
R7	470 Ω resistor
R8	270 Ω resistor
R9	3.3 kΩ resistor

are then boosted by a high gain amplifier stage (IC1). The pulses are shaped up into nice clean square waves by IC5. The squared pulses are fed to another counter (IC3). The counter counts the pulses, and feeds the value out in binary form through outputs A, B, C, and D. The digital value can then be fed to an appropriate gating circuit, so that each possible value can drive a different function.

Fiberoptics

All light based systems suffer from relatively limited transmission ranges. Moreover, they are strictly line of sight systems. Light beams cannot travel around corners. (You could set up mirrors, but alignment tends to be difficult. This is generally impractical for most control systems.)

If an object (including a person, or the family cat) gets between the transmitter and the receiver, the signal will be blocked. (This is true even if mirrors are used, and will probably be even harder to avoid in a mirrored system.)

Often the best solution is to use a fiberoptic cable. In a fiberoptic system, connecting cables are strung from the transmitter to the receiver, but they carry light pulses, rather than electrical signals.

Fiberoptics are small, slender tubes, which are quite flexible, so they can be bent any way needed to conduct the light signal to its destination. The light will follow all of the twists and turns of the fiberoptic cable, even if it's tied in a knot. The light at the output is unchanged (except for a slight attenuation due to the cable length) from the input.

Obviously, if you use a fiberoptic cable, you lose the wireless advantage. So why bother? Fiberoptic cables offer several advantages over ordinary electrical wiring. Because no electrical signal is carried through the cable, it is inherently safer. There is no way for anyone to get shocked or for a fire to start because of a worn insulation or short.

A fiberoptic cable of a given thickness can carry more independent signals than a comparably sized electrical cable. Telephone lines, for example, are using more and more fiber optics.

Fiberoptic cables tend to be more flexible than comparable electrical cables. If a bend in an electrical cable is made too sharp, an internal break in a wire may result.

Fiberoptic cable is more expensive than ordinary electrical

214

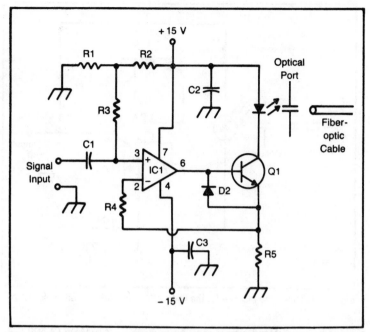

Fig. 12-20. This remote transmitter circuit is designed for use with a fiberoptic cable.

wire, so it is only practical for the hobbyist to use it in applications in which its special advantages are significant.

PROJECT 52—FIBEROPTIC TRANSMITTER

A practical application for fiber optics is illustrated in Fig. 12-20. This is a remote control transmitter specifically designed for fiberoptic transmission. The parts list for this project is given in Table 12-11.

Table 12-11. Parts List for the Fiberoptics Transmitter Circuit of Fig. 12-20.

IC1	LF356 op amp
Q1	NPN transistor (2N2222 or similar)
D1	LED
D2	1N914
C1-C3	0.1 μF capacitor
R1	220 Ω resistor
R2	1.2 kΩ resistor
R3, R4	1 kΩ resistor
R5	47 Ω resistor

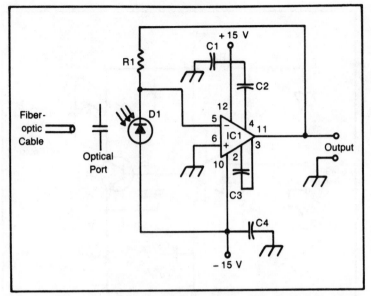

Fig. 12-21. This is the receiver for the fiberoptic transmitter circuit of Fig. 12-20.

The modulated signal may be as high as 3.5 MHz (3,500,000 Hz). When no input signal is applied, the LED current will be 50 mA (0.05 amp). The input signal should be kept within the 0 to +5 volts range. The current across the LED will vary from 0 to 100 mA (0.1 amp).

PROJECT 53—FIBEROPTIC RECEIVER

A fiberoptic receiver to use with the last project is shown in Fig. 12-21. The parts list is given in Table 12-12. The sensitivity of the photodiode listed in the parts list is 0.5-amp per watt. The op amp boosts this small signal to a usable level, which is passed on to the output. This system can be used for simple on/off con-

Table 12-12. Parts List for the Fiberoptics Receiver Circuit of Fig. 12-21.

IC1	LH0032 op amp
D1	Photodiode (HP5082-4220)
C1, C4	0.1 μF capacitor
C2	1000 pF capacitor
C3	4.7 pF capacitor
R1	100 kΩ resistor

trol, or a modulator and demodulator can be added to allow multichannel control, or voice communications.

CARRIER CURRENT CONTROL

It is often convenient not to have connecting wires between the controller and the controlled device in a remote control system. However, such systems are rarely truly wireless. Except when portability is an absolute must, batteries tend to be too expensive, bulky, and generally inconvenient for use in a home control system. Most practical devices will have a power supply that derives its operating (dc) voltage from the ac electrical wiring that is run through the halls of almost all modern buildings.

You can't really call any ac powered system "wireless," because the controller and controlled device are connected to the same (usually) ac wiring. There is a physical connection between the two units. So what? The ac lines just carry the operating power. True. But we can modulate the 60 Hz ac power line signal with a control signal. This is called carrier-current control.

There are certain limitations to this convenient system, which is why it isn't universally used. The designer must be extremely careful to isolate any part of the circuitry the user might come into contact with from the ac line. (Optoisolators are often utilized.)

Another problem stems from the simple fact that the ac house wiring was never designed for communication of modulated signals. Noise and interference is inescapable to some degree. In some cases it can be so severe that the carrier current system may be rendered useless. Such problems may or may not be temporary. It all depends on what else happens to be using the same ac power lines.

Even so, the convenience of carrier-current control certainly makes it a viable alternative to consider when designing a control system. A typical carrier current control system is illustrated in Fig. 12-22.

Now, let's consider how to put the idea of carrier-current control into actual practice.

Figure 12-23 shows a simplified diagram of a home wiring system. Notice that there are actually two separate circuits here. The power line entering the home is a cable made up of three wires. One of these is a common line. The voltage between either of the outer wires with the common is approximately 120 Vac. (The actual voltage varies from time to time, depending on the current load

217

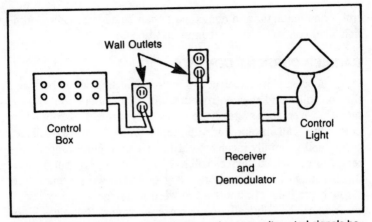

Fig. 12-22. Your ac house wiring can be used to transmit control signals between remote devices.

on the system, and from location to location, depending on the specific equipment used by the power company.) Simple math tells us that the voltage between the two outer lines must be about 240 Vac.

You may run into problems with a carrier-current remote control system. The transmitter may be plugged into one line and the receiver may be plugged into the other. There may not always be a direct connection available. In large buildings with multiple fuse-boxes, there may even be more than two circuits to contend with. A second potential problem is that there is no way to determine

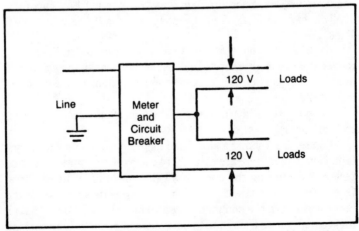

Fig. 12-23. This is a simplified diagram of a typical home wiring system.

what else might be plugged into the circuit when the system is in use.

Many of these seemingly impossible problems can be dealt with by selecting the proper frequency for the carrier-current signal. When this fails, it is often possible to condition the wiring so that it will carry the control signals.

There is no way to specify a general purpose optimum frequency for a carrier current system. Every wiring situation will be different. A few rules of thumbs may be suggested, however.

A high frequency (rf—radio frequency) transmission line should be terminated in its characteristic impedance, or potentially problematic standing waves could be created along the length of the line. Standing waves mean that the voltage and current will vary throughout the line. For lower frequency signals, this isn't as great a problem. The line length will not be particularly important with low frequency signals.

This is not to imply that a low frequency system is problem free. At low frequencies the ac line looks like a random network of various resistances, capacitances, and inductances. There is no way to predict the exact electrical characteristics of the ac line. But these problems also exist at higher frequencies, along with the standing wave problems. In other words, using a low-frequency signal will usually be the lesser of two evils. If high frequencies are used, there might also be problems stemming from rf interference with broadcast signals.

Now, what low frequency should be used? We can narrow the choices down a little further. The ac power lines in the United States carry a strong (*very* strong) 60 Hz. This means you should not use a signal close to 60 Hz. It would just get lost in the power signal. By the same token, you should avoid the harmonics of 60 Hz (120 Hz, 180 Hz, 240 Hz, 300 Hz, 360 Hz, etc.). Any low frequencies in this range will have to be extremely powerful not to get buried in the noise.

The carrier-current signal should not be too low or too high in frequency. While the wiring situation can vary considerably, generally you'll have the best chance of success using frequencies in the 60 kHz to 180 kHz range. This is high enough that the harmonics from the power line itself should be reduced to an insignificant level, but low enough that rf interference and transmission line problems shouldn't give you too much grief. For our discussion we will arbitrarily select a carrier frequency of 100 kHz, primarily because it's a nice neat value.

The carrier frequency is not the only frequency of importance in a carrier current system. Control signals are tone encoded. The encoded tones are used to modulate the carrier signal. Either amplitude modulation (AM), or frequency modulation (FM) may be used. FM systems are more complex and expensive, but tend to be less noisy. (Tone encoding will be discussed in more detail later in this chapter.) The tone encoding frequencies should be selected to avoid 60 Hz, and its harmonics, to limit interference from the power line itself.

If you need several control frequencies, you can save yourself a lot of trouble and calculating by adopting the dual tone frequencies used in Touch Tone™ telephones. These frequencies were carefully chosen after a great deal of study. They are probably as close to optimum as you're likely to get.

In order to deal with any problems and spurious signals that might be in the power lines, you obviously need to know what they are. This is easier said than done in many cases. For one thing, making measurements is made difficult by the huge 60 Hz power signal. This will be tens or even hundreds of times stronger than potentially significant interfering signals.

If you try to measure the signal on the ac power line with an oscilloscope, or other test instrument, all you'll see will be a 60 Hz, sine wave. Not very informative.

You must filter out the 60 Hz signal (and possibly some of its lower harmonics) in order to accurately and meaningfully monitor the ac power line. You do this with a narrow band-reject (or notch) filter. The simplest type is illustrated in Fig. 12-24. This is called

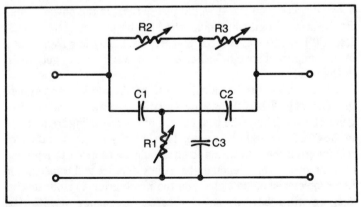

Fig. 12-24. The 60-Hz power line frequency can be cut down with a twin-T network filter.

a twin-T network (or parallel T), because the schematic looks like it's made up of two Ts. One is comprised of C1, C2, and R1, while the second contains R2, R3, and C3. To center the rejection band around 60 Hz, the following component values could be used:

R1	147 Ω
R2, R3	295 Ω
C1, C2	9 μF (at least 600 volts)
C3	18 μF (at least 600 volts)

The rather oddball resistance values can best be obtained with trim pots (small, screwdriver adjusted potentiometers).

The requirements for maximum attenuation at the center frequency are as follows:

$$R2 = R3 = 2 \times R1$$
$$C1 = C2$$
$$C3 = 2 \times C1$$
$$R1 = \frac{1}{2 \pi C3F}$$
$$C1 = \frac{1}{2 \pi R2F}$$

where F is the desired center frequency. Pi (π) is a constant with an approximate value of 3.14. Pi turns up quite frequently in electronic equations.

The trimpots must be tuned precisely, because the rejection band is quite narrow, and any deviation from the calculated values will alter the center frequency. You may not attenuate the frequency you want to cut down.

PROJECT 54—CARRIER FREQUENCY GENERATOR

A carrier current transmitter is generally made up of three primary stages, as shown in Fig. 12-25:

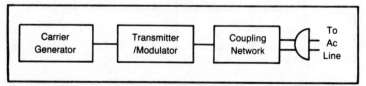

Fig. 12-25. A carrier-current transmitter is made up of three basic stages.

221

- ☐ Carrier frequency generator.
- ☐ Transmitter.
- ☐ Coupling network.

A typical carrier frequency generator circuit is illustrated in Fig. 12-26. The parts list is given in Table 12-13. Basically this circuit is a VCO (voltage-controlled oscillator). The input signal modulates the output frequency. This is frequency modulation (FM).

The nominal (zero signal) output frequency can be calculated with this formula:

$$F = \frac{1.44}{(R1 + R2)C1}$$

The component values listed in Table 12-13 will allow output frequencies from about 1 kHz to over 100 kHz.

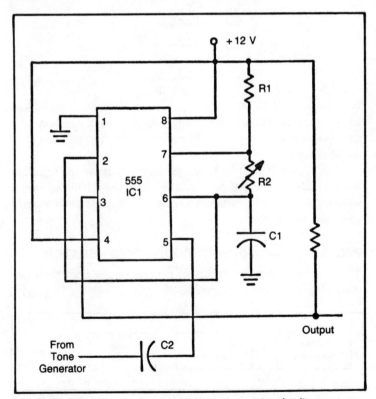

Fig. 12-26. This is a typical carrier-frequency generator circuit.

IC1	555 timer
C1	0.1 μF capacitor
C2	0.01 μF capacitor
R1	1 kΩ resistor
R2	100 kΩ potentiometer

The input frequencies should be significantly lower than the carrier frequency to avoid aliasing problems.

Coupling Network

The coupling network scarcely calls for a project of its own. This is just a Twin-T filter, as discussed earlier in this chapter, and a few coupling capacitors. A simple coupling network circuit is illustrated in Fig. 12-27. Suitable component values are listed in Table 12-14.

PROJECT 55—FIRST CARRIER-CURRENT TRANSMITTER

Now comes the transmitter section. One suitable circuit is

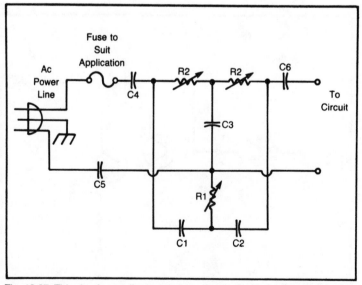

Fig. 12-27. This simple coupling network can be used with the following carrier-current transmitter projects.

Table 12-14. Parts List for the Coupling Network Circuit of Fig. 12-27.

C1, C2, C4, C5, C6	0.1 μF, 600 V capacitor
C3	0.2 μF, 600 V capacitor (may be two 0.1 μF capacitors in parallel)
R1	26,539 Ω resistor (50 kΩ potentiometer)
R2, R3	53,078 Ω resistor (100 kΩ potentiometer)

shown in Fig. 12-26. The parts list for this project is given in Table 12-15.

This circuit will present a very low impedance to the ac power line, which is highly desirable. The same basic circuit could be used with either AM or FM signals.

If the carrier current signal must be transmitted over a large distance (say, in a large building), more powerful transistors than the ones specified in the parts list may be required.

PROJECT 56—SECOND CARRIER-CURRENT TRANSMITTER

An alternate carrier-current transmitter circuit is shown in Fig. 12-29, with the parts list given in Table 12-16. This circuit is suitable for low-power signals.

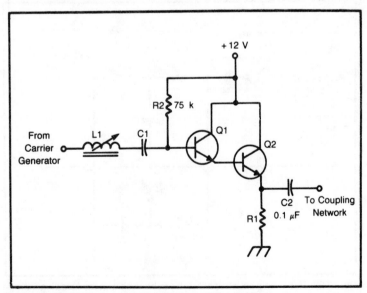

Fig. 12-28. The first carrier-current transmitter circuit.

**Table 12-15. Parts List for the First
Carrier-Current Transmitter Circuit of Fig. 12-28.**

Q1, Q2	NPN transistor (2N4401 or similar)
L1	5-30 mH coil*
C1	0.0002 μF capacitor
C2	0.1 μF capacitor (500 volts or more)
R1	1 kΩ resistor
R2	75 kΩ resistor

*The coil is adjusted to provide maximum drive for Q1. (A TV width
coil may be used for L1.)

PROJECT 57—THIRD CARRIER-CURRENT TRANSMITTER

A final carrier-current transmitter circuit is illustrated in Fig.
12-30. It is built around the 555 timer. The complete parts list for
this project is given in Table 12-17.

PROJECT 58—FIRST CARRIER-CURRENT RECEIVER

Obviously, a carrier-current transmitter isn't going to be good
for very much beyond paper-weight duty without a comparable receiver unit.

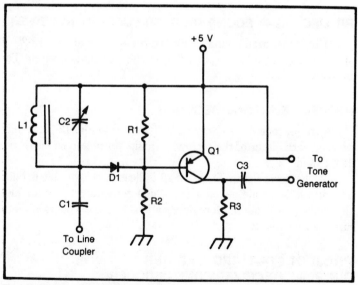

Fig. 12-29. The second carrier-current transmitter circuit.

225

Q1	PNP transistor (GE53 or similar)
D1	SK3091 diode (or similar)
L1	Ferrite rod antenna*
C1	0.1 μF 600 V capacitor
C2	730 pF variable capacitor
C3	0.012 μF capacitor
R1	10 kΩ resistor
R2	220 kΩ resistor
R3	47 kΩ resistor

*May be salvaged from an old AM radio.

Figure 12-31 shows a receiver circuit intended to be used with the carrier-current transmitter of Fig. 12-28. It may be used with other transmitters as well.

Reception may be improved by adding an impedance matching network at the input. It would not be very practical to go into specifics on this here, because the requirements will vary from location to location. The tone decoder will be shown shortly. The parts list for this project is given in Table 12-18.

PROJECT 59—SECOND CARRIER-CURRENT RECEIVER

A receiver circuit suitable for the transmitter of Fig. 12-29 is shown in Fig. 12-32. The parts list for this project is given in Table 12-19.

PROJECT 60—TONE DECODER

A simple tone decoder circuit is illustrated in Fig. 12-33. It may be used with either of the receiver circuits presented so far (Figs. 12-31, and 12-32).

As the parts list in Table 12-20 indicates, this circuit is built around the 567 tone decoder IC, which is manufactured for just this type of application. More information on tone decoders is given later in this chapter.

PROJECT 61—THIRD CARRIER
CURRENT RECEIVER/TONE DECODER

One final carrier-current receiver circuit is illustrated in Fig.

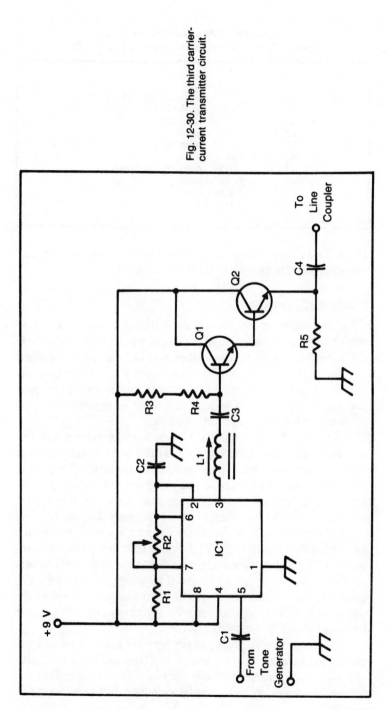

Fig. 12-30. The third carrier-current transmitter circuit.

Table 12-17. Parts List for the Third
Carrier-Current Transmitter Circuit of Fig. 12-30.

IC1	555 timer
Q1, Q2	NPN transistor (SK3122 or similar)
L1	32 mH adjustable coil
C1	0.01 μF capacitor
C2, C4	0.1 μF capacitor
C3	250 pF capacitor
R1	100 Ω resistor
R2	100 kΩ potentiometer (tune)
R3	68 kΩ resistor
R4	6.8 kΩ resistor
R5	1 kΩ resistor

12-34. This circuit incorporates its own built-in tone decoder. The parts list for this project is given in Table 12-21.

TONE ENCODING

Using different frequencies for different functions is a convenient way to combine multiple control signals on a single channel. Almost any transmission method may be used, including direct connection through wires, rf (radio frequency) signals, optical signals, or ac carrier currents. Another transmission method is sonic. Just send out the sounds with some kind of loudspeaker and pick them up with some kind of microphone.

In some cases, audio control tones could be annoying or distracting. Ultrasonic signals (above 20 kHz) will function in pretty much the same way, but will not be audible to humans. (They might drive your dog or cat crazy, if you're not careful, though.) Ultrasonic transducers (speakers and microphones) may be more expensive and harder to find than af (audio frequency) devices.

Very simple single on/off control can be accomplished with a simple burst of sound and a VOX (voice-operated switch) circuit, but may succumb to false triggering due to environmental noises.

Better accuracy can be achieved by assigning a specific frequency to the control function. The controlled device will be designed to recognize only its assigned frequency. Sounds at other frequencies will be ignored.

Well, once you've gone this far, why not assign a second frequency to a second control function. And then add a third, a fourth . . . the possibilities are virtually limitless. This is called tone encoding. The tones are generated by a circuit called a tone encoder.

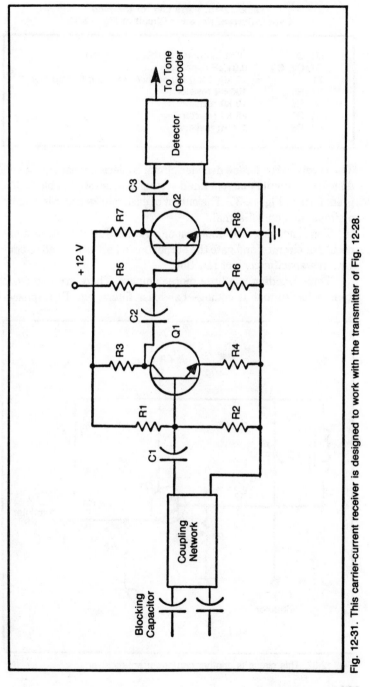

Fig. 12-31. This carrier-current receiver is designed to work with the transmitter of Fig. 12-28.

229

Table 12-18. Parts List for the First
Carrier-Current Receiver Circuit of Fig. 12-31.

Q1, Q2	NPN transistor (2N2222 or similar)
C1, C2, C3	0.01 μF capacitor
T1	10 kΩ: 3.2 Ω impedance matching transformer
R1, R5	100 kΩ resistor
R2, R6	10 kΩ resistor
R3, R7	22 kΩ resistor
R4, R8	1.2 kΩ resistor

The receiver has a tone decoder circuit to decide what signal will do what. A simple tone-operated system is illustrated in block diagram form in Fig. 12-35. The output of each tone decoder is usually a simple dc control signal.

Tone encoding is a simple enough matter. Just use one or more oscillator circuits, and gate the output on and off as desired to activate the specific control function.

Tone decoding is a little more complex. There are two basic approaches to tone decoding—bandpass filters, and PLL (phase-

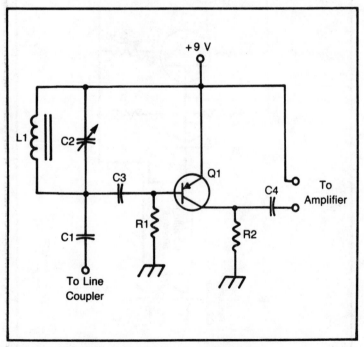

Fig. 12-32. This circuit is another carrier-current receiver.

**Table 12-19. Parts List for the Second
Carrier-Current Receiver Circuit of Fig. 12-32.**

Q1	PNP transistor (GE-53 or similar)
D1	SK3088 diode (or similar)
L1	Ferrite rod antenna*
C1	0.1 μF 600 V capacitor
C2	730 pF variable capacitor
C3	0.18 μF capacitor
C4	0.12 μF capacitor
R1	100 kΩ resistor
R2	1 kΩ resistor

*May be salvaged from an old AM radio.

locked loops). Each of these approaches will be discussed in the
following pages.

Filter Decoding

Probably the most obvious approach to tone decoding is the
filter method. A band-pass filter is a circuit that passes only those

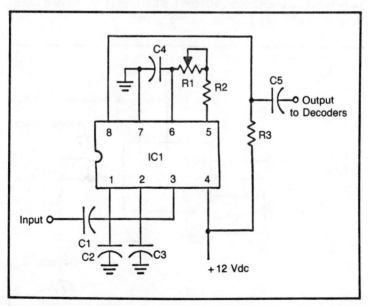

Fig. 12-33. This simple tone decoder can be used with either of the receiver
circuits (Figs. 12-31 and 12-32).

Table 12-20. Parts List for the Tone-Decoder Circuit of Fig. 12-33.

IC1	567 tone decoder IC
C1	0.1 μF capacitor (500 volts or more)
C2, C5	0.1 μF capacitor
C3	25 μF 35 volt electrolytic capacitor
C4	0.005 μF capacitor
R1	20 kΩ potentiometer
R2	2.2 kΩ resistor
R3	4.7 kΩ resistor

frequencies which lie within a specific band (or range). Any signals with frequencies outside that band will not reach the output. A graph illustrating the action of an ideal band-pass filter is shown in Fig. 12-36.

Practical circuits can not distinguish quite so sharply between frequencies. Instead of a sharp, instantaneous cut-off, there will be a more gradual slope. The frequency response of a practical band-pass filter is illustrated in Fig. 12-37.

The action of a bandpass filter is defined primarily by two specifications. The center frequency (F_c) is the midpoint of the passed band. The bandwidth (BW) is the size of the passed band. That is, how many frequencies are passed.

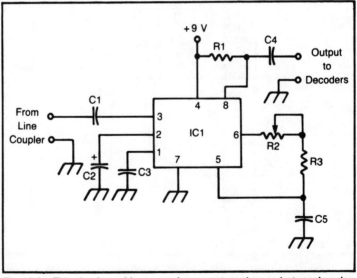

Fig. 12-34. This circuit combines a carrier-current receiver and a tone decoder.

**Table 12-21. Parts List for the Third
Carrier-Current Receiver/Tone Decoder Circuit of Fig. 12-34.**

IC1	567 tone decoder IC
C1	0.1 μF 600 V capacitor
C2	22 μF 35 V electrolytic capacitor
C3, C4	0.1 μF capacitor
C5	0.005 μF capacitor
R1	3.9 kΩ resistor
R2	25 kΩ potentiometer
R3	22 kΩ resistor

For example, let's consider an ideal band-pass filter which passes only those frequencies between 2300 Hz and 3700 Hz. The center frequency is 3050 Hz, and the bandwidth is 3700 − 2300 = 1400 Hz.

Frequencies close to, but outside the pass-band of a practical filter will get through to the output, but will be attenuated to a degree proportional to the distance from the pass-band.

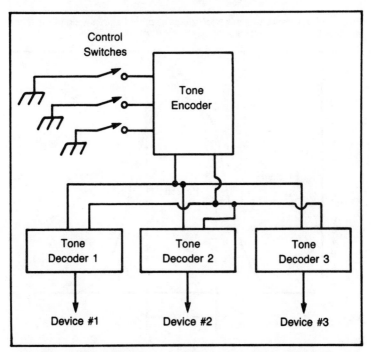

Fig. 12-35. A simple tone-operated system permits multiple functions to be controlled from a single channel.

233

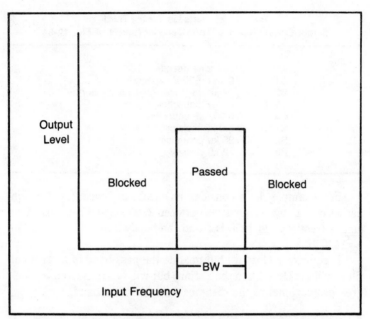

Fig. 12-36. An ideal bandpass filter rejects all other frequency signals that are outside its specific passband.

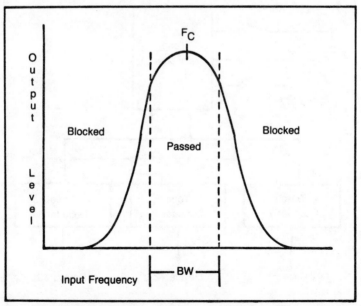

Fig. 12-37. A practical bandpass filter has a gradual slope between the pass-band and the rejection bands.

234

Obviously, the steeper the rolloff slope, the better the selectivity of the filter will be. Very steep rolloff slopes are possible with op-amp based circuitry, such as the one illustrated in Fig. 12-38. The bandwidth of this circuit is quite narrow. The center frequency (F_c) is determined by the values of coil L and capacitor C, according to this formula:

$$F_c = \frac{1}{6.28 \times \sqrt{L \times C}}$$

Let's assume that L = 1500 μH (0.0015 henry), and C = 0.0022 μF (0.0000000022 farad). In this case, the center frequency works out to:

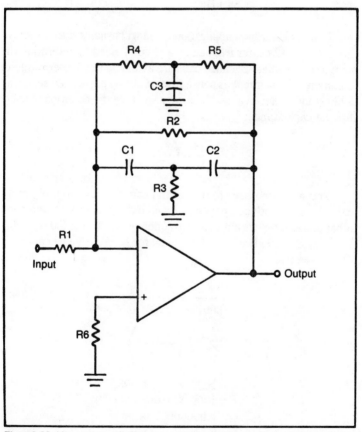

Fig. 12-38. Very steep rolloff slopes can be achieved with an op-amp based filter circuit.

$$F_c = \frac{1}{6.28 \times \sqrt{0.0015 \times 0.0000000022}}$$

$$= \frac{1}{6.28 \times \sqrt{0.0000000000033}}$$

$$= \frac{1}{6.28 \times 0.0000018}$$

$$= \frac{1}{0.0000114}$$

$$= 87{,}656 \text{ Hz}$$
$$\approx 88 \text{ kHz}$$

In practical design applications, you will usually start off knowing the desired center frequency, and you'll need to determine the component values. Because coils are available in a lesser range of common values, it makes sense to start out by arbitrarily selecting a likely inductance value. Then we rearrange the equation to solve for the capacitance:

$$C = \frac{1}{L} \times \left(\frac{1}{6.28 \times F_c} \right)^2$$

You will often have to try several combinations to find practical values for both components. As an example, let's say we need a bandpass filter with a center frequency of 50 kHz (50,000 Hz). Let's try a 1000 μH (0.001 henry) coil for L. What value capacitor should we use?:

$$C = \frac{1}{0.001} \times \left(\frac{1}{6.28 \times 50000} \right)^2$$

$$= 1000 \times \left(\frac{1}{314000} \right)^2$$

$$= 1000 \times (0.0000032)^2$$
$$= 1000 \times 0.00000000001$$
$$= 0.00000001 \text{ farad}$$
$$= 0.01 \ \mu\text{F}$$

There are other components in the circuit, besides the capacitor and coil. The resistor values determine the gain of the passed frequencies. The formula is:

$$G = -\frac{R2}{R1}$$

The negative sign simply indicates that the output will be 180° out-of-phase with the input. In most control applications this will be totally irrelevant.

Once again, we'll make things clearer with a simple example. Let's say that R1 = 22 kΩ (22,000 ohms), and R2 = 220 kΩ (220,000 ohms). The gain would be equal to:

$$G = -\frac{220000}{22000}$$

$$= -10$$

An input of 1 milliwatt should result in an output of 10 milliwatts, as long as its frequency is within the passband. Resistor R3 should have a value equal to, or slightly less than that of R1.

Other bandpass filter circuits can also be used, but we don't really need to go into them here. Filter design is covered extensively in many other electronics texts.

In a multichannel filter decoding receiver, several separate bandpass filters are used one for each encoded frequency (and for each independent controlled function). A block diagram of such a system is illustrated in Fig. 12-39. The control signal triggers the appropriate device if (and only if) there is an output from the appropriate filter. Obviously, this will happen only when the input frequency is within that filter's pass band.

Each encoded frequency must be carefully selected so that it is within the pass band of one and only one of the filters. Remember the gradual nature of the rolloff slope. Even a partially attenuated signal within the slope region could cause false triggering. Be very, very careful when choosing your encoding frequencies.

If the proper encoding frequencies are selected, such a system can be reasonably reliable and efficient. Only a relatively small number of control lines will be practical for most filter decoding systems.

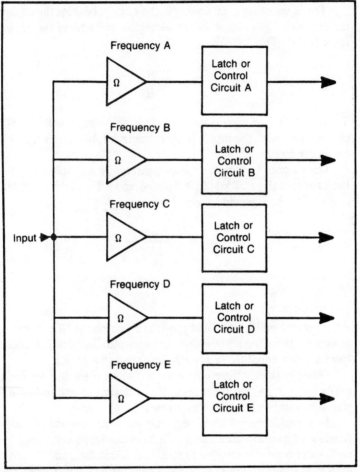

Fig. 12-39. In a multichannel filter decoding receiver several separate band-pass filters are used; one of each encoded frequency.

PLL Decoding

The other method of tone control uses the PLL (phase-locked loop). PLLs have a largely undeserved reputation for being extremely complicated. Actually, they are conceptually quite similar to the closed loop automation system discussed at several points throughout this book. The basic components of a PLL are illustrated in block diagram form in Fig. 12-40. As in the closed-loop automation system, the key to the PLL is the feedback loop.

A PLL circuit is made up of three basic stages:

☐ Phase comparator.
☐ Low-pass filter/amplifier.
☐ VCO (voltage-controlled oscillator).

In most modern cases, all three stags are generally contained within a single IC chip.

Two signals are fed into the phase comparator. One is the external input signal. The other is the output of the VCO (and the PLL itself)—this is the feedback loop.

If these two signals are perfectly in step with each other, and 90° out-of-phase, there will be no output from the phase comparator. The output of the PLL (the VCO's frequency) will not be changed.

If the two signals are not locked together, however, the phase comparator will produce an output called the error signal. This signal will be fed through a low-pass filter for smoothing, and to prevent oscillation within the closed-loop system. The error signal is then amplified, and fed to the control input of the VCO, changing its phase, and possibly its frequency, until it is locked onto (and 90° out-of-phase with) the external input signal.

A popular PLL IC is the 567. It was designed with frequency sensing and tone decoding applications in mind. A block diagram of this device is shown in Fig. 12-41.

Notice that the 567 also contains a second (quadrature) phase detector which is fed to a power output stage. When the input fre-

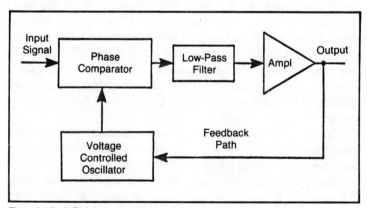

Fig. 12-40. A PLL is a simple closed-loop system.

239

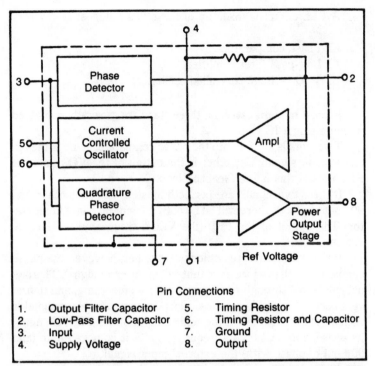

Fig. 12-41. A popular PLL device for tone decoding applications is the 567.

Pin Connections

1.	Output Filter Capacitor	5.	Timing Resistor
2.	Low-Pass Filter Capacitor	6.	Timing Resistor and Capacitor
3.	Input	7.	Ground
4.	Supply Voltage	8.	Output

quency is close to the center frequency of the device (determined by external components), pin 8 will go to ground level (0 volts). At all other times, this pin will be kept floating.

A simple tone decoder circuit built around the 567 is illustrated in Fig. 12-42. Resistor R1 and capacitor C1 set the free-running (center) frequency of the current-controlled oscillator. With the component values shown, this frequency will be about 50 kHz (depending on the setting of the potentiometer). This will be the frequency detected by the tone detector. Unless the external input frequency is close to the oscillator frequency, pin 8 will be floating, and no current will flow through the load.

If the correct frequency is applied to the input, the quadrature phase detector turns on the power output stage, grounding pin 8, and allowing a current (of up to 100 mA) to flow through the load.

Noise immunity of this tone decoder is achieved by adjusting the amount of time required for it to respond to a tone. Slower reaction times will allow the circuit to ignore brief transients that might otherwise confuse it. The response time can be adjusted by changing the circuit's bandwidth. The wider the bandwidth, the quicker the response. For slower, more noise immune response, a narrow bandwidth should be used. The bandwidth is determined by several factors, primarily, the applied signal voltage, the center frequency, and the value of capacitor C2.

The center frequency, as mentioned earlier, is set by the values of R1 and C1. The formula is:

$$R1 = \frac{1}{F_c C1}$$

The usable range of center frequencies for the 567 runs from 0.01 Hz to 500 kHz (500,000 Hz). This range should take care of almost any control application you're likely to need.

TOUCH-TONE ENCODING

If you are using more than just a few control functions in a tone

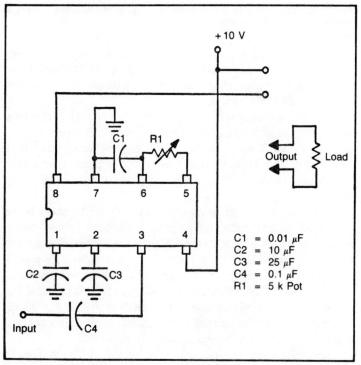

Fig. 12-42. This is a typical tone decoder circuit built around the 567 PLL IC.

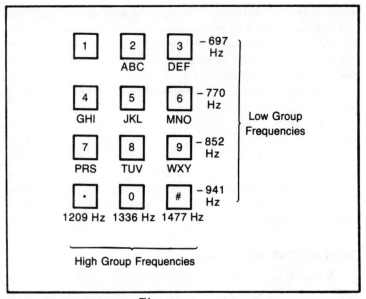

Fig. 12-43. The Touch Tone™ system is made up of 12 control signals arranged in a column/row matrix.

encoding system, greater reliability can be achieved with complex tones. Each frequency must be selected to avoid harmonics that could cause false triggering, and to avoid 60 Hz (the power-line frequency) and its harmonics.

The phone company has already done a lot of work in this area, so we might as well take advantage of their extensive research and use the Touch Tone™ system. Each digit is represented by a combination of two tones. Both tones must be present for a valid control signal to exist. This greatly limits the chances for false triggering.

A big advantage of using the Touch Tone™ system is the availability of preconstructed devices. A standard Touch Tone™ telephone set can be used to generate all of the tones. Circuits and ICs for generating the Touch Tone™ signals are also widely available, and can be easily incorporated into your control projects.

The Touch Tone™ system is made up of twelve control signals arranged in a column/row matrix, as illustrated in Fig. 12-43. Whenever one of the buttons is depressed, a low frequency and a high frequency will be simultaneously generated.

Several manufacturers make ICs for use in Touch Tone™ systems. A typical example is the MC14410 tone encoder IC from

Motorola. This device is illustrated in Fig.12-44. All of the component tones are derived from a 1 MHz crystal oscillator. This base frequency is divided down digitally to create each of the component frequencies. An additional column is supported by this device, permitting a total of sixteen control switches, as shown in Fig. 12-45. A tone-encoding circuit built around the MC14410 is illustrated in Fig. 12-46.

At the receiving end, a tone decoder for each of the seven (or eight) component frequencies must be provided. Gates are used to combine the tone decoder outputs appropriately. A circuit for a standard 4 × 3 keypad system (12 signals—7 frequencies) is shown in Fig. 12-47. The output of each NOR gate will be high if and only if both of its inputs are low. Each input goes low when the appropriate tone decoder is turned on (pin 8 of the 567 grounded).

RADIO CONTROL

When wireless control is mentioned, most people immediately think about radio control. While radio control may be a desirable choice in some applications, in most cases it introduces more trouble than it's worth. Interference problems are almost inevitable. Radio circuits are usually quite critical in terms of component selection, placement, and shielding. Radio frequency circuitry tends to be rather expensive. In addition, you can easily (perhaps inevitably) run into problems with legal restrictions on radio transmissions. Still, despite these problems, there are certainly applications in which radio control may be the best (occasionally the only practical) choice, so we can't afford to ignore it here.

The first things to consider are the legal restrictions. All rf (radio frequency) transmitters come under the jurisdiction of the FCC (Federal Communications Commission). Don't try to cheat here. The hefty fines if you get caught make this a very poor gamble. The FCC's detection equipment is surprisingly accurate, and many an experimenter has been caught for violating the FCC's rules and regulations.

Don't suffer from the misapprehension that if the power level is low enough it is not considered a radio transmitter. If it transmits rf signals at all, it is a radio transmitter, and that's that. The power level is irrelevant to the definition of a radio transmitter.

In most cases, radio transmitters must be licensed by the FCC to be legally used. There are a few exceptions, which are described in Part 15 of the FCC rules. (If you are considering using radio control at all, you should carefully read the FCC rules, which are available from the local branch office of the FCC.)

The FCC assigns specific functions to various frequency bands in the radio spectrum. Three bands have been assigned to radio control devices:

☐ 27 MHz
☐ 50 to 54 MHz
☐ 72 to 76 MHz

The highest (72-76 MHz) and the lowest (27 MHz) of these bands do not require an operator's license. This is not to imply there aren't any legal restrictions on their use. Read the FCC rules before using these frequency bands for a control system.

Each band is divided into several channels:

27 MHz band
26.995 MHz

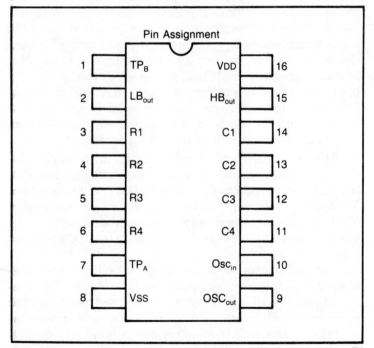

Fig. 12-44A. The MIC14410 tone encoder IC is used in Touch Tone™ systems.

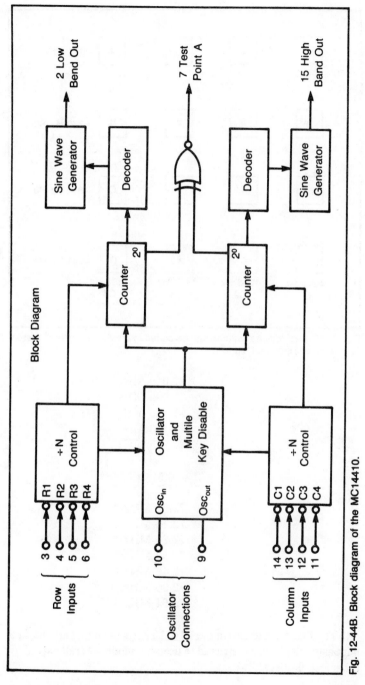

Fig. 12-44B. Block diagram of the MC14410.

245

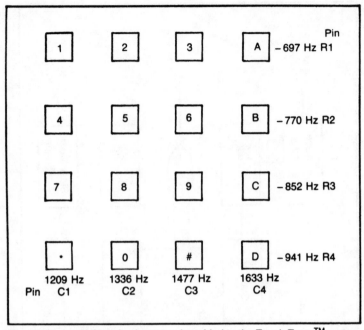

Fig. 12-45. An additional column can be added to the Touch Tone ™ system for a total of 16 control signals.

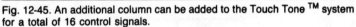

27.045 MHz
27.095 MHz
27.145 MHz
27.195 MHz
27.225 MHz

72 - 76 MHz band

72.08 MHz *
72.16 MHz
72.24 MHz *
72.32 MHz
72.40 MHz *
72.96 MHz
75.64 MHz *

The four frequencies in the 72 to 76 MHz band that are marked with asterisks (*) are restricted to use with model aircraft *only*. Any other use is illegal.

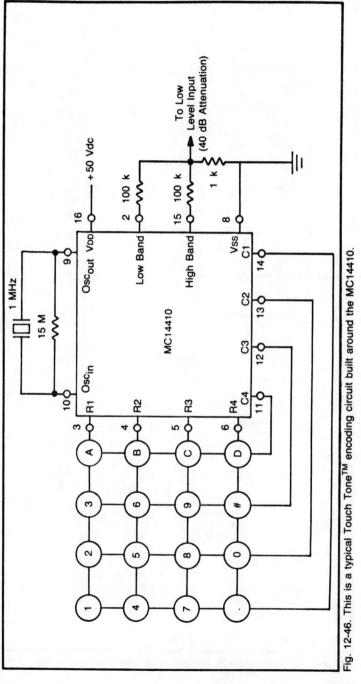

Fig. 12-46. This is a typical Touch Tone™ encoding circuit built around the MC14410.

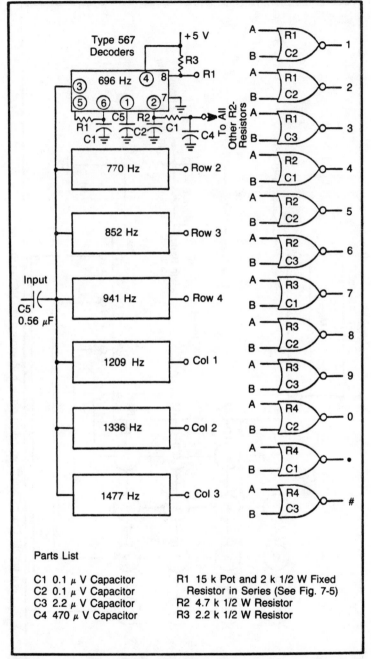

Fig. 12-47. This is a receiver/decoder for the tone-encoder circuit of Fig. 12-46.

An amateur radio technician class license (or better) is required for the 50-54 MHz band. The assigned channels in this band are:

51.20 MHz
52.04 MHz
53.10 MHz
53.20 MHz
53.30 MHz
53.40 MHz
53.50 MHz

Notice that many of the channel assignments in each band are closely spaced. This means that highly selective receivers (usually superheterodyne type) must be used.

Probably the easiest approach to using radio control in your projects is to use a transmitter from some commercial device such as a garage door opener or model airplane. These transmitters are already Type Approved, Type Accepted, or Certified by the FCC. While you can modify the receiver any way you'd like to suit your application, it is illegal to make any modification to such a trans-

Table 12-22. Parts List for the
Low-Power AM Transmitter Circuit of Fig. 12-48.

IC1	CA3140 op amp
Q1, Q2	NPN transistor (2N3904 or similar)
D1	1N914 diode
C1	0.22 μF capacitor
C2	1 μF 35 V electrolytic capacitor
C3	5 μF 35 V electrolytic capacitor
C4	10 μF 35 V electrolytic capacitor
C5	0.05 μF capacitor
C6	1000 pF capacitor
C7	500 pF capacitor
C8	33 pF capacitor
C9	270 pF capacitor
C10	330 pF capacitor
R1	4.7 kΩ resistor
R2, R3	1 MΩ resistor
R4, R5, R6	2.2 kΩ resistor
R7	560 Ω resistor
R8	270 Ω resistor
R9	33 kΩ resistor
R10, R11	100 kΩ resistor

mitter. That includes adding a longer antenna! If you are unsure about the legality of anything you might have in mind, check with the local branch office of the FCC, or change your plans. Do not risk a large fine, or possible jail sentence.

If possible, you should avoid opening the transmitter housing, unless you are licensed for working on radio transmitters, and definitely know what you're doing.

Actually, this isn't too significant a limitation for most control applications. A control signal is a control signal. It's what the receiver does with the control signals that matters. There are no legal restrictions on modifying a receiver.

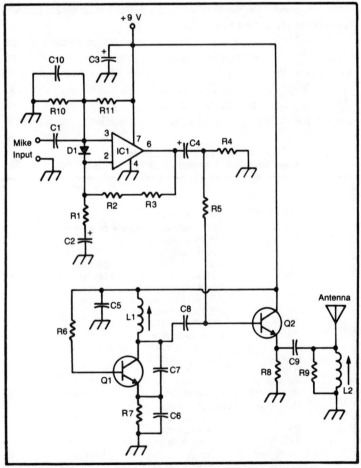

Fig. 12-48. This small transmitter will send signals to any AM radio.

PROJECT 62—LOW-POWER AM TRANSMITTER

It is legal to build a small unlicensed transmitter for the AM broadcast band (54 kHz to 160 kHz). The transmitted signal may not cover more than a fifty foot range.

A simple AM wireless microphone circuit is shown in Table 12-22 and Fig. 12-48. Instead of a microphone (voice) input, you could use control tones. The signal can be picked up by a nearby standard AM radio, tuned to the transmitter frequency. Be aware that there may be considerable interference within this band, limiting its usefulness for control applications.

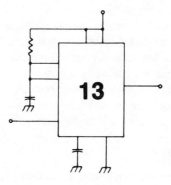

Computer Control

T HE ULTIMATE IN AUTOMATION SYSTEMS IS TO EMPLOY
computer control. A computer can be programmed for a wide
variety of automated control patterns, simple or complex, open-
loop or closed-loop. The biggest advantage of computer control lies
in the programmability. The control pattern can be altered at any
time, just by reprogramming the computer. No physical rewiring
of the hardware circuitry is required.

Just a few short years ago, few hobbyists could reasonably afford to dedicate a computer to automation tasks. Now, microcomputers are widely marketed almost everywhere. Many are available for under $100. You could almost get one for each automation
system, and not use it for anything else, and still get your money's
worth.

Even if you already own a fancy microcomputer, you might
want to consider buying a budget model for your automation sys-
tem(s). Automation applications will rarely call for heavy-duty com-
puting ability, super-fast calculations, or large memory banks. A
budget microcomputer will do the job just fine, and you won't have
to tie up your main computer for the automation tasks.

If you have a strong backgrcund in electronics design, you
might want to consider building a dedicated computer system. A
CPU (central processing unit) can be purchased for $10 to $20. You
don't need to pay for a fancy case, or any circuitry you don't really
need in your system. If you are interested in taking this approach,

I recommend you read my earlier book, *30 Customized Microprocessor Projects* (TAB book 2705).

If your technical expertise isn't quite up to the challenge of designing a computer-based system from scratch (or just don't want to bother), you can accomplish pretty much the same things by using the I/O (input/output) ports of a full microcomputer. In this book we will concentrate primarily on this second, somewhat simpler approach. Much of what is said here will also apply (with minor modifications) to a completely home-brew CPU based system.

PROGRAMMING

Virtually every microcomputer in existence requires somewhat different programming than every other microcomputer. There will be some degree of overlap in techniques. We will just discuss the general basics in this chapter.

There are many different programming languages around today. These are analogous to languages like English or French or Turkish. A programming language is just the way you tell the computer what you want it to do.

Ultimately, any computer only understands one language. This is called machine language. (Different CPUs usually understand different forms of machine language. They can't directly "talk" to each other.) Machine language is made up of binary numbers. Binary numbers contain only 1s and 0s. You can think of each binary word, or "byte" as a string of switches, as illustrated in Fig. 13-1. If a given switch is open, that binary digit (or "bit") is a 0. If the switch is closed, the bit is a 1. Different combinations of 1s and 0s mean different things to the CPU.

Fortunately, almost all commercial microcomputers come supplied with a built-in translator program, so the computer can understand a "higher" (more English-like) language. BASIC is by far the most popular language. This is not the place to go into the debate of whether or not it's the best choice. In today's market, it is definitely the most readily available and convenient choice. In some cases, it is the only available choice.

BASIC is so popular because it is such an easy language to learn and work with. English-like commands are used. In many cases, the meaning of the command is perfectly obvious. For example:

PRINT 2 + 3

would tell the computer to display a "5" on its video screen.

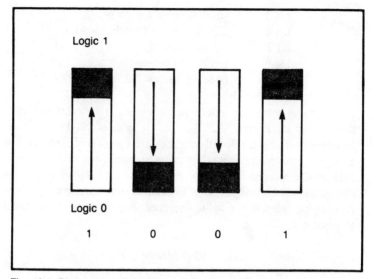

Fig. 13-1. Binary words (bytes) can be thought of as a series of switches.

It would not be appropriate to cover BASIC (or any other programming language) in depth here. Many fine books on learning BASIC have been written.

INPUT SIGNALS

In most automation systems, the computer will need to sense various conditions in the outside world. Many sensors can be connected directly to an Input Port of the computer. Almost any device that performs a switching function can be used in this manner. The computer can tell if each switch connected to its input port(s) is open or closed.

Several switching type sensors can be connected to a single input port. Each switching device is one bit of the incoming binary word. For most inexpensive microcomputers, each port can handle one byte, or eight bits. Therefore, eight switching sensors can be fed into a single input port, and the computer will be able to individually distinguish between them.

To see how this is done, let's look at a typical example. The following devices are connected to input port "A":

bit 0	door intrusion switch (front)
bit 1	window intrusion switch 1
bit 2	window intrusion switch 2

bit 3	window intrusion switch 3
bit 4	door intrusion switch (back)
bit 5	smoke detector
bit 6	temperature sensor
bit 7	flooding sensor (basement)

Now, the computer will be programmed to periodically check the value at input port "A." If it finds a value of 0000 0000, it assumes everything is OK (all switches are open), and moves on to other programming. Any other value at input port "A" will indicate an alarm condition (one or more switches is closed), and the computer will be programmed to take an appropriate action, depending on the specific value detected. For instance if the value at input port "A" is:

1000 0000

The computer may display a message reading, "Flooding In Basement." In addition, it may feed out some control signals to the output ports (which work in the same, but opposite manner as the input ports). These control signals could activate a sump pump, and possibly trigger an audible alarm.

Now, let's say the incoming value at input port "A" is:

0010 0000

This code would trigger an intrusion alarm. The computer can even pinpoint the location of the intrusion. For example, the display might read "Intrusion—Master Bedroom Window." A light could be turned on at the appropriate location to startle the intruder.

With a little more advanced programming and hardware, the computer could automatically dial the phone number of the local police department, or a neighbor, then activate a tape recorder to play a prerecorded message giving your address and requesting assistance. As you can see, computer control can range from very simple to quite complex.

It is also possible for the computer to be programmed to respond only when a specific combination of input switch sensors are activated. For example, an input value of:

0110 0001

might trigger a special action that is not activated by any other input value.

The possibilities are limited only by your imagination and programming skill.

D/A CONVERSION

A computer can recognize and put out only digital signals, for simple on/off functions. This is quite sufficient for a great many applications. Other real world applications aren't quite so cooperative. A continuous range of values might be needed either as an input or an output signal.

A computer cannot input or output a continuous range analog signal. But all is not lost. It is certainly possible to convert between analog and digital signals. We will look at digital to analog (D/A) conversion first, because it is somewhat simpler.

Remember the individual bits of a byte do not have to be treated like independent entities. Each bit has a value dependent on its position within the byte. Each bit's value is a power of 2. That is:

BIT	Value
0	1
1	2
2	4
3	8
4	16
5	32
6	64
7	128

But, 0 is the right-most bit. Bit 7 is the left-most. That is:

$$7\text{-}6\text{-}5\text{-}4\text{-}3\text{-}2\text{-}1\text{-}0$$

Bit 7 is worth much more (has greater weight) than any of the other bits. Bit 0 is worth the least (the least weight).

To find the total value of a binary word, you just add together the place values of all bits that are 1s, and ignore the 0s. For example:

$$0101\ 1001 = 0 + 64 + 0 + 16 + 8 + 0 + 0 + 1 = 89$$

In other words, 0101 1001 is eighty-nine times as great as 0000 0001.

We could try summing together the bits of an output port. Let's say each bit switches between 0 and +1 volts. In this case 0000 0001 would become an analog output of +1 volt, which is fine. But 0101 1001 would be a mere +4 volts, because all of the bits have equal weight. This is obviously not at all what we're looking for. We need some way to weight each bit.

A simple solution is to put a resistor with an appropriate value in series with each bit, as shown in Fig. 13-2. Only four bits are shown here for simplicity. The digital bits are represented as SPDT switches that individually select +V or 0 volts.

The most significant bit (MSB—largest value) passes through the smallest resistance. Lesser bits pass through greater resistances that are multiples of two of the minimum (MSB) resistance value. Obviously, the least significant bit (LSB—smallest value) should pass through the largest resistance. This technique works in accordance with Ohm's law:

$$E = IR$$

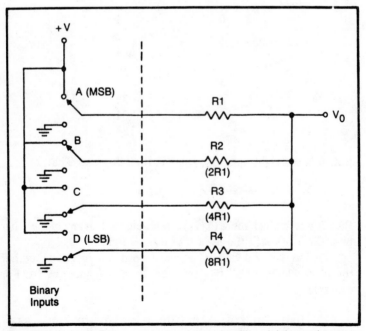

Fig. 13-2. A simple D/A converter can be made with weighting resistances.

If we choose a value of 10 kΩ for resistor R1, then R2 will be 20 kΩ, R3 will be 40 kΩ, and R4 will be 80 kΩ. Holding the current constant, the amount of voltage drop across each resistor will be weighted proportional to its binary value.

For our discussion, we will assume a logic 0 equals 0 volt, and a logic 1 equals +5.0 volts. We will assume the current drawn by the output load circuit gives the following voltage drops across each of the resistors (for a +5.0 volt input):

R1	1.0 volt
R2	3.0 volts
R3	4.0 volts
R4	4.5 volts

If all of the input bits are at logic 0, the output will obviously have to be 0 volts. If one and only one of the input bits is at logic 1, the output voltage is simply the difference between the input voltage (+5.0 volts) and the appropriate resistor. For instance, let's say the full input value is 0010. Only input C is a logic 1. Therefore, the output voltage will be:

$$V_o = 5.0 - 4.0 = 1.0 \text{ volt}$$

Each weighted bit works out to a voltage that is exactly twice its predecessor:

Bit	Voltage
D	0.5 volt
C	1.0 volt
B	2.0 volts
A	4.0 volts

This is the same weighting used in the binary numbering system.

Thanks to the consistency of the weighting scheme, intermediate values (two or more bits at logic 1) will also work out right:

Binary Input	Decimal Value	Output Voltage
0000	0	0 + 0 + 0 + 0 = 0 volt
0001	1	0 + 0 + 0 + 0.5 = 0.5 volt
0010	2	0 + 0 + 1 + 0 = 1.0 volt

Binary Input	Decimal Value	Output Voltage
0011	3	$0 + 0 + 1 + 0.5 = 1.5$ volt
0100	4	$0 + 2 + 0 + 0 = 2.0$ volts
0101	5	$0 + 2 + 0 + 0.5 = 2.5$ volts
0110	6	$0 + 2 + 1 + 0 = 3.0$ volts
0111	7	$0 + 2 + 1 + 0.5 = 3.5$ volts
1000	8	$4 + 0 + 0 + 0 = 4.0$ volts
1001	9	$4 + 0 + 0 + 0.5 = 4.5$ volts
1010	10	$4 + 0 + 1 + 0 = 5.0$ volts
1011	11	$4 + 0 + 1 + 0.5 = 5.5$ volts
1100	12	$4 + 2 + 0 + 0 = 6.0$ volts
1101	13	$4 + 2 + 0 + 0.5 = 6.5$ volts
1110	14	$4 + 2 + 1 + 0 = 7.0$ volts
1111	15	$4 + 2 + 1 + 0.5 = 7.5$ volts

The output increases in 0.5 volt (LSB) steps. The analog output is directly proportional to the digital input value. That's exactly the result we were looking for.

But there are still problems. Uneven loading by the output could cause the current draw to vary, which affects the voltage drops. To head off loading problems, a buffer amplifier stage should be added to the simple D/A (Digital to Analog) converter, as illustrated

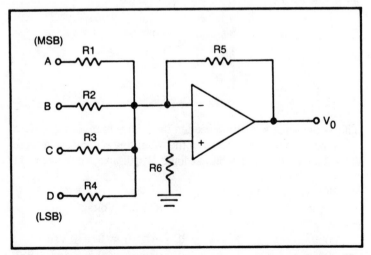

Fig. 13-3. A practical Direct Weighting D/A converter includes a buffer-amplifier stage to limit loading problems.

in Fig. 13-3. This buffer stage could also amplify the signal, if desired.

This system is simple and direct, but it can have a number of problems if more than just a few input bits are to be converted. With more than just a few bits, the resistances will have to cover a fairly large range. Rather oddball (not standardly available) values will be called for. In addition, the resistors have to be closely matched. Wide tolerances in the value could completely upset the accurate weighting of the bits.

The most obvious way to obtain the oddball resistances required, would be to put several standard value resistances in series (or sometimes in parallel). Unfortunately, the tolerances add. Let's say we want to make up a 40 kΩ resistance from four 10 kΩ resistors in series. If each 10 kΩ resistor has a tolerance of 5%, the total resistance will have a tolerance of 20%. That is, its value could be anything from 32 kΩ to 48 kΩ.

The wide resistance range can also be problematic. Consider the resistances for an 8-bit D/A converter of this type. If we use a 10 kΩ resistor (R) for the most significant bit (MSB), the other resistances will be as follows:

Input Bit			Resistance Value
7 (MSB)	R1	1R	10 kΩ
6	R2	2R	20 kΩ
5	R3	4R	40 kΩ
4	R4	8R	80 kΩ
3	R5	16R	160 kΩ
2	R6	32R	320 kΩ
1	R7	64R	640 kΩ
0 (LSB)	R8	128R	1280 kΩ = 1.28 MΩ

Obviously, this direct approach is awkward at best. A more convenient type of D/A converter is the R-2R ladder network that is illustrated in Fig. 13-4. Only two resistance values are needed—R and 2R. These two values are used repeatedly throughout the circuit. By using the combination scheme shown in the diagram, each incoming bit will be properly weighted. This system can be extended to accept as many bits as you need.

Practical R-2R ladder D/A converter circuits should also include a buffer amplifier stage to prevent loading problems. This is shown in Fig. 13-5.

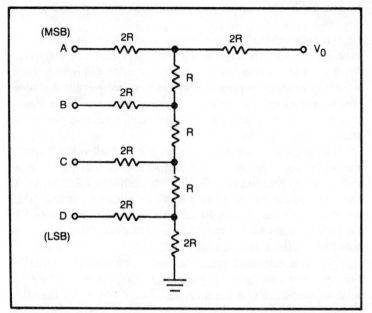

Fig. 13-4. A better approach to D/A conversion is to use a R-2R ladder network.

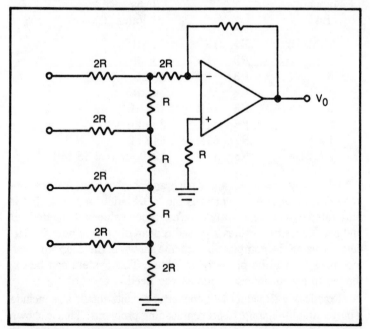

Fig. 13-5. Practical R-2R D/A converters also include a buffer-amplifier stage.

A/D CONVERSION

In the last section, we adapted the computer's digital output to the analog world. In many practical applications (especially closed-loop automation systems) it is necessary for the computer to examine and interpret analog input data. The analog input signal must be converted to digital form to be usable by the computer.

This is done with an A/D (analog-to-digital) converter, which is just the opposite of the D/A converters described in the last section of this chapter. Unfortunately, A/D conversion is more complicated than D/A conversion. There are several possible approaches.

In most A/D converters, the input signal is sampled at a regular rate (typically several hundred or thousand times per second). Each sample is then individually converted into a proportional digital value.

The conversion isn't perfect, of course. Digital values change in a stepwise manner, rather than a smooth linear spectrum. Intermediate values must be rounded off. For example, if we set up a system of 1-volt per bit, the recognized values are as follows:

0000	0 volts
0001	1 volt
0010	2 volts
0011	3 volts
0100	4 volts
0101	5 volts
0110	6 volts
0111	7 volts
1000	8 volts
1001	9 volts
1010	10 volts
1011	11 volts
1100	12 volts
1101	13 volts
1110	14 volts
1111	15 volts

If the sampled value is 3.5 volts, the computer will have to see this as either 0011 (3.0 volts) or 0100 (4.0 volts). We are locked into the step units of the conversion factor.

If we need greater resolution, we need to reduce the step value

(value of each bit). Let's say we make it 0.20 volt, instead of 1.0 volt. Now, the recognized values will be:

0000	0 volts
0001	0.2 volt
0010	0.4 volt
0011	0.6 volt
0100	0.8 volt
0101	1.0 volt
0110	1.2 volt
0111	1.4 volt
1000	1.6 volt
1001	1.8 volt
1010	2.0 volts
1011	2.2 volts
1100	2.4 volts
1101	2.6 volts
1110	2.8 volts
1111	3.0 volts

Notice that the range has been sharply reduced by the change in the step value. (Everything in life is a compromise, isn't it?) Instead of 0 to 15 volts, we can now only cover 0 to 3 volts with the same four bits.

There is only one way to increase the resolution without reducing the range (or vice versa). That is to increase the number of bits. If we use eight bits instead of four, we have 256 steps, rather than the 16 we get with the four-bit system. If the step value is 1 volt, the eight-bit range will be from 0 to 255 volts. If a 0.20 volt step value is used, the range will run from 0 to 51 volts. Again, there is a price. Increasing the number of bits increases the cost and complexity of the A/D converter circuitry.

There is no law that says that the range has to start at 0 volts for a digital value of 0000. In the following examples, the step size is 0.15 volt. A starts at 0 volts, B starts at 2.50 volts, and C starts at −1.00 volt:

Digital Value	A	B	C
0000	0.00	2.50	− 1.00
0001	0.15	2.65	− 0.85

Digital Value	A	B	C
0010	0.30	2.80	− 0.70
0011	0.45	2.95	− 0.55
0100	0.60	3.10	− 0.40
0101	0.75	3.25	− 0.25
0110	0.90	3.40	− 0.10
0111	1.05	3.55	0.05
1000	1.20	3.70	0.20
1001	1.35	3.85	0.35
1010	1.50	4.00	0.50
1011	1.65	4.15	0.65
1100	1.80	4.30	0.80
1101	1.95	4.45	0.95
1110	2.10	4.60	1.10
1111	2.25	4.75	1.25

All three of these examples have the same step and range size, but the range is shifted.

One of the most common forms of A/D converter circuits is the single-slope circuit, shown in block diagram form in Fig. 13-6.

The analog input signal is fed to an op amp, which is wired as a comparator. The input signal is compared to the output of the D/A converter, which comes later in the circuit (a feedback loop).

The comparator puts out one bit, which is a one if, and only if, the input is greater than the output from the D/A converter. This bit is inverted and fed to an AND gate, along with the clock signal. There are four possible input combinations to this gate. Each input combination and its resulting output is as follows:

Comparator	Clock	Gate Output
0	0	1
0	1	0
1	0	0
1	1	0

Notice that the gate output is a 1 if, and only if, both the clock and the inverted comparator output are at logic 0. (The direct converter output is a 1, meaning the analog input signal is greater than the D/A output.)

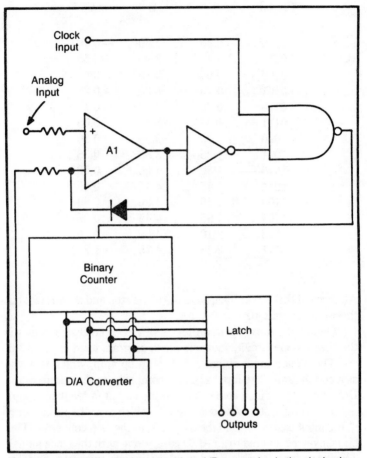

Fig. 13-6. A relatively simple approach to A/D conversion is the single-slope converter.

As long as the inverted comparator output is high, the clock signal is ignored. When the inverted comparator signal is low, the clock signal passes through the gate. The pulses are counted by the binary counter. The output of the counter is converted into analog form by the D/A converter. This analog value is fedback to the comparator.

The counting continues until the D/A output exceeds the external input. The gate is now cut off, so no further clock pulses get through to be counted. The counter now holds a digital value that is proportional to the analog input voltage. This binary number is fed out to the computer input.

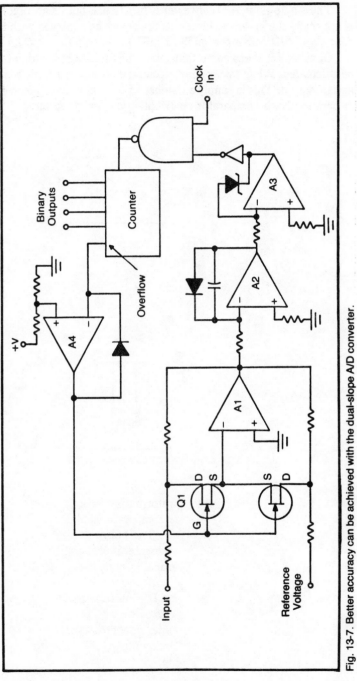

Fig. 13-7. Better accuracy can be achieved with the dual-slope A/D converter.

267

The single slope A/D converter is functional, but its accuracy is not really the greatest. Better accuracy can be achieved with a dual slope A/D converter, as illustrated in Fig. 13-7.

Obviously it takes some finite time for each sample value to be calculated. When faster conversions are required, a flash converter is used. This is simply a number of comparators connected in parallel. Each comparator contributes one weighted bit.

Index

A

ac motor, 133
A/D conversion
  computer, 263
adjustable light-controlled relay, 200
air conditioner humidity control
  circuits
  table of, 89
air conditioner humidity control, 86
alarm system
  complete entry, 67
am transmitter
  low power, 251
American Design Components, 28
astable multivibrator, 165
autodialer
  telephone, 123
automated guest greeter, 46
automatic caller, 123
automatic door opener, 62
automation, 1
  simple, 4

B

band pass filter, 231
base bias voltage, 155
BASIC, 254
bistable multivibrator, 165
boiler controller, 75

C

C&H Sales, 28
capacitance
  calculations for, 32
  parallel, 32
capacitor-start ac motor, 133

capstan, 17
carrier current control, 217
carrier frequency generator, 221
carrier-current receiver I, 225
carrier-current receiver II, 226
carrier-current receiver tone
  decoder, 226
carrier-current transmitter I, 223
carrier-current transmitter II, 224
carrier-current transmitter III, 225
cascading timer, 187
clocks
  24-hour, 192
closed loop system, 4
compound dc motor, 130
computer control, 253
control initiator, 2
control systems
  applications for, 6
  carrier current, 217
  radio, 243
controlled device, 2
controlling motors, 127
coupling network, 223
cross-fader, 55
crystal sensor, 23
customizing the projects, 33

D

D/A conversion
  computer, 257
dc controlled switches, 159
dc motors, 127
diode sensor, 21, 70
door indicator, 57
DPDT switch, 138, 147

E

electronic switching, 145
electronic thermostat
  simple, 75
emitter voltage source, 155
encoding
  touch tone, 241

F

FCC regulations, 243
FET switches, 156
fiberoptics, 214
fiberoptic receiver, 216
fiberoptic transmitter, 215
field-effect transistors, 138
filter
555 timer, 163
  band pass, 231
filter decoding, 231
flood alarm I, 94
flood alarm II, 94
frequency
  calculating the, 173
friction, 14

G

gas sensor, 22

H

Hall effect sensor, 23
heater humidifier, 82
Herback & Rademan
  Inc., 28

I

inertia, 14
infrared receiver, 207
  multifunction, 212
infrared transmitter, 207
  multifunction, 208
input signals, 255

L

LASCRs, 198
latching light-controlled relay, 200
LED, 199
lever, 10
light dimmer, 41
light interruption detector, 203
light relay switch, 35
light-beam control, 193
  LASCRs, 198
  LED, 199
  optoisolator, 199
  photoresistors, 196

photovoltaic cells, 194
light-beam receiver, 205
light-beam transmitter, 204
light-controlled relay III, 202
lighting projects, 35
linear motion, 17
liquid control, 91
liquid probes, 91

M

magnetic reed switch, 19
mechanical devices, 8
mechanical interfaces, 8
mercury switch, 20
moisture detector, 95
monostable multivibrator, 165
motor controller, 133
motors
  ac, 133
  capacitor-start ac, 133
  comparison of ac, 134, 135
  compound dc, 130
  controlling, 127
  dc, 127
  permanent-split capacitor ac, 133
  series ac, 133
  series dc, 130
  shaded pole ac, 133
  shunt dc, 130
  split-phase ac, 133
  synchronous ac, 133
  two-value capacitor ac, 133
  universal ac, 133
  using, 15
  wound-rotor ac, 133
multifunction infrared receiver, 212
multifunction infrared transmitter,
  208
multiple 555 ICs, 176
multiple light controller, 43
multivibrator
  astable, 165
  bistable, 165
  monostable, 165

O

open loop system, 4
optoisolator, 199

P

permanent-split capacitor ac motor,
  133
phase-locked loop decoding, 238
photocells, 22
photoresistors, 22, 196
photosensitive automatic light
  switch, 48

270

phototransistors, 22
photovoltaic cells, 194
plant monitor, 91
precision timers, 176
probe assemblies, 73
programming, 254
project
  air conditioner humidity control, 86
  multifunction infrared receiver, 212
projects
  2240 programmable timer, 181
  adjustable light-controlled relay, 200
  am transmitter, low power, 251
  autodialer, telephone, 123
  automated guest greeter, 46
  automatic caller, 123
  automatic door opener, 62
  boiler controller, 75
  carrier frequency generator, 221
  carrier-current receiver I, 225
  carrier-current receiver II, 226
  carrier-current receiver tone decoder, 226
  carrier-current transmitter I, 223
  carrier-current transmitter II, 224
  carrier-current transmitter III, 225
  cascading timer, 187
  complete entry alarm system, 67
  cross-fader, 55
  electronic thermostat, 75
  fiber-optic receiver, 216
  fiber-optic transmitter, 215
  finding parts, 26
  flood alarm I, 94
  flood alarm II, 94
  heater humidifier, 82
  infrared receiver, 207
  infrared transmitter, 207
  latching light-controlled relay, 200
  light dimmer, 41
  light interruption detector, 203
  light-beam receiver, 205
  light-beam transmitter, 204
  light-controlled relay III, 202
  lighting relay switch, 35
  moisture detector, 95
  motor controller, 133
  multifunction infrared transmitter, 208
  multiple light controller, 43
  photosensitive automatic light switch, 48
  plant monitor, 91

  recorder timer switch, 108
  remote lamp dimmer, 42
  sequential controller, 54
  sound compressor circuit, 107
  speed controller, 140
  stereo, 101
  stereo advanced auto shut-off, 102
  stereo automatic shut-off, 101
  substituting electronic components, 29
  sump pump controller I, 95
  sump pump controller II, 99
  telephone, 115
  telephone-activated relay, 115
  telephone-activated relay, improved, 116
  telephone off-hook alarm, 121
  telephone recorder controller, 121
  television, 101
  television auto-off circuit, 110
  television remote control mute, 113
  temperature equalizer, 81
  time activated automation, 48
  tone decoder, 226
  touch switches, 160
  triac remote light control, 39
  VOX recorder controller, 103
  VOX relay, 105
pulley, 12
pulley size
  calculating, 16

R
radio bands, 244
radio control, 243
recorder timer switch, 108
relays, 145
remote control, 1
  simple, 2
remote control and automation
  basics of, 1
remote lamp dimmer, 42
resistance
  calculations for, 30
  parallel, 31
  series, 31
rotary motion, 15

S
SCR switches, 158
semiconductor switching devices
  other, 156
semiconductors, 32

271

sensors, 18
  crystal, 23
  diode, 21
  diode temperature, 70
  gas, 22
  Hall effect, 23
  input signal, 255
  photcells, 22
  photoresistors, 22
  phototransistors, 22
  switches, 18
  temperature, 69
  thermistor, 22, 70
  thermocouples, 69
  VOX, 22
sequential light controller, 54
series ac motor, 133
series dc motor, 130
shaded pole ac motor, 133
shunt dc motor, 130
signal path, 2
silicon-controlled rectifier, 158
snap action switch, 19
sound compressor circuit, 107
SPDT switch, 147
speed controller, 140
speed reduction
  calculation of, 15
split-phase ac motor, 133
stereo advanced auto shut-off, 102
stereo automatic shut-off, 101
stereo projects, 101
substituting electronic components,
  29
sump pump controller I, 95
sump pump controller II, 99
switches
  dc controlled, 159
  DPDT, 138, 147
  FET, 156
  magnetic reed, 19
  mercury, 20
  SCR, 158
  snap action, 19
  SPDT, 147
  touch, 160
  transistor, 148
  UJT, 157
synchronous ac motor, 133

T
telephone-activated relay, 115
  improved, 116
telephone off-hook alarm, 121
telephone projects, 115
telephone recorder controller, 121

television auto-off circuit, 110
television projects, 101
television remote control mute, 113
temperature control, 69
temperature equalizer, 81
temperature sensors, 69
thermistor, 22
thermistor sensor, 70
thermistors
  negative temperature coefficient,
    71
  positive temperature coefficient,
    71
thermocouples, 69
time-activated automation, 48
timers, 163
  555, 163
  cascading, 187
  precision, 176
timing period
  calculating the, 167
tone decoder, 226
tone decoding, 230
tone encoding, 228
touch switches, 160
touch-tone encoding, 241
transistor circuit component value
  calculation of, 151
transistor switches, 148
transistors
  avalanche mode, 156
  current mode, 154
  saturated mode, 149
triac remote light control, 39
24-hour clocks, 192
2240 programmable timer, 181
two-value capacitor ac motor, 133

U
UJT switches, 157
universal ac motor, 133

V
VOX recorder controller, 103
VOX relay, 105

W
weighting computer bits, 259
window indicator, 57

V
VOX sensor, 22

W
wireless control, 193
wound-rotor ac motor, 133

Edited by Roland S. Phelps